Sun on the Water

Sun on the Water

The Brilliant Life and Tragic Death of Kirsty MacColl

Jean MacColl

with John Dalby and Fred Shortland

JOHN BLAKE

Published by John Blake Publishing Ltd,
3 Bramber Court, 2 Bramber Road,
London W14 9PB, UK

www.blake.co.uk

First published in hardback in 2008
Hardback ISBN: 978-1-84454-549-0

First published in trade paperback in 2008
Trade paperback ISBN: 978-1-84454-596-4

British Library Cataloguing-in-Publication Data:
A catalogue record for this book is available from the British Library.

Design by www.envydesign.co.uk

Printed in the UK by CPI William Clowes Ltd, Beccles, NR34 7TL

1 3 5 7 9 10 8 6 4 2

Papers used by John Blake Publishing are natural, recyclable products made
from wood grown in sustainable forests. The manufacturing processes
conform to the environmental regulations of the country of origin.

Every effort has been made to contact relevant copyright holders. Any
omission is inadvertent; we would be grateful if the appropriate people
could contact us.

This book is dedicated to my son Hamish; to my grandsons Jamie and Louis; to all those throughout the world who have never stopped fighting for justice; and to my darling daughter

Contents

Preface and Acknowledgements

During the long years since Kirsty's death, I have received hundreds, if not thousands, of kind, warm and supportive messages from all around the world. It was those expressions of love and support that kept me going through the darkest days. It is a tribute to Kirsty's enormous gifts that her music and spirit continue to inspire such admiration, respect and love. 'It's hard to be brief about a talent as great as Kirsty MacColl,' wrote one of her fans, Wes Eichenwald, to me from America:

> Perhaps the most important thing about Kirsty's music is that she was able to capture emotions – jealousy, regret, joy – in a way that few artists have done. Sometimes it was with quiet vulnerability, other times with wicked wit, but always with honesty. It is this combination of intelligence and sincerity that makes Kirsty's music special. She recreated snapshots of her life and, in doing so, gave us a clearer picture of our own.

In some ways this book is another collection of 'recreated snapshots' from my daughter's life; it certainly contains a wide range of emotions: joy, pride, love, anxiety, anger... and it is my anger at Kirsty's loss, and at the failure, now nearly seven years after her death, to achieve justice in her name, that has led to my writing this book. In telling the story of our campaign for justice over Kirsty's death, however, I have also chosen to tell for the first time the story of her life – of *our* life together, from the days before I first cradled her in my arms in the maternity ward of the Mayday Hospital in Croydon, to the time I scattered her ashes in the seas off Cuba.

Sun on the Water is therefore as much a celebration of my darling daughter's life as it is a manifesto of the grievous wrongs associated with her death. In writing this book, I have been overwhelmed by the enduring friendship, love and practical assistance offered me by the many kind souls without whose assistance, so freely given and in so many different ways, this book would never have been written. So in addition to my beloved son Hamish, and my darling grandsons Jamie and Louis, I would especially like to thank Nick de Somogyi for his practical advice, sympathetic ear and constantly supportive encouragement to 'just keep on writing'; my great friend Denise Keir, who kindly volunteered to take over the typing when my eyes deteriorated in the latter stages of the book (making me grandly feel rather like Barbara Cartland as I relaxed in an easy chair, dictating to my 'secretary'); and my agent Robert Smith, who took me on trust, but believed, as we all do, that this is a story that needed to be told.

The profound gratitude I feel both to John Dalby and Fred Shortland is recorded in the pages that follow. Further thanks are due to Stuart Robertson, Lucian Randall and all at John Blake Publishing; and, finally, to the following close friends who, in their many different ways, have helped me to keep going over the last few years:

Preface and Acknowledgements

Danny Assadourian – Sarah Aucott – Eddie Beck – Ann Beach – Art Bennett – Alison Boberg – Bono – Boz and Lyn Boorer – Billy Bragg – Viv Bridson – Jo Briscoe – June Brown – Carl Chase – Philip Chevron – Jono Coleman – David Coolidge – Rosemary Cooper – Ivan Diaz – Charlie Dickins – Michele Drees – Keith Dyson – Donna and Wes Eichenwald – Marcia Farquhar – Jem Finer – Jenny Frankel – Pete and Leni Gillman – Pete and Ingrid Glenister – Demetrio Guerra – Ginger Halstead – Ronnie Harris – Philip Hedley – Alan Herdman – Nick Hern – Jools Holland – Wolfgang Hoss – Claire Iden – Tommy James – Julian Jones – Miriam Karlin – Dr Sabjit Kaler – Lee Kent – Alix Kirsta – James Knight – Olivia Lichtenstein – Steve Lillywhite – Janice Long – Shane MacGowan – Louise McLean – Tracey MacLeod – Johnny Marr – John Miranda – Mitch Mitchelson – Frank Murray – Mark Nevin – Pip Newlove – Alan Officer – Stella Powell – Philip, Jann and Georgia Rambow – Peter Rankin – Tosh and Judy Rapoport – Nigel Reeve – Lindsay Royan – Dave and Jen Ruffy – Peter Schaufler – Victor Spinetti – Margaret Spurring – Spider and Louise Stacy – Alison Steadman – Sonja Wallis – Jill Welfare – Matthew Westwood – Tom Willingson.

I hope I haven't overlooked anybody, but if I have, I offer them my apologies – and my thanks.

'Thanks for being Kirsty's Mom,' wrote my American e-mailer in a PS to his message: 'Girls don't get to be as cool as Kirsty unless they have a great role model'. I really don't know how true that is, but my constant role model in writing this book has been Kirsty herself and the honesty, warmth, passion – and rage against injustice – she always brought to her life, to the music and to our world.

Jean MacColl
March 2008

Prologue

Days

And though you're gone,
You're with me every single day, believe me...
'DAYS', THE KINKS, RECORDED BY KIRSTY MACCOLL, 1989

18 December 2000

It had been a great evening at the theatre. As soon as I arrived home, I was on the phone to my old friend and close colleague John Dalby to tell him about it. My friend Denise Keir and I had been to see the ballet *The Car Man*, a new production based on the Carmen story, and it had exceeded all my expectations. Later, after making myself a cup of tea, I noticed the shopping list of vegetables Kirsty had left for me when she went on holiday – along with her instructions not to get them too soon. I smiled to myself. Perhaps she thought that, in my enthusiasm for a family Christmas, I would buy them too early. Although she'd written her phone number in Mexico at the top of the page, I decided I wouldn't ring her just then.

She had been busy promoting her latest CD, *Tropical Brainstorm*, and had only just returned from a lengthy trip to Cuba, where she had been preparing a musical history of the island for the BBC. She had gone away with her two sons – Jamie and Louis – and her new partner, James Knight, and she had earned those few precious days. They were holidaying on the Mexican island of Cozumel and there would be time enough to share our news.

The night before they flew, I joined them for supper and Kirsty ran me home. Our last words had been 'I love you'.

Lost in my thoughts, I was suddenly brought up by the telephone. Surprised that anyone should ring me so late, I spoke with James, Kirsty's boyfriend. I immediately felt a slight pang of unease – why hadn't she rung me herself? Perhaps she was busy cooking and had just asked James to place the call for her. But he wasted no time.

'There's been an accident – Kirsty is dead, but the boys are all right.'

'No – oh, no... Tell me Kirsty is just injured...'

'No. Kirsty is dead. The boys are all right. A powerboat hit her while she was in the water.'

I don't remember the rest of the conversation. What I do remember is that I screamed, once, from the terrible well of grief that had opened up under me. I tore at my earrings and threw them down. If only she had just been injured, I could cope with that – but 'dead' was so shocking, so unexpected. Beautiful, witty, talented Kirsty – her life cut short by some dreadful accident.

I needed to tell people who were close to me. I was immediately back on the phone to John, to whom I had only just been speaking after the show, and he promised they'd be right over.

Denise, who had just returned home to Croydon, said she would drive over.

How could it be that I had sat through and enjoyed an evening at the ballet while my daughter had lost her life? Why had I not felt anything, sensed no inkling of this tragedy? I tried to ring Hamish, Kirsty's brother, who was then living in Stroud, Gloucestershire, but the line was engaged. I knew that the news would soon break, so I rang my nephew to warn my brother Pip and inform the rest of the family. Then John arrived with his partner John Thompson; we could only hug one another. They made more tea, taking my now-cold mug away – containing tea made long ago, it seemed, when the world had been a very different place.

It was a long time before I finally got through to Hamish. His phone had been engaged because he'd been on the internet.

'Hamish,' I said, 'I am so sorry, sit down – I've got bad news.'

His relaxed manner changed in an instant.

'What is it?'

'I'm sorry, Mish, but Kirsty has been killed by a powerboat. I'm so sorry you are alone. The boys are okay.' I don't remember what, if anything, was said after that. All I know is that my other child, grown-up as he was, was left alone to grieve.

Before long, Denise arrived, prepared to stay overnight, and the two Johns left, promising to return the following day and to keep in touch by phone. Steve Lillywhite, Kirsty's ex-husband and father of her boys, rang from New York sometime in the early hours to say he was flying out to Cozumel, where the accident had happened. Denise was by now asleep.

Switching on the TV, I caught the first public announcement of Kirsty's death. I remember seeing '1959–2000' on the screen, underneath Kirsty's picture. Both then and in later broadcasts, and for weeks, even months, afterwards, I could not relate the two dates to each other. '1959' was meaningful: it was my daughter's birthday. But '2000'? Although I knew in my head that she had died, it seemed the sort of inscription to be found on headstones or in obituaries, and usually for old people, people of my own age.

I couldn't bring myself to understand it. And it gave rise to the inevitable and futile wish in me that I should have died in her place. And now came the realisation that she would need her mother to make life tolerable for her own children.

The phone started ringing very early. I was told people were gathering outside the house and being politely asked to go away.

Someone called Sarah, who worked at Kirsty's record company, rang regularly to inform me of what was going on. I had rung Ronnie Harris, Kirsty's good friend and, as it turned out, one of those appointed executor for her, just as he was flying out to South Africa on his holidays. He said he would try to deal with things and, somehow, he did.

After the pathologist's initial report (which ended with the words 'this is an accident that should never have happened'), Ronnie arranged for Kirsty's body to be flown back to Croydon immediately after Christmas. But meanwhile there was Christmas itself to get through.

Christmas 2000

There was the Christmas tree, propped against the back door. I let myself into the silent house, Kirsty's house, picking up her Christmas cards as I stepped onto the doormat. I could feel the desolation, the abandonment. Presents left on the office floor were waiting for her to wrap and put them with cards. The gifts she had already decorated had been put to one side. An atmosphere of loss filled every room. The hands that had been busy with so many preparations in the run-up to Christmas would never return to complete these celebratory tasks. It was a horribly vivid demonstration of a life suddenly cut short.

I put the kettle on and switched on the hall light so that the house might seem a little more welcoming, and waited for the taxi to arrive.

The doorbell rang, and through the glass I saw four figures peering in. I opened the door wide and hugged Louis first, and then Jamie, who winced – he was still recovering from abrasions and bruising to his side. Nobody seemed to want anything and the boys quickly disappeared into the lounge and started to play a game on the computer. James disappeared upstairs and Steve told me a little of what he knew. He said that Louis had cried on the flight home. I hoped this would help him – anything was better than this terrible numb sense of shock that had left us all like automatons.

Hamish came later, and James's mother also arrived from the north. Steve's new partner Patti and their young son arrived a day or so later. Then the boys' friends from Bedales School started coming. I bless the school and the parents for letting their children come and stay over until Christmas Eve and return again later. I am sure their presence was vital to the boys in those early days of their grief. They slept in their bedrooms, which gave them the opportunity to talk if they wished.

The horror was still present in all our thinking and emotions were raw. Endless cups of tea and coffee were made, but many went untouched. I remember making shortbread with Louis and his friend Cosmo – anything to keep us busy. When the biscuits came out of the oven, one of them said, 'Look, I've made a sun! Look at his smiling face,' and sure enough there was a gingerbread man with a grin from ear to ear. I felt like hugging them.

Mutual friends started to arrive. James's brother and the two Johns came over, and we ordered pizza for everyone, squashed around the dining table. It seemed right to me that all these people should be here. I am sure Kirsty would have wanted it.

Their love for her and the boys will be something I shall always be grateful for. But the time eventually came, on

Christmas Eve, when everyone rejoined their own families and we were left alone.

The boys put up the tree and decorations without any help from the rest of us, following their mother's example from previous years. Presents were put underneath the tree. Now what? We were all battling individually with tremendous grief and no-one seemed able to decide what we should do next. I took my strength from Kirsty, trying to imagine what she would want.

'Why don't we all sit around in a circle,' I suggested, 'put the tree lights on, and turn off the main lights? Let's light a candle to Kirsty - she's here with us. And, maybe, each of us in turn, can choose one of her songs.'

Hamish thought he wouldn't be able to do that, but he joined in when the others agreed. Steve was the DJ. We each chose a favourite song as we went round the circle. After we'd finished, I commented on the quality of the sound. My own CD player, ancient and noisy, had recently packed up and we'd been using Kirsty's equipment. I was surprised when some of them laughed.

'It's beginning to feel a little bit like Christmas now,' said Jamie, quietly.

As the family members moved about, I think there was a slight easing of tension. Hearing Kirsty sing had been very therapeutic.

Louis was sitting next to me on the sofa. He asked me if I knew what had happened. I said I didn't, but that I would be grateful to hear - but only if he wanted to tell me.

'It will make you sad, Granny,' he said.

'I'm sad already, Louis,' I replied.

It was then that he told me for the first time what had actually happened.

'It was wonderful.' Louis's eyes lit up briefly at the memory of his first scuba dive. 'Mummy loved the moray eels and the shells. I saw a lobster the size of my arm,' and he measured it in imagination against his arm. 'Then it was time to come up.' They had all been given instructions by Ivan, the dive-master, and Kirsty had warned them to follow his rules precisely.

'I was the first to come up,' continued Louis, 'then Mummy, and then Jamie. I looked at Mummy and she smiled and said, "Wow!" And I said, "Great!"'

Jamie had surfaced just as a warning shout alerted all four divers. Kirsty, with her back to the danger, turned her head to see the powerboat almost upon them. Louis said it was travelling at high speed and high enough out of the water for its propellers to be visible. Kirsty managed to push Jamie and Louis out of the way before the boat struck her. She saved their lives. Louis turned around and followed in the wake of the boat.

'I was swimming in Mummy's blood. I heard Jamie calling out, "Where's Mummy? Where's Mummy?" I told him not to look. "Don't look, Jamie! Get back to our boat, look the other way!"'

That was all I could take in at the time. I was to find out later that Guillermo Gonzalez Nova, one of Mexico's wealthiest businessmen, was the owner of the powerboat, and had been on board with his two grown-up sons. Witnesses later told me that my grandsons' cries of distress were clearly heard as they were left bobbing in the water with their mother's body. It was others who called for assistance: the first to do so was the captain of a fishing boat who had tried without success to divert the course of the powerboat. I thanked Louis for telling me, and we sat together for a while. It was to be several years into our investigation before I heard how the boys had been left alone, ignorant of what was going on.

Kirsty's partner James had stayed behind to do some reading at their rented accommodation and, having been under the impression there had been a minor accident, he took the car to the harbour. When he arrived he was not allowed to go too close to the water's edge. No one would answer his questions as to what had happened, and in desperation he had got out of the car and screamed, 'What the hell is going on? Why doesn't anyone tell me something?' Hearing his voice, the boys suddenly ran into his arms, telling him that Kirsty had been killed, and Jamie cried, 'What will become of us now?'

James took them home – but still no one came to tell them anything at all. (Presumably, it was at this point that Guillermo Gonzalez Nova was busy sending for his lawyers from Mexico City to fly in and give evidence on his behalf. Ivan, Kirsty's diving master – not being a wealthy 'Don' – had to wait over 24 hours before being allowed to give his evidence.)

It was now almost midnight on Christmas Eve, 2000. Soon it would be Christmas Day, and I dreaded it. I looked for the large turkey we always had, thinking to prepare it for the oven and was surprised to find a box containing a smaller bird than I'd expected. It turned out that the butcher had changed the order after hearing the news. I went to bed. This turkey would only need a couple of hours at most.

The presents under the tree were handed out, as usual, at around ten o'clock on Christmas morning. I had two presents from Kirsty. The first was a large box which turned out to be a new portable hi-fi system. So *that* was why everyone had laughed the previous night: she had decided to replace my defunct machine and the boys had known about it. Her other present was a pair of non-slip socks for my tiled kitchen floor.

The television channels played 'Days', over and over again, in Kirsty's memory and I felt comforted to know that other people cared. Somehow we got through the day, pulled our crackers, briefly wore the silly paper hats and raised a glass to Kirsty. Afterwards everyone disappeared, perhaps to try to catch up on their sleep.

Days

On Boxing Day morning my old friend Joan Littlewood, godmother to both Kirsty and Hamish, came to see us. We had first met when I visited the Theatre Workshop company, which she and Ewan MacColl had founded – as its director and playwright respectively – in 1946. Both were fascinated by Rudolf Laban's ideas on movement, and had written to Laban himself, asking if he might spare someone to train their actors. As his assistant, Laban asked me to visit the company. Joan and Ewan had been briefly married before the war, but when I met them, Joan had begun an enduring relationship with Theatre Workshop's business manager, Gerry Raffles, and Ewan was unattached. He and I fell in love, and were married in April 1949.

Joan talked in typical fashion about everything except the accident – that was too hard for her to confront. She brought me a beautifully bound book on French dance. I knew that the book represented everything she felt unable to say in words. She had always, whenever possible, been there for Kirsty during her childhood, and had later chosen to spend a period of convalescence with Kirsty and Steve. Now 85 years old, she looked frail. I encouraged her to have a snack and a glass of wine, and then Steve offered to drive her home. By the time he returned, the boys' friends were back for an overnight stay – I think they had organised a visiting rota among themselves.

Musician friends came and went over the next few days, during which the phone seemed to ring constantly – Sarah, from the music company, Ronnie, Kirsty's friend and executor from South Africa, the funeral directors and crematorium, friends, many from overseas and an engagement in Chicago that had had to be cancelled. There were many loving letters and cards that had to be answered and many more, I'm afraid, that weren't. The postman handed me his own bouquet of flowers.

January 2001

It was necessary to make preparations for the funeral, and Hamish and I decided to leave most of the details to James, who would know Kirsty's closest friends, particularly those in the music world. We were able to help with relations and family friends who had been in constant touch over the years. It was during this time that I was informed that Kirsty's body had been brought back to a funeral parlour in Croydon. With Kirsty's co-executors Kieran and Annie, who were also the boys' godmothers, I made the journey from my home in Ealing to Croydon on a cold, wet, dreary January day.

I went in alone. There lay my beautiful daughter, with her red hair surrounding her unmarked face. I felt the tears stream down my cheeks. As I gazed at the still figure, so unnaturally silent, I begged for a miracle, hoping for those lovely eyes to open and for her smile to return to me. But her spirit had flown elsewhere. I talked quietly to her, as I had done so many years before and in the silence of the room I promised to look after her boys and to do my best to take care of things. I told her how much she was loved. Touching her hands gently, and kissing her for the last time, I left the room.

On the journey back I vowed to find out the truth about this accident 'that should never have happened'. Stupidity and recklessness had cheated my daughter of a full life. She would never see the sons she loved so much grow into manhood. I had no idea then that my quest for the truth would come to involve both the British and Mexican governments and thousands of people from around the world.

Kirsty's funeral took place on Friday, 5 January 2001 at Mortlake Crematorium. The cars arrived, we took our places, and as the drivers moved off, I remembered my visit two days earlier to the funeral parlour and realised that this was the last farewell.

Days

The queue outside the chapel stretched down the path and out of sight. These silent figures seemed momentarily motionless to me, as if in a Lowry painting. And I felt for them, as their grief-stricken faces turned towards us. A friend of Kirsty's – not a musician, just a good friend who had always been a treasured guest at her parties – was sobbing uncontrollably inside the chapel and I tried to comfort him and put my arms around him, but I was somehow unable to cry myself. I just gave what help I could.

The chapel was full, as expected, and outside its open doors stood many more. I remember seeing Sasha, an old playmate of Kirsty's, who had come with her new baby. The coffin area was decorated with fairy lights and Kim and Lesley, Ealing florists, had been there very early, arranging exotic blooms from warmer climes. In the centre, by contrast, was placed a bunch of sweet-smelling freesias. I had asked for them specially. Years before, when Kirsty and I were living in Selsdon, I had attempted to make a small rockery with alpine plants. Each year the freesias would grow among them, and I would weed them out and put them somewhere else, only to be surprised to find them springing up again. Kirsty told me, much later, that she had always put the freesias back – they were her favourites.

The first piece of music was Fauré's 'Requiem'. Kirsty had loved this piece, and at the age of about 12 had put a note on the record sleeve that she wanted it played at her funeral. We wanted someone who could talk about Kirsty with some understanding and, after speaking to her friends, Glen Colson recommended a humanist officiant to take the part played by religious figures in traditional ceremonies.

Kirsty's friend Ronnie Harris also spoke. He said that Kirsty had always given a percentage of her earnings to charity and always checked the annual accounts. He had a collection of toy frogs and wherever she travelled, she always managed to return with a new one for him. I had recorded my own contribution on tape, a memory of Kirsty's childhood, when she had insisted on feeding foxes and badgers, and this recording was played. Hamish, much more bravely than me, spoke live but couldn't finish his tribute. The Beach Boys' 'Good Vibrations' was played.

In a moving address, James spoke of their love, quoting Tennyson's lines:

''Tis better to have loved and lost

Than never to have loved at all.'

'All I have are photos, records, memories,' wrote James:

but mine are so strong that they're burning a hole through my head and my heart. We promised each other we would be together until the very end, that we would never break each other's hearts. Well, my heart is broken, Kirsty: the only promise of yours that somebody else broke for you. And I know how angry you are because I can still feel you inside me, but I know you died safe in my love for you – knowing you were cherished and admired and most of all loved completely by me and the boys.

I want to be anecdotal, but there are too many and this is too hard. I'll just read what I wrote in my Valentine's card to you last year. 'Kirsty, I love waking up with you (like now). I love going to bed with you. I love holding you, touching you, being fiercely protective of you, being proud of you, being part of your life. I love you with everything I am and everything I hope to be. Yours always, James.'

I'll leave Kirsty to tell you how she felt about me. This song was the last she wrote, and the only one we ever wrote together. I'll end by saying that no matter how many years go by, I'll always love you, Kirsty. You were the one for me, and I the one for you.

Kirsty's recording of 'Good For Me', with James on the saxophone, was then played, reinforcing in music our sense of that loving relationship as words alone could not. The ceremony ended with 'Remember Me' by the Blue Boy Band.

After the service, as I looked at the flowers outside, a line of people formed, wishing to shake my hand and offer words of comfort. Among the many faces in the line, I seemed to recognise one elderly gentleman in particular, but could not put a name to him. When he came up to greet me, however, I realised with a shock that it was my own brother Pip. Then 84 years old, he was wearing a thin summer's suit, having just disembarked from a Saga cruise ship a few hours before. I think Hamish, James and I were all operating on autopilot.

Back at home, we had arranged for a marquee to cover the back of the house and part of the garden. There were many guests I didn't know - mostly people working in the music industry - and there were also many guests that James didn't know, such as old family friends, and so on. There was such a strong sense of belonging, however, that many introductions and a good number of friendships were forged that day. I was surprised to see the actress June Brown among the crowd. When we shook hands, she told me she and Kirsty had once worked together.

The long and difficult day came to an end. We had done our best, but I knew we had also been sustained by the love and generosity of so many of Kirsty's friends. Meeting and talking with them, sharing stories and even a few jokes, was a very healing experience. I think we must all have slept a little better that night.

April 2006

Five years after Kirsty's death, when my grandsons had left school, I asked them where they would like to see their mother's ashes scattered. 'Cuba,' they replied, a country she had loved and had visited many times, taking the boys with her on two occasions. And so at last in April 2006, a small group of us went to Havana on our special pilgrimage – Kirsty's partner James, her brother Hamish, her son Louis, then 19, and my old friend Denise. Kirsty's close musician friends Pete Glenister and Dave Ruffy – who had worked with her on *Tropical Brainstorm* and knew of her great love for the island – also joined us with their wives. I also invited Nigel Reeve from EMI, who had worked so hard to put together the 2005 anthology of Kirsty's music, *From Croydon to Cuba*.

As the boat travelled out to sea for a short distance and then drew parallel to the distant Havana coastline, we were suddenly aware that we were being followed by a flying fish, which caused great excitement among the otherwise silent crew. Flying fish had never been seen in that area before. We were all of us conscious that the cover art of Kirsty's last CD, *Tropical Brainstorm*, had featured a flying fish under a sunny sky and over turquoise waters. We all felt that she was with us. A voice whispered in my ear: 'Granny, how much further do we have to go? I don't like boats.' It was then that I realised how truly courageous Louis had been to come out with us on this boat.

The boat came to a stop. I said a few words, and as the close family scattered her ashes into the sea, her friend Omar played a piece he had specially written for Kirsty on his violin. Pete and Dave were wearing the Havana shirts Kirsty had bought them. Louis spent a long time looking down into the water and then turned to me with a glowing smile on his face. With this sudden change of mood he had become more relaxed as he tried to explain that he had seen an extraordinary vision. I think it affected him profoundly and I am sure it is an experience he will treasure for the rest of his life. The rest of us were strangely comforted by the flying fish, and our dark mood lightened a little. The gentle breeze, blue sky and warm sun on the way back encouraged us to reminisce over happier times with Kirsty and on reaching the shore we raised our glasses to her and her shimmering, flying spirit.

Chapter One

Innocence

1959-1963

'Mummy, was I born in Octember or Noctover?'

<small>KIRSTY MACCOLL TO JEAN MACCOLL, 1963</small>

The glorious Indian summer of 1959 came to an end late in the Saturday afternoon of 10 October, when I remember hearing the rumble of thunder. It heralded the birth of my baby and by early evening I was the proud mother of a beautiful eight-pound baby girl. I had already chosen a name: Kirsty. I asked the nurse to be sure to put the name band on her immediately, but I needn't have worried: there was no mistaking the soft, reddish down on her head.

That evening our doctor friend Arron dropped in to admire the new arrival and report back to Hamish. Ewan visited the following day. After a difficult few years when he was in denial over his true feelings – wanting to work in the folk-song world after giving up the theatre, but at the same time wanting to save our marriage – he and I had become reconciled. We planned a future together, and I became pregnant. But Ewan had struggled with his conflicted feelings, as became clear when Peggy Seeger gave birth to his son in early 1959. Now committed to an American tour with

1

Peggy and their baby, he made plans to return to the three of us after the tour. I was not optimistic, however, and so it proved. After a brief stay, we separated for good. I knew that events had overtaken him, and I had to get on with my new life.

My next visit was from the three Rapoport families. The three brothers – Wolf, Arron, and Michael Rapoport – were all doctors in the same practice; I sometimes think of them as the Marx Brothers!

Ewan and I had got to know Arron and his wife Sylvia before we moved to Croydon (they had been at parties where Ewan sang, and Sylvia joined a dance class I was running), and Arron was our own GP for a time.

Later, I also became friendly with Arron's elder brother Wolf and his wife Annie and their children Tosh (short – sort of – for 'Patricia'), Judy and David. David was Hamish's age and they went to grammar school together (and he was later Hamish's best man) and Tosh and Judy babysat for me regularly. Kirsty was a great favourite with all of them. Linda (Arron's younger brother Michael's daughter) was Kirsty's age and they were later at primary school together.

The hospital decided to send me home after three days and Ewan's mother said she would like to stay with me until he came back from his tour. Hamish, now nine years old, was thrilled to have a little sister and was very helpful fetching and carrying for her. The next morning he sat on my bed covered in spots: chicken pox! Fortunately, the baby was immune, but despite having gone through it myself as a child, I succumbed again a few days later and remained very poorly for several more.

So when visitors arrived to 'wet the baby's head', glasses were raised to my recovery as well, though I couldn't myself partake. Among the well-wishers was Joan Littlewood, who had rung to say she was hoping to visit with the Irish playwright (and notorious drinker) Brendan Behan. She eventually turned up rather late and somewhat apologetic. It seemed Brendan had celebrated Kirsty's birth at every hostelry on the way to the station, and she had finally left him at the last one, as she thought I would not be best pleased for him to be breathing boozily over my baby – she was right! The large bottle of champagne she brought was nevertheless shared out among my other visitors and made for a proper party atmosphere.

Joan also told me that my actor friends from the Theatre Workshop, Yootha Joyce, her husband Glynn Edwards and Stella and Howard Goorney, had stayed up all night playing cards to pass the time while waiting to celebrate the baby's arrival. Yootha rang the hospital several times that evening asking for news on 'Jean Newlove' and at last wailed in desperation, 'Well, she *must* have had it by now!' It was only when the hospital thought to ask if 'Miss' Newlove might have a married name that the penny dropped.

Hamish and I recovered over the following weeks and life took on a daily routine. When the local nurse called in to see how we were getting on, she took one look at Kirsty and exclaimed, 'Oh, she's a redhead!' then sought to reassure me by adding, 'Never mind, dear. They're *all* nice.'

Ewan had made noises about the two of us getting back together after his trip and while I would have wanted us to put recent traumatic months behind us, I had few expectations of a future together – after all, while I had just given birth to his daughter, he had a child with Peggy. Though part of me felt sorry for him, torn between two young families, I knew that events had overtaken him and I had to get on with my new life. In a single year I had lost the three most important men in my life: my father had died, my husband Ewan had left me and my spiritual mentor, the great choreographer and theorist of dance Rudolf Laban, died in 1958.

• • •

I can't remember a time when I did not want to dance. At the age of seven, taking my first ballet examination in 1930, I was offered a scholarship by the celebrated international dancer Espinosa. Then retired, he was running his own ballet school in London. However, my parents thought I was too young to leave home and were also concerned about my wider education. I continued with my dance classes in the local area and at the same time started reading all about the subject in the public library. I worked my way through the classical ballet section, where I learned about the great Bolshoi. I decided I should learn Russian with a view to visiting that country one day; I only managed to get as far as mastering the alphabet.

Then I came across a book on 'modern' dance and first encountered the name of Rudolf Laban. It seemed that he was the founder of an entirely new dance form that eschewed tutus and block ballet shoes and that his ex-pupil, Kurt Jooss, ran his own modern dance company and had just won an award in Paris for his great piece of anti-war choreography, *The Green Table*. Laban was also described as a crystallographer, artist, architect, dancer and philosopher. I had to learn more about this man and his type of dance at the earliest opportunity.

The outbreak of war in 1939 seemed to put paid to my plans. I was then 16, and my brother Pip was in the British Expeditionary Force in France and soon to be evacuated from Dunkirk. One year later, I heard that Jooss was living in Cambridge. It was too good an opportunity to miss, and I successfully petitioned him for an audition. He invited me to join the company as a student dancer.

It seemed that the company would attempt to go abroad. I spoke to my father, who advised me not to take up the offer for two reasons. One was that the war was going badly for Britain and plans could change without warning; many foreigners were being interned. Secondly, within a year I would have finished my Higher Certificate and could finish school. Hopefully, things might have improved by then. And so I took his advice.

I remembered that my father had himself won an art scholarship as a boy, which he had similarly been unable to take up, through no fault of his own. As a young man he had worked in Paris for many years, spending his spare time watching and learning from the artists there. My mother was also living in Paris, where she was working as a nurse. They used to meet in the Parc Monceau and in due course became engaged and got married before returning to England soon after the start of the First World War.

In the spring of 1941, I heard that Laban himself was staying at Dartington Hall in Devon, the guest of Dorothy and Leonard Elmhirst. During his convalescence from one of many bouts of illness, he met FC Lawrence, a trustee of the Dartington estate. Lawrence, a factory consultant and engineer, had become fascinated by Laban's movement theories, and suggested that Laban should apply his theories of movement to the war effort and increase production in industry. Many women had taken over heavy work from their menfolk. A creative partnership had been formed. I travelled to Dartington, danced for Laban and he asked me to train with him and become his assistant. Third time lucky!

I became a pioneer in helping women improve their skills and increase production. At the end of the war, Laban received a letter from a young woman who said she was a great fan of his work. Her name was Joan Littlewood. She wondered whether he might be able to recommend someone to come and train a company of young actors in movement, someone who would be both a performer and a choreographer. Laban, knowing that my ambition was to work in theatre, recommended me, and suggested I visit them on a part-time basis.

After the dreadful war years, it was a fascinating experience for me to return to dance professionally and work with other artists. I discovered that the company was called Theatre Workshop, and met its founders, Ewan MacColl and Joan Littlewood, the company's playwright and director respectively. I was soon required full time, and went with Laban's blessing.

I also made discreet enquiries about the playwright's availability. It seemed that he and Joan had married when they were both 19, but the marriage had not lasted more than a few months and Joan now had an enduring relationship with Gerry Raffles, the company's business manager. Ewan was unattached! We married in April 1949.

Ewan was born of Scottish parents in Salford, near Manchester and was their only child. His mother often had to support the family because of his father's ill health due to asthma. Ewan was greatly influenced by his father's politics: he was a staunch trade unionist who frequently found himself on strike for better conditions and was consequently a thorn in the flesh of the management. I never got to meet him, but Joan told me that he was a very good singer of traditional Scottish songs and an extremely popular figure with his colleagues. As a child, Ewan learnt much of his father's repertoire.

Ewan left school at 14 and went through a variety of jobs. I don't imagine he was cut out for any of them. Like me, he spent hours in the public library catching up on his reading, starting (as he told me) with 'B' for Balzac, and gradually working his way through the alphabet. I have no idea if he got to the end (or what happened to the 'A's, for that matter) but he was exceptionally well-read.

At around the same time, he became involved with agit-prop

theatre, the European movement that disseminated a socialist message through theatre. Often using the back of a lorry for a stage, the young left-wingers acted to as many local audiences as possible.

It was during this period in the 1930s that Ewan started writing, and not surprisingly, songs were included to drive home the message. A later fairly regular source of income was as an actor in Manchester's BBC radio programme, *Children's Hour*.

By the time Joan Littlewood arrived in Manchester from London, Ewan had assembled a group of dedicated and fairly experienced performers. I think that Joan herself had taken on some acting roles at the BBC before meeting him. Together they planned a theatre based on the great popular theatres of the past, where playwrights such as Aristophanes, Shakespeare and Molière produced plays dealing with the dreams and struggles of the people. The new plays would be fast-moving, with singing and dance-movement as an integral part of the action. Lighting and sound would meld into the whole, operated by the very best technicians. The cast would train daily in movement and dance and the company would build their own sets and make the costumes. There would be no 'stars' in the cast.

A start was made in Kendal in the Lake District – not exactly ideal for a people's theatre, but the rehearsal premises were cheap. The company soon disbanded because of the outbreak of war, but immediately peace was declared, Ewan and Joan sent out a rallying call to the company members, while Gerry Raffles looked for a permanent 'home'. Only one thing was missing: the actors needed movement training, and Joan, hearing that Laban was in Manchester, lost no time in writing to him.

Looking back, it seems a strange coincidence that the three of us had all refused scholarships. Ewan was given the opportunity to study singing in Italy; Joan refused the Slade. Luckily, I was finally able to accept Laban's offer, which eventually led me to join the Theatre Workshop company.

By 1958 Ewan and I were living in London with our eight-year-old son Hamish, having moved down from Scotland with the company in 1952. It had been a controversial move, but financial problems and continual touring had taken their toll. Then we heard about a derelict theatre in London's East End available at a peppercorn rent. We were tempted by the sound of it, the Theatre Royal. Some of our company thought we were 'selling out' and left. Ewan agreed with them and left the company after the move south, while I stayed on. He worked with Humphrey Lyttleton and Alan Lomax in the BBC's *Ballads and Blues* radio series but in order to start a new career using all his previous theatre experience, Ewan needed the help of a trained musician. A young backpacker, Peggy Seeger, arrived from America in 1955 – and immediately fell in love with him. Ewan admitted that he was flattered (he was twice her age) by the trained musician.

After a difficult few years when Ewan was in denial, it was me who made the decision to part. Ewan would not hear of it. We were temporarily reconciled and made plans for our future together. I became pregnant, my baby due in late 1959. In March that year, however, I heard that Peggy herself had given birth. Our marriage ended.

•　　•　　•

When Kirsty was about three months old, in early 1960, I went back to work and started rehearsing *Fings Ain't Wot They Used T'Be* at the Theatre Royal at Stratford East. It was a long journey from Croydon and back, but Kirsty was an excellent traveller and spent most of the time asleep. She lay in a carry cot in the wings when I was working onstage. By now her hair was beginning to curl and was a lovely russet-gold colour. (She was lucky in later life not to suffer the perennial fate of redheads: her skin tanned, but did not burn.) Someone in the cast – it may have been Victor Spinetti, or else our musical director Lionel Bart – nicknamed her 'Our Reet', after that other glamorous redhead Rita Hayworth.

Following his return from the latest tour, Ewan visited us, on average, once a week. From the very first, though, he never made a single mention of his other family: it was as though he were a sailor between ports and whenever he spoke of his work he always did so in the first person singular. This behaviour, which I happily accepted, persisted for several years. Indeed, I only knew that he and Peggy Seeger had another child when noticed a little boy of four or five years old sitting in the passenger seat of Ewan's car when Kirsty was about nine.

Kirsty was a very sociable child, enjoying her stayovers at Joan's flat in Blackheath, or visiting my mother in the Midlands. (I still hadn't told her of my marriage breakup because she was still grieving over the loss of my father.) Nor was there any shortage of babysitters from among the Rapoport family – Wolf's children Tosh and Judy being in their early teens when Kirsty was born. I remember my brother coming over to see his new niece one day and teasing her by taking her bowl from the high chair and pretending to go away with it – but the joke was on him. Although Kirsty must have been hungry, there were no tears. Instead, she looked at him with a wide-eyed and serious expression which I can only describe as 'weighing the strange man up'. Suitably ashamed, he returned the bowl, but she continued to observe him with solemn curiosity.

Ewan's visits were usually at weekends, when I would make Sunday lunch. This arrangement became a routine which seemed to suit him and I went along with it as much for

Hamish's sake as anything. In the summer of 1961 Ewan told me he had some royalties due to him in Poland but that he couldn't get them out of the country since (according to the powers that be) 'owing to the exchange rate, it would undermine the economy of the country'. We had both worked in Warsaw in 1955 and had become friendly there with George, an Englishman with a Polish wife. Ewan suggested that I should accept their offer of hospitality and take a holiday with the children, using the Polish royalties as funds. With the money we were able to travel first class by train via Holland and East Germany, stopping over in Berlin and taking the night train from there to Jelenia Góra near the Karkonosze mountains on the Czechoslovak border. Armed with all the necessary visas and passports – or so I thought – we set off from Victoria.

We had a leisurely breakfast in Holland, and Kirsty enjoyed herself greatly. She attracted attention, I think, because she smiled back when people smiled at her, and showed no shyness – sizing them up as she had done my brother. In Berlin we were met by an actress from Bertolt Brecht's Berliner Ensemble and taken to a flat to await the arrival of other members of the company. As it was such a nice day and there was a park nearby, we were asked if we would like to go for a walk and I took Kirsty in her pushchair. She saw an elderly man pushing an empty wicker pram and leading a child rather older than herself by the hand. Without a word, Kirsty got out of her pushchair, crossed over to the stranger and climbed into the wicker pram. He smiled and pretended to go off with her, but Kirsty remained unfazed as the distance increased and equally unfazed when she was at last returned to her nearest and dearest.

That evening there was quite a celebratory dinner before we had to catch our midnight train to the border town of Görlitz. Kirsty was the centre of attention, as usual, looking on with interest, always smiling and seeming to enjoy the company. When it was time for us to leave, the whole party said they would see us off, and as the train pulled out under a starlit sky their voices rang out, 'Goodbye, Kirsty! Come again!', gradually fading into the distance until we could hear them no more.

We had reserved our apartment, but it was no longer first class. An apparently friendly conductor came in to check our tickets, and told me that I needed a transit visa as well as a tourist visa, so I bought one and then settled the children down for the night. This transit visa was to cost me dear on the return journey. The night was freezing cold and I piled clothes over the children and shivered in my summer dress. Just as I was dropping off to sleep the train came to sudden stop and there was George, our host, banging on the window – 'Only two minutes before it leaves!' I grabbed children, pram and clothes and lugged our huge suitcase onto the platform just as the whistle announced the train's departure.

George lived in a spacious farmhouse called *Owczy Dwor* (or 'The Sheep-House'). As well as being a writer, he kept chickens and sheep. He wrote during the day and his wife translated his work into Polish. Most of his publications were about English history. Hamish loved his library and soon found a copy of Arthur Ransome's *Swallows and Amazons* to keep him happy. George and his wife Anna had two daughters, Sybill and Cricky. Cricky was more or less the same age as Hamish, Sybill about three years older. As George's Polish was poor, both children were brought up bilingual and spoke perfect English. Summoned to breakfast on our first morning, the three of us went into the dining room where I put Kirsty into a high chair. She noticed two visitors, a young married couple called Bronka and Gidek. For some reason bursting out laughing at Gidek, she pointed to him and said, 'Oh boy!' None of us could explain this but from then on, and for many years, Gidek was known to us all as 'Oh Boy'.

We had a marvellously relaxing time collecting wild strawberries, swimming in a little pool and enjoying the company of the other guests. When the time came for Bronka and Gidek (alias Oh Boy) to leave, he gave me a note with a telephone number on it and told me if I ever came to Warsaw to ring them. I thanked them but couldn't imagine an occasion when I would use it. I put the scrap of paper in my blouse pocket.

Finally, with all the other guests gone, it was our turn to leave, but George had a surprise in store for us. Instead of the long train journey to Poznań we had expected, he now offered to drive us there himself, promising a picnic on the way. I put some paper napkins, together with a glass bottle of Ribena in a small bag which George, in holiday mood, slung into the car rather too forcefully. Imagining the worst, my heart sank, but there was no time to waste – the picnic basket was put in the boot, Anna rushed out issuing final instructions to her children, got into the car, and we were off. The countryside was at its best and we sat under the shade of some trees at the edge of a vast forest to have our lunch – a splendiferous affair indeed!

We arrived in Poznań barely ahead of the Moscow to Hook of Holland train, and Anna insisted that we took the remainder of the picnic with us. Our train departed as quickly as it had arrived. The sleeper compartment was spacious and extremely comfortable. I prepared the top bed and tidied up our cases before relaxing with Kirsty. Hamish meanwhile discovered that the restaurant car sold chocolate. With almost our last Polish coins, he bought a cheap bar, returning in triumph at having negotiated the transaction. I was looking forward to a glass of hot tea later served by an attendant from the *samovar* – a kind of Russian hot drink urn – installed at the end of the carriage.

We arrived at the East German frontier amid a lot of noise and banging of doors as the guards came on board demanding to see our passports, visas and other documents. George had heard on the radio that the Cold War had suddenly heated up but he was sure that I would not be affected. He was wrong.

Unlike the Poles, the German guards and police were curt and officious. Although my German wasn't perfect, I understood that I was somehow missing an important piece of paper. The passports and tourist visas were in order, but 'Where are your transit visas?' I showed him the document I had bought on the incoming journey but this turned out to be only a one-way visa. Without a return visa, I would have to get off immediately.

I said I was willing to buy the necessary visa, as I had done before, but this was apparently impossible: they were only issued on entering the Eastern section. The guard tried to intimidate me, ordering me to leave the train then and there. Annoyed at his manner, I protested that we weren't going to set foot on East German soil since we were merely travelling through his country. Even though my German was poor, there was no mistaking his determination to get us off. A fine was incurred for every minute the train was delayed. He demanded I left the compartment immediately; my luggage would be seen to 'later'. And have it disappear along the German–Polish border? No thank you!

Hamish was meanwhile being very helpful, hauling a rucksack onto his back as I refused point blank to leave the train until they allowed us to take our luggage. No help was forthcoming from the guards, who looked on impassively as we struggled to collect our things and install ourselves on the platform. I was taken aback to see my fellow passengers pressing against the windows of their compartments – perhaps they thought some spies had been caught.

I rather hoped that Kirsty would be so upset and look so forlorn and unhappy that the senior guard would change his mind – but there she was, smiling happily and waving from her pushchair to all the passengers, who now even started to wave back at her. Had the question been put to the popular vote, Kirsty would certainly have won our case hands down – but then free elections were scarcely an East German speciality.

The train slowly started to move on, leaving us stranded with our luggage on the platform. We were taken to a large and hastily erected tent on another platform, with a Red Cross over the entrance – presumably prepared for refugees like ourselves. Obviously, more 'truants' were expected. I asked if I might phone my friends in East Berlin, or indeed anyone in authority, for help. This request was met with a blunt refusal. The tent already had one guest: a kindly Polish farmer. I gathered he had been on a group passport, hoping to visit relatives in Holland but had also fallen foul of the transit visa problem. We sat there for several hours until we were told to collect our things and board a train for Warsaw – argument proved futile.

Hamish's eyes were by now a little watery, and so I smiled at him encouragingly, gave him a hug and said, 'This is a *real* adventure.' Luckily, he didn't know how far east we were going. We found the first-class carriages where I invited our Polish friend to join us. Then it seemed time for a banquet. I spread out the picnic food, Hamish's chocolate, and some other delicacies. Looking for Kirsty's Ribena I realised my earlier fears had been justified, but at least the paper napkins had soaked up all the spilt juice. The Polish gentleman offered me his cigarettes. It was actually quite a happy occasion, despite there now being no sleeper accommodation.

At some point in the early hours of the morning a Polish ticket collector arrived on his rounds. I knew very well what he was telling me – that I was going in the wrong direction with the wrong tickets and that the fine alone would be double the cost of the ticket. But apart from two little coins, I didn't have any zlotys and so smiled in blind incomprehension. After a time he gave up.

I suddenly remembered Oh Boy's note and realised I was still wearing the same blouse. I felt inside the breast pocket and there was the telephone number.

We arrived in Warsaw at around 7am. Porters rushed to help me but quickly disappeared when the ticket collector told them I had no funds. Hamish shouldered the big rucksack and between us we managed the suitcase. I rang the number and someone answered in Polish. All I said was, 'Oh Boy!' and like a password it solved our dilemma. He promised to be there as soon as he could. His famous last words were: 'Don't go away.' With a bag full of nappies, a pushchair, luggage and two small children, I wasn't going anywhere.

We stayed with Gidek and Bronka for three days while we waited to find out what to do and had time to go around the restored Jewish ghetto and see some of the sights I remembered from my previous visit a few years before. Kirsty was on baby-reins some of the time, much to the amusement of the Poles, who had never before seen such a thing. While we enjoyed our enforced tourism, Oh Boy arranged for us to go to the German Embassy to procure the required documents.

There was one man in the room for our interview, sprawling back in his chair with his feet on his desk. I disliked his superior attitude and his apparent enjoyment of my predicament. Oh Boy addressed the man politely, but whatever it was that he replied, it immediately changed the atmosphere. Oh Boy suddenly became every inch the aristocratic Polish officer, drawing himself upright and making a curt remark that seemed to drive home a point. When we got outside I asked him what had happened. He told me not to worry: he had merely reminded the gentleman that he was a guest in his country (with an emphasis on the word 'guest'). All the Poles I met treated such Teutonic precision about transit visas with equal disdain and humour, saying that if they had been so rigid, I might have ended up, through no fault of my own, a stateless person.

Oh Boy saw us off from Warsaw station. It was a comfortable compartment and the seats slid down to form a bed. Hamish and I studiously ignored those getting on the train, hoping to keep our compartment to ourselves, but we underestimated Kirsty's charm as she smiled at a young man waving to her through the glass door. He entered apologetically, saying he had simply fallen for my daughter. He told me he was a school teacher and after amusing Kirsty for several hours, he got off the train, leaving me his address.

This time round, the German and Dutch borders were passed safely and we pulled into Rotterdam with time in hand to make the Channel ferry. The rest of our journey thankfully passed uneventfully (except for both children throwing up into the Channel during the crossing).

Autumn came all too quickly in 1961. Hamish started grammar school, we celebrated Kirsty's second birthday in October and I returned part-time to the theatre as a choreographer. Wolf Mankowitz's play *Make Me an Offer* was in production, with Daniel Massey and Dilys Laye in the cast. When it transferred to the New Theatre, Frank Norman's *Fings Ain't Wot They Used T'Be* followed, and then William Saroyan's *Sam the Highest Jumper of Them All*.

Kirsty was meanwhile developing something of a free spirit. My middle-aged baby minder, Suzanne, was very concerned when she took Kirsty to the park and the child ran off such a long way that she had been afraid of losing her. I took Kirsty to the same park, telling her not to run away. When she saw a young priest sitting on a nearby bench with a book on his lap, she toddled over to him, climbed companionably onto the seat beside him and politely asked him what he was reading. Whether he was shy, preoccupied, or simply absorbed in his studies, I just don't know, but he scrupulously ignored her and his eyes remained glued to the book. I went over to take her away.

'Mummy,' she said loudly, looking at his book with great interest, 'this man won't tell me what he is reading.' It wasn't that she was upset at being ignored so thoroughly: she was just curious to know, at the age of two or three, what was interesting him so much in the book.

After being quite poorly with measles, Kirsty developed a chest infection and I rushed her to hospital. I was not prepared to wait and told the probationer she had to fetch the doctor immediately. She picked up the phone, slightly tentatively since she knew that she would be interrupting the doctor's lunch. In a few moments a young doctor came hurrying towards me, wiping his mouth with his hand. He gave Kirsty a quick examination, and then turned to me.

'You have a very sick little girl here,' he said. It was clear what he was trying to tell me, but I refused to acknowledge the implications. I just stood there silently, willing him to do something.

Kirsty was put in an oxygen tent and the nurse kindly found a camp-bed for me in another part of the hospital. I made the short trip to and from Kirsty's bed throughout the night, on one occasion asking her how she felt.

'Fine,' she replied, though I'm not sure she was. But the infection cleared up in due course and she returned home.

I read to Kirsty most days before I left her in the morning and usually left the story at a particularly exciting part, promising to finish it when I got back. When I returned one day and said I would finish reading her the story, Kirsty looked at me with some slight annoyance. 'Well, I've read it now, haven't I?' she said. She was well aware of my ruse, but I don't remember her ever actually being taught to read.

Kirsty's lifelong friend Sasha, the daughter of my friend Denise, would also come over and read to her as she was still confined to bed. She was only four years older than Kirsty and had a wonderful bedside manner, picking up the book and saying 'Well now, where have we got to?' I would arrange a bedside tray of delicacies – little sandwiches, and perhaps a small chocolate cake decorated on the top with crystallised violets. This was to thank Sasha, but I also hoped that Kirsty would eat something, though her appetite was poor and I was lucky if she ate a sandwich.

As I came to collect the tray one afternoon, I overheard the following conversation.

'What does your Daddy do?' asked Sasha.

'He's a folk singer,' replied Kirsty. 'What does yours do?'

'Oh! He's at university,' said Sasha, in a rather lordly manner.

'Yes, I know,' said Kirsty, 'but what will he do when he grows up?'

It was decided that Kirsty should go into hospital for a series of tests, and on one of my visits I was told she could come home the next day. The results would be sent to my GP. As I left a cheerful-sounding Kirsty, I noticed an open window behind her bed and my instinct was to close it for fear of draughts. Not wishing to appear a paranoid parent, though, I did nothing. Next day, as I was parking my car, I saw Judy Rapoport coming down the hospital steps from the ward, tears streaming down her face. She told me she had never seen Kirsty so depressed. It seems she had caught cold and would not now be leaving. She had also been given a grey skirt to wear which made her feel, she said, 'like a grey elephant'. She at last came home a couple of days later, but I did feel guilty about that open window.

Ewan visited as usual during these difficult months, but was unable to offer any practical help. I was pleased that he took Hamish out on trips, but to Kirsty, at this age, he remained a stranger. When he came one day, she even asked, 'Who is this man?'

On my birthday Hamish came home and banged on the front door as he couldn't open it himself: he was carrying a huge bunch of flowers, and a package which seemed to be caught up in his schoolbag. Both were for me. I unwrapped the package, and discovered that it contained a half-bottle of gin. He had gone into the off-licence and said that it was his mother's birthday and the manager recommended the gin. I sometimes wonder if he thought his mother was an alcoholic.

In 1963 I was working on Joan Littlewood's *Oh What a Lovely War* and teaching movement at the East 15 Acting School. Although the journey between Croydon and Stratford East was long, I generally managed to get home in the early afternoon. My mother had moved to live nearby and she and Kirsty got on very well. But there was still a great deal to do. Hamish had out-of-school activities and homework. I would prepare an early evening meal and then get on with the daily domestic chores, washing, ironing and so on.

Hamish would often get hungry again later so I taught him how to cook simple meals for himself. This seemed to work perfectly, and our evenings were frequently filled with the aroma of some new delicacy the chef had cooked up. And when I came into the kitchen in the morning there wasn't even any washing up to do. After a few days of this perfect arrangement, however, I began to notice I was running short of pots and pans – they were nowhere to be found. Then I had the bright idea of looking under Hamish's bed and the mystery was solved!

One day at around this time Joan treated Kirsty and me to the ballet to see *Cinderella*: it was Kirsty's first visit to the theatre. We sat in the front row of the dress circle. Kirsty was very quiet until the interval, and as the lights came up she looked around her with interest. At the start of the second half, when Cinderella was distraught at the thought of losing her prince, a small clear voice pronounced clearly, 'Hamish is a naughty boy.' It had broken the silence in the auditorium and then everybody in the dress circle tried to suppress their laughter. I was about to suggest she might like to leave, but she was happily absorbed in the ballet again.

Joan's birthday was very close to Kirsty's and the three of us were usually together during Joan's celebrations at her house in Blackheath. The singer Alma Cogan was at one of these parties, I remember, which she had attended with Lionel Bart. She was wearing a glittering dress, very tight-fitting at the waist and with a voluminous skirt: Kirsty was most impressed by that dress.

Summer came, and Ewan said there were still further royalties due to him in Poland and suggested we once again take advantage of George and Anna's hospitality. They were looking forward to our visit. Anna had a cook and apart from anything else, I knew it would be a real holiday for all of us, with country walks, collecting wild strawberries – and a huge library with many English books for Hamish to enjoy. He had been disappointed when the new form library in his school opened because he had already read every book in it, so each week he was given money by his teacher to buy an addition on approval. We had all enjoyed our last visit and, politically, things had eased in the last two years – at least as far as travelling was concerned.

When the woman sitting next to Kirsty in our compartment asked her what her name was, she answered, 'Kirsty Anna Louisa MacColl,' and asked the woman's name in return. The reply seemed to be double-barrelled, a mixture of German and Polish, and was quite incomprehensible to our English ears. Giving her a direct look, Kirsty said, rather severely, 'I don't believe you,' leaving the woman in tears of laughter.

This time the journey passed uneventfully and in due course we were once more in Poland, piling out of the train quickly before it moved on. Hamish had his old job back, collecting the eggs each morning and Kirsty picked the cherries and wild strawberries. To Anna's delight, I had brought her two stone-removers for the cherries. Chilled cherry soup was promised for the following day.

That evening we went to bed early, but during the night I was woken by the sound of Kirsty fighting for breath. She looked dreadful and could hardly speak. I sat her up in her cot and alerted Anna and George. We agreed that a doctor was needed urgently but would take quite some time from the hospital in Poznań.

After a long and anxious wait, the doctor examined Kirsty and then asked me if she was allergic to any medication. I didn't know for certain, but thought not. To be on the safe side, she said she would give Kirsty an injection and we would need to wait a few hours. If everything was all right, she would then administer a much larger dose.

She went downstairs for some food and – as I only subsequently learned – told Anna that it was a severe case of asthma, and that I would have many difficult years ahead of me. I had never seen anyone with asthma before, though I knew that Ewan's father had suffered severely from the affliction and had died at 60.

I wondered what I could do to amuse Kirsty. She asked for a story. This was when 'Horatio' was born: a story that was only told when things were really desperate. Later, I secretly came to hate Horatio, knowing that Kirsty only ever asked for him when she was feeling very poorly indeed.

Making it up as I went along, I told her about Horatio, a handsome white horse who lived in the mansion house of a beautiful village and drove a Rolls-Royce. Horatio was the village squire, and his best friend was French, Penelope Poodle. She enjoyed visiting him, and always wore the most beautiful Parisienne hats with flowing veils when she drove out with him. (I gave all the characters their appropriate voices.) Horatio had a cherry tree in his garden and every year the local villagers would come to his open day to pick the fruit and enjoy a wonderful party. The story grew, and in later years she drew pictures of him, and of the other animals in the village (there were no humans), all of whom had names, families and personalities.

Breaking into our story, the doctor now returned, and after an examination decided to give Kirsty the full injection. When I saw the needle I was shocked, the syringe being far larger than any I had seen at home. Kirsty protested at the size, so I suggested we went on with the story and we would both look away. I was told that this injection would keep her well until she got home. She was given vitamins in the shape of crispy little chocolate-flavoured bits which were much appreciated by the patient. She had another day-and-a-half to recover before getting up and we spent the time happily drawing and reading books.

Hamish took Kirsty up the hill to visit some children he had met in a neighbouring house. But within 20 minutes they were back – both white as sheets and spattered with blood. Hamish carried Kirsty into the house. He told me she had fallen and hit her head on a rusty iron gate. I bathed the cut with Dettol and hoped for the best. Shaken though I was by these setbacks, most of all by Kirsty's asthma attack, the rest of our holiday was enjoyable. We toured the countryside around Zakopane, the winter ski resort, where we visited a retired writer and priest. He lived in a beautiful, secluded area close to a large forest and offered to take us all on a day's trek but I quietly declined, indicating Kirsty and saying there was 'a problem' with this plan. She overheard me and immediately spoke up: 'I'm not a problem, I'm a little girl.'

When the time came for us to leave for home, George said he had arranged for us to travel overnight by train instead of the long car journey we had previously made to Poznań. Much as we had all enjoyed it, he thought it would be a safer bet. So midnight saw us in a second-class berth on a Polish sleeper. Cramped though the space was, we slept cosily enough and by morning we were pulling into Frankfurt-an-der-Oder – only to see our connecting train pull out from another platform. We caught another one a couple of hours later to East Berlin, and I was assured we could still make our train in West Berlin. They didn't reckon on the German guards at the entrance to the U-Bahn: the Berlin Wall had gone up in 1961 and the deliberately slow investigation of each traveller meant that even the short journey by tube to West Berlin wasn't fast enough and once again we missed our connection.

Both children were fine after a good night's sleep, but we still had a lot of luggage and Berlin was experiencing a heat wave. I deposited everything but the pushchair and my handbag in left luggage. Impressing on the kindly official that I *must* be on the platform in time for the trans-European express train that evening, I was reassured that everything would be ready.

I had a little 'emergency money' and thought this was as good a time as any to enjoy it. We were in a smart part of Berlin, near the zoo in the Kurfürstendamm district. We came across a very smart, newly renovated hotel for the day. The room seemed palatial: single and double beds, chaises longues, a table and easy chairs. The en suite bathroom was brand new, with white fleecy towels, shower-caps, shampoo and sachets of bath foam. Being the youngest, Kirsty was the first to enjoy these luxuries. Wearing a shower-cap she almost disappeared under the foam. I rang room-service and ordered four Coca Colas and two lagers. They came beautifully chilled.

After our bath we relaxed on our beds with our drinks – but this had to be a day to remember, so Kirsty got a toy tiger which she called 'Benji from Berlin'. (I still have it.) Hamish, our resident DIY expert, chose a Scalextric model to build. We went back to our room and while Hamish worked on the model, Kirsty and I amused one another with stories.

At about five or six in the evening, we all began to feel very hungry. Reluctantly leaving our room for the last time, we went down to the dining room and were shown to our table for three. The children ordered fish and chips and I was delighted to see Kirsty display a healthy appetite and finish her meal. She and I chose ice cream for dessert; Hamish chose crêpe suzette. The trolley rolled its way past the diners, the waiter settling it by Hamish's chair. With a full house of spectators looking on, the waiter played to the gallery. As the flames rose high from the pan, he turned to face his audience, shaking a bottle of liqueur around his head before taking out the cork and liberally splashing it into the pan. A murmur of approval met his antics and he smiled, supplying an encore with another bottle, and finally a third, before placing the plate, by now swimming in alcohol, before my son. I hoped Hamish wouldn't like it; he assured me it was excellent. I asked him only to eat a small portion as I needed him to help with the baggage and I didn't want him to be worse for wear. Regretfully he agreed, but Kirsty had listened in on the conversation: she volunteered to finish the crêpe and swallowed a spoonful before I could stop her. She pronounced it 'very nice'. In desperation, I finished it. They were both right – it was the best I ever tasted.

After settling our bill, we went into the well-lit streets. Passing the famous Gedächtniskirche, recently rebuilt after the Allied bombing, we saw crowds waiting outside, the doors opening every ten minutes to let another lot of visitors come in as the others went out. Before I knew it, Kirsty had gone in with the waiting group and we were just too late. We followed with the next crowd and met up with her inside, standing in front of a new piece of artwork. There was no doubt even then of her independent spirit: unafraid, affectionate and interested in everything.

Once at the station, my kindly official in the left-luggage department waved to me and said that he would bring our luggage to us himself when the time came. He had also asked his wife to escort us to the right platform. We were duly introduced to an elderly smiling woman, walking painfully on swollen feet, whose shoes were distorted by her bunions. My protests were politely turned down and she walked over the bridge with us to our platform. I was slightly concerned not to see my luggage following but she told me 'her man' would bring it in time.

The express was now due, and as it noisily came in, I heard the rattle of a trolley and there was our friend – and our luggage. We packed it all into our sleeping quarters which, like those of our first visit two years before, were spacious and clean. We all stood around on the platform for a while, like some family group. I thanked them profusely for their help. They were all smiles as we shook hands and then embraced one another.

We waved until the train turned a corner and our brief friendship was gone for ever. The beds in our compartment had already been made up and looked very inviting. An attendant came by and asked me for our passports and documents which I was happy to give him, knowing that we would be in Holland by morning. We all slept well – perhaps the crêpe suzette had something to do with it. By the following evening we were back home in Croydon.

A friend of mine recently told me that he had once read Kirsty's contribution to an article about celebrities and their earliest experiences of foreign holidays. In typically forthright fashion, she had said that I had taken her and Hamish to Poland by train because I was afraid of flying. I'm not sure that statement is quite true; or if it is, I might have wanted to modify or qualify it.

I suppose I was, at that time, slightly anxious about the whole business of flying, but that was because of something of a lucky escape earlier in my life when Ewan and I had been offered a flight back from Moscow after I took part in a dance competition. We had refused, since I preferred (or perhaps simply thought it was better form) to travel back with the others in the company by train. By the time we arrived at the Channel port, however, I noticed that many people in the British contingent had bought the newspapers and were crying over what they were reading. It seems that the Aeroflot flight that we would have taken had been due to land in Copenhagen, but had overshot the runway and plunged into the sea, with the loss of the Russian crew and their passengers.

•　　•　　•

Safely back home in England with my children, I brought up my concerns over Kirsty's health with our GP, who referred her to a chest specialist. Over the next few months she had a number of further attacks and was monitored regularly by our doctor and the specialist. It was only after several months, however, that she was formally diagnosed as asthmatic. This was surprising for all of us, as none of my family had ever suffered from the disease. It was then that I remembered Ewan's father.

We nevertheless wondered whether the condition might be psychosomatic: could there be a link with her high IQ and the frustrations this caused her? The consultant found us a psychiatrist and Kirsty took her black-and-white Dalmatian pyjama case to the first appointment. 'That's a nice Dalmatian,' said the psychiatrist to her. 'What do you call it, Kirsty?' Kirsty's voice rang out quite clearly: 'His name is Alfrige Hitcock.' The other patients, who had been silent up till now, began to titter. The psychiatrist was taken aback, and so was I. I had no idea where she had heard that name and she certainly hadn't seen any of 'Alfrige Hitcock's' films. There were a few further visits, each of which ended with Kirsty going to sleep. Later she told me that she had only pretended to go to sleep since that was what seemed to be required. She had really only wanted to get on with other, more important things.

The results of Kirsty's tests were no real surprise to me. I was told she was very bright, which I already knew, and when I pressed them for more information about her asthma attacks, was told that they might ease by the time she was seven years old. (In fact it was much longer.) I would meanwhile simply have to grit my teeth.

Over the next few years she became a regular patient under the care of Mr Norman, head of the asthma clinic at Great Ormond Street Hospital for Children. Kirsty started primary school, but she was only able to attend for three days before once again becoming ill and being rushed to hospital. She didn't return that school year. Indeed, her total attendance during the second year amounted to only three weeks and in the third year three months.

This time, the oxygen tent in the hospital distressed her. A Nigerian couple who had been standing by the cot next to Kirsty's, looking at their beautiful little boy, left silently. This waiting period is so hard; one never gets used to it. I sat next to Kirsty, improvising more adventures for Horatio and his friends until dusk. The little boy with the black curly hair quietly died, the sudden flurry of urgent activity all to no avail.

I moved my chair to a position where Kirsty would only be able to see me and I continued with the story while the dead child in the next cot was laid out. Later, leaving to go home to collect some essential belongings for Kirsty, I saw the little boy's parents dragging themselves so wearily up the stairs to the ward that I wanted to say something, anything. I said nothing, however, afraid of intruding on them; I didn't even know if they had been informed of the news.

That evening, a telephone operator at the hospital gave me a sort of priority on incoming calls. At midnight there was 'no change'. The following morning, Ewan joined me at the hospital and the doctor told us that Kirsty was suffering from asthma and pneumonia: it was 'early days yet'. Both our cars had collected parking tickets. Ewan and I said our farewells and went our separate ways. I sent off an explanation to the car parking authority for both of us; Ewan would never have remembered.

Kirsty's condition slowly improved, and in time she came home. It was clear to me that my theatre work and movement classes at the East 15 Acting School would have to take second place from now on. The children got on very well with my mother, who had recently moved down to Croydon. She was a reliable babysitter but there were occasions when I would ring home on my way to work, learn Kirsty wasn't well and turn round and come home to spend the day trying to amuse her. My mother also had some good ideas, like buying a bag of coloured wooden beads and getting Kirsty to make necklaces and bracelets.

One Christmas many years later, when Kirsty was healthy, successful and herself a mother, I wrote to Mr Norman, a lovely caring man, to thank him for all his help and support during those difficult years. A letter came back in a spidery hand: now semi-retired, he thanked me for my letter, said it was probably one of the nicest presents he could hope to receive and that he remembered Kirsty very well. Rejoicing in her recovery, he also reflected on his less successful cases, adding sadly, 'It's the *failures* you know that haunt one.'

Chapter Two

My Way Home

1963-1968

JEAN: Do go to sleep.
KIRSTY: I can't.
JEAN: Well, count sheep.
KIRSTY: All right. One, two, three... thirty-five... forty.
Oh, there's a sweet little black one. He can't get over
the hedge to join the others. He's running away.
He's going to get... oh, now I've lost count.
JEAN: There aren't any black ones, and they can all
go through the gate.
KIRSTY: The black one couldn't.

<small>BEDTIME CONVERSATION, C. 1965</small>

In the early days of my separation from Ewan and, before my second trip to Poland, I read in the local newspaper that a large area of Croydon, including my road, was due for demolition. The large old Victorian houses and their mature if somewhat unkempt gardens would give way to smart new estates for London commuters.

Numerous architects' sketches showed that the detached properties would be surrounded by communal gardens

31

comprising mostly of lawn and a few carefully arranged shrubs – a 'tasteful' look that would require all the old fruit trees to be cut down and disposed of with the rest of the rubble. One thing was plain: the available properties would be too expensive for me, and I would have to start looking for alternative accommodation for the three of us, near enough for Hamish to travel to his new grammar school. After living in a sizeable flat which, although very difficult to keep warm, had the great advantage of a large garden, I was looking for a smaller place but still with a garden. After weeks of looking at various properties, however, I realised that not only did I not particularly like what was on offer but all the prices were beyond my means. It was time to put Plan B into operation.

I had always dreamed of finding a plot of land on which to build my very own house and this seemed the opportunity I had been waiting for. I went with Kirsty in her pushchair to Croydon Town Hall and asked to look at the large-scale planning maps of the region to find out if there was any vacant land for sale. They were neither entirely helpful nor particularly optimistic and so I started to widen my search, scouring the southern outskirts of Croydon. Whenever I came across a likely piece of land, I would return to the planning department to ask who owned it and whether it was for sale. The regular replies either pointed out that there was no public access, or else there were electrical substations on the site.

After working my way through the first of these maps, I asked if I could look at the adjoining one. It was obvious they were getting tired of my search for land when they told me that the map I wanted was stored in the cellars and they couldn't get it out. However, quite by chance, I bought the local paper on the way home, and there I found an advertisement of a plot of land for sale. I phoned them up, took down the details and within a few hours travelling with Kirsty to Beech Way, an unmade road in Selsdon, about four miles south of the centre of Croydon. Here was the plot of my dreams.

We looked across acres of woodland that dipped into a valley before rising again to the skyline. It was so exciting that we both attempted to walk through the briars for a little way. Kirsty was a willing little companion but very soon we had lost sight of civilisation - our car, the road and a nearby house had all disappeared. With more luck than judgement I eventually found our way back to the car, excitedly returning home to tell Hamish all about it.

We were eventually the owners of an acre of land - now all I had to do was find an architect and see if my small budget would be sufficient to build a house for the three of us. When I took Joan Littlewood to see the land, she told me, in typical Joan style, that she knew just the man for the job. If my long association with her had taught me anything, though, it was to add a smidgen of caution to her wonderfully exuberant remarks - and so it proved.

The design her architect came up with was for a five-storey building that would have completely blocked out the view for the two houses on the other side of the road. Joan had told her architect, Cedric Price, that I needed a studio and this had been designed for the fifth floor: there was a ground floor, a mezzanine, then the children's bedrooms, then my bedroom, and finally my grand fifth-floor studio. He had also proposed under-drive heating, after I had told him of the difficulties with ice in bad weather. Alas, I was not ready for Cedric Price's vision of my future - and nor, more to the point, was my bank balance. I later learned that my neighbours had complained to the planning office. Joan's architect subsequently went to America, where he collected a number of awards.

I was driving with Kirsty through Biggin Hill in Kent one day when we caught a glimpse of a very nice chalet-type house, set back from the road. A large notice announced: Eric Mayne, Architect. Without thinking twice, I turned into his driveway, Kirsty and I got out of the car and we rang the bell. The door was opened by a bearded man. 'I like your house,' I said.

'And I like you,' he replied with a smile. 'Come in.'

I had found my architect.

And it was in this utterly random way that I eventually realised my dream of a warm house with large garden – and the total cost came in at only a fraction of the price of the properties for sale in Croydon. The house was scheduled for completion by May 1965, but in the event it was another four months before we moved in. The three of us, along with our cat Solomon, briefly joined my mother in Croydon.

I found a little time for my own leisure activities. Tosh Rapoport was a willing and reliable babysitter and I would occasionally go out for dinner, but usually preferred to invite friends over. Once a week I would go with a friend to classes in central London to continue my study of the Russian language – a discipline I had imposed on myself as a child, when I thought my ballet studies would take me to Moscow. But the Russian classes stopped abruptly when Kirsty fell ill again. When things temporarily improved, I tried a life class at Croydon Art College. Tosh's brother David joined Hamish in babysitting Kirsty. They got on very well. At the age of twelve, David asked his mother if it was possible for a man to marry a woman ten years younger than himself. Many years later, when both he and Kirsty were each married with children of their own, David and his wife Sandy came to a party Kirsty held for me. When I reminded them of this, Kirsty laughed and turned to Sandy with a single word: 'Jezebel!'

Hamish invited me to a social event at Trinity School – a film show – and we sat together on hard benches to watch Alec Guinness in *Kind Hearts and Coronets*. In the interval between reels, Hamish bought me a cup of tea and a biscuit, and after the show he escorted me home. We had both enjoyed the outing tremendously and his manners had been meticulous. Ewan bought him a motorised go-kart at around this time, and I remember a few exciting rides on it, whizzing round a track in the old school playground.

• • •

The three of us – four, with Solomon II the cat – said our goodbyes to my mother and finally moved into Coombe Cottage, as our new house in Selsdon was to be called, in the summer of 1965. Hamish carried Solomon in his basket and settled him comfortably near the central heating boiler in the laundry room. Meanwhile I carried Kirsty into the house, encouraging her with tales of the foxes and badgers that lived in our new garden. But she was not well enough to respond with her usual enthusiasm. Under normal circumstances this would have been a joyous day and I would have attempted some small celebration to mark the occasion – but Kirsty was clearly unwell, and I began to worry that we were now five or six miles further out from Croydon, and I would need to change to a local GP.

I got her to bed as soon as possible in her new bedroom and was delighted that the house was warm throughout – unlike our old draughty flat. Kirsty lay down facing the large windows that overlooked the garden, which stretched for an acre or so before disappearing into woodland. I left the curtains open so that she could look out, and I talked to her not only about the animals she would be able to see in the morning but also about the stars. My knowledge of astronomy was not great but I could still show her the North Star and the Plough. I also told her about the small shed in our garden which I promised to clear out, and which would be for her use only: she would have to think about what she wanted to put in it.

The bedrooms were on the ground floor, and Hamish and I went upstairs to the lounge to start some unpacking. He was very impressed with his new surroundings. Would Kirsty and I mind spending the night with my mother, he asked casually, so that he and David could have a party there? I thought about it, and agreed – at least someone was in a celebratory mood. It was a couple of weeks before everything was in place and I kept my promise, though I must say I was rather nervous that things might get broken or damaged. In fact, everything went very well: those 60s teenagers all had a good party – and the girls loved playing house, continually wiping up and tidying in the kitchen. I was quite impressed – and quite relieved too.

There is no doubt that Kirsty was frustrated at not being able to explore her new surroundings as much she would have wished. I remember looking at her pale, slight figure, in her blue dressing gown, as she fought for breath. It didn't seem fair that all her friends were outside playing while she had to spend so much time in her bed. I kept reminding myself that Kirsty was physically strong: it was just this crippling asthma that was holding her back. Sitting on the end of her bed, I sensed her weariness and determined to try some gentle encouragement. While eager to learn, she had been disappointed with school. I started to talk about people's talents. Some were good at music, I said, others at mathematics; some could design houses and others became surgeons. Some people were born lucky, with more than one talent, and I told her I thought she was one of them: it was important for her to enjoy trying out anything that interested her. We would get over the asthma eventually, I said; nothing was impossible. I tried to encourage her by telling her about Albert Schweitzer, explaining that he worked as a doctor in Africa but was also a famous musician who toured the world, playing the organ to fund his medical work. This mixture of music and politics, as it turned out, seems to have stuck in her mind. A few years ago I came across an interview she gave in a German magazine where she recalled the story and ended by reflecting, 'I didn't know who the hell Albert Schweitzer was, but I thought, if it's good enough for Albert, it's good enough for me!'

• • •

Kirsty returned to her primary school in September 1965. In her first year at her previous school she had only attended three full days. Mr Norman at the Great Ormond Street clinic wrote to the headmistress of the new school advising her not to send Kirsty out during inclement weather, but the advice of the top consultant in the country was apparently ignored. Kirsty, who had been very keen to go back to school, now became a very reluctant pupil. She seemed extremely nervous and during the car ride and walk to the school gates Horatio came to my aid once more. Again, I promised to carry on with the story on the return journey. When I saw the headmistress I asked her if she had taken note of Mr Norman's letter. She laughed rather unsympathetically and said, '*I* know how to treat these children – they're sent out with a coat on.' I began to realise why Kirsty was so fearful, for she was clearly not ready for the rough and tumble of school life.

Leaving Hamish in charge one night, I attended a parents' evening at the school. Chatting to her form teacher, a middle-aged woman, I found myself listening to her complaint that Kirsty was 'always asking questions'. I sympathised with her, knowing that, if she had a large class, such behaviour might be difficult. I therefore suggested she might ask Kirsty to wait until the end of the lesson and have her questions answered then. I told Kirsty what the teacher had said. I knew she was used to having my complete attention at home, so I asked her if she expected the same from her teacher.

She looked me in the eye and said scathingly, 'Certainly not! If she'd told me exactly what she wanted me to do, I'd do it – but she waffles! Also, if I've been away, she won't give me the book the class is working from until the end of the lesson – so even when I *am* there I don't have the right book!' As far as I could see, Kirsty's description caught the teacher's attitude perfectly.

At the end of her second year in 1966, Kirsty's attendance totalled three weeks. She didn't return as I had lost all confidence in the establishment and it was obvious to me that her well-being was more important than anything else. Without the burden of getting an unwilling child to school I was now able to enjoy her company and introduce her to all sorts of stimuli. We would go into the garden and look at the wild flowers, discover slow worms, enormous snails and, miracle of miracles, at night we had glow worms in the garden near the front door. Kirsty wanted to know much more about these creatures than I was able to tell her, so we would go to bookshops and she was allowed to choose more or less any book that interested her.

She once chose a textbook which was meant for GCSE biology students. I asked her if she was sure that this was the book she really wanted. After all, she was only seven and it was written for 16-year-olds. But no, she assured me that this was the one she wanted. I'm not sure she could follow it all, but I know that it gave her a great deal of satisfaction and she used it for several years. Soon she was able to tell me about the habits and behaviour of slow worms.

Once when I was looking out of the window and saw Kirsty

playing in the garden I was thrilled to see a little fox cub only a yard or two from her also playing with a piece of stick. They suddenly turned to face each other and I wished I had a camera to catch that moment of surprise before the little fox cub ran away. As I was writing this book, I read in the papers that a vixen had made a home of Kirsty's memorial bench in Soho Square: the locals christened her Kirsty – 'She's even got the same colouring,' said one of them.

In bad weather we had a lot of activities to keep her interested. She experimented with paint, gouache and watercolours; as I had never painted with oils, I thought we should try that too. She made collages and wrote her first little book and illustrated it (I still have it). When she heard that Arthur Ransome had died without finishing one of his books, Kirsty wrote a letter to his publishers volunteering to finish the book on his behalf – though I didn't send it.

When she wasn't feeling very well, there was a thunderstorm which seemed to be immediately overhead as it was deafeningly loud. I thought Kirsty might be rather apprehensive and so I told her what little I knew about forked and sheet lightning. This didn't satisfy either of us and so I went upstairs to find an encyclopaedia and we sat in bed together and read all about the causes of thunderstorms and the difference between sheet and forked lightning. She was also interested to know if thunder preceded the lightning and became quite an authority in our household.

Life now slowly became a little easier. Kirsty had been promised a dog when she was able to look after it and the time seemed appropriate. Anya, a honey-coloured Labrador joined our family; Hamish's black cat Solomon was not impressed and showed his superiority whenever he could. He would hide behind the ceiling-to-floor curtains and stick out a front paw as the unsuspecting Anya went by, making her yelp in surprise, or he would sit high up on a glass shelf above the fireplace and push ornaments over the edge when she passed below. She was sweet-natured dog, though, and never retaliated by growling or chasing her antagonist. With hindsight it seems surprising that the medical authorities didn't warn me against allergies caused by the dander from animals, but Solomon hadn't affected Kirsty and during our first visit to Poland we had been constantly accompanied by our hosts' family dog with no problems at all.

What the specialist did recommend was that Kirsty, now six, would be better off if she went to a school for physically handicapped children. 'Let the other schools wait for their bright child,' she said. I thought this was a good idea, since Kirsty would have the companionship of other children. She seemed to settle into her new routine of school life quite well. A car collected and returned her each day, which took some pressure off me, and there was also the reassurance of knowing there was always a nurse on hand at the school itself. Each child's health was tested weekly. I was also told that it was customary for every new child to have an IQ test, but their policy was not to advise parents of these results. When the child had been at the school for about a month, the head would invite the parents in.

On my day I was greeted by a smiling headmaster. 'Kirsty is quite a character, isn't she?' he said. After my previous experience with school teachers I was not sure whether he looked upon this as a bonus or a hindrance. Fearing the worst, I started to apologise but he interrupted me by saying, 'Oh no! If we could run the school exactly as she would wish it would be excellent, but we can't. Her complaint is that they start a subject and get very interested in it, but then the bell goes and they have to change and do something quite different. Her idea would be to do the same lesson all day and make real progress.' He understood that Kirsty would be a real asset, and not a problem. The only thing I was told about the IQ test was that her standard of reading was already up to that of a nine-and-a-half-year-old. I came home greatly reassured that people were friendly and that despite her long absences, her reading age was ahead of her peers. I was not entirely surprised at this, since I had seen Kirsty with my copy of *Male and Female*, Margaret Mead's book about sexuality.

I felt confident enough in the summer of 1966 to arrange a summer holiday at Renvyle on the west coast of Ireland for Kirsty and my 77-year-old mother, while Hamish went camping with a friend. Our animals were looked after by friends. It was a great holiday, as Kirsty was completely healthy throughout the trip, which I put down to the clean air and outdoor activities. As it happened, no dogs were allowed in the hotel although she did play with one outside and I didn't see any cats. We would go out in the hotel's rowing boat and attempt some primitive fishing and other days were spent on the seashore collecting shells or touring the area. In the early evening Kirsty socialised a lot with the guests and told them about her granny's forthcoming birthday. One evening, a cake with lighted candles was carried into the dining room and everyone sang 'Happy Birthday'.

In 1967 I read in the *Observer* that they were holding a writing competition for children aged 11 to 19. The title was 'The school that I'd like': the children were encouraged to write about their own schools in a critical fashion and to make suggestions as to how things might be improved. Kirsty was under the age but entered just for fun. We did not expect to hear anything, but when she was nine her piece was published as part of a collection of the best. She even received a postal order for her contribution. When we bought the book, though, she was mortified to spot mis-spellings. I had not attempted to change anything because this was her own work, even if 'poem' was spelled 'poim'. Kirsty was the youngest contributor to the book. Its editor, the great champion of children's literature Edward Blishen, said he couldn't resist including her piece, and nor can I:

I would like a school that did not tell you off much and when it did tell you off theyd only tell you what youd done wrong and not do it again. They only say your nauty you shouldnt have done it but quite often we don't know what weve done wrong.

I wold like a school that some times let you writ out work for other children in other schools. I wold like it espesherly becos I get tiyed of having work givern to me to do and I think as i am a child that I now how other children feel and so i can make it eseyer for them and its youshuly only seniers that visit other schools and hospitals and places but we now just as much as seniers and if we cold visit all these places wed now how other children feel a lot more and I think it wold be nice if we cold sugest things for ourselves to do.

Wy cant we have one lesson for each day and coldent we keep our own clay and stuff, and coldent we have classes of speshel things lik modling, music, poims, and dansing of diforent cinds wich we cold chos to do. Id like us to have mor nature lessons out side and id prefer not to keep together as animals don't come out wen thers lots of people.

Her seven-year-old spelling may have been 'creative', but the voice can only have been Kirsty's – feisty, anti-authority, sympathetic to the needs of others, independent-minded and in love with 'modling, music, poims, and dansing'.

Chapter Three

Things Happen

1967-1968

'I watch you lie asleep, watch you breathing.'

KIRSTY MACCOLL, 'TOMORROW NEVER COMES', 1994

I was no longer able to work full time, but I did take on occasional day or weekend courses. The National Association for Gifted Children wrote to me one day, asking if I might like to take some movement classes for them at weekends. I jumped at the chance and took Kirsty with me.

She seemed to enjoy these trips and participated in the various activities laid on. I hadn't worked with children before and found them very receptive, enjoying the sessions immensely. There was one youngster who was musically gifted, but was unable to use his imagination in anything other than his music. So in my movement class he floundered, and the other children seemed surprised at his inability to enjoy creating a different world. It later transpired that all his time was spent playing the piano: when required to move along the floor like some strange creature, he said his mother wouldn't like him to get dirty. He found it very difficult to mix. Kirsty, on the other hand, had no problems mixing and took a serious interest in everything. She also expected very high standards from those in charge.

One weekend course was held at the Yehudi Menuhin School and I was taking another movement class. I had asked the children to move like various creepy crawlies, either real or imaginary, and we would turn it all into a dance. I gave encouragement where necessary to make those imaginative 'creatures' come alive. I noticed that Kirsty was standing upright, though everyone else was down on the floor, crawling along. As the session ended, I went up to her and asked what kind of insect or small animal she was. She replied, 'An elephant'! On the way back I apologised for not giving her more help or attention, but said I felt the other children needed me more. She said she understood that, but I shouldn't have ignored her completely; she had a point. With only a little help from me, at the next session, the 'elephant' turned into an exotic insect along with the others.

It was partly as a result of these classes and of my hearing of the difficulties that some parents had, that I decided to have an independent IQ test for Kirsty. A psychologist was recommended to me and we drove to Essex for our appointment. Kirsty had not had a good night and because of heavy traffic through London we arrived late for the test. The psychologist explained that her fatigue had affected the result and that the assessment represented only a minimal level of her actual reasoning ability. For all that, seven-year-old Kirsty achieved the very high IQ score of 168, which represented a mental age of 11 years and 8 months. Tests vary, of course, but the psychologist said she was the brightest child he had ever tested.

'This much is certain,' he said. 'Kirsty is a charming personality of extremely high intelligence who is unlikely to have all her academic and intellectual needs met by the provision currently made in the ordinary school.' He also raised an issue that I had been concerned about myself. 'She needs,' he continued, 'especially in view of her extended absence in the past, opportunities to grow in the social and emotional senses as well.'

It was this comment that made me finally decide not to take advantage of a scholarship to Millfield School. Like most parents, I wanted the best for my child and would have felt very sad if she had gone away to board at such an early age. I felt she was too young to leave home and I also heard that the young boarders were expected to care for a variety of animals such as rabbits and gerbils. I was beginning to associate animals with the asthmatic attacks, although Kirsty's doctors had not yet reached that conclusion since, confusingly, she sometimes had attacks when she was nowhere near an animal.

I felt reassured and justified that what I had been doing over the previous few years to help Kirsty through her illness had been the right approach. Academic studies were not important for the moment: so long as she was interested in something and was free to work at her own pace, she seemed not to suffer any stress. I also wanted to share as much time with her as possible, since her illness had so often robbed her of the friendship and companionship of her contemporaries. I also made a decision that I would never foist my views on her. I would always say what I thought but at the same time try to leave things open for her to form an opinion for herself.

Ewan was politically biased and had strong ideas about music. (According to him, there were only three types of music: folk, classical, and jazz. He hated 'pop'.) Although I shared some of his views, I would often argue about others. I also felt strongly that children should be able to make up their own minds; after all, with time, they would do so anyway. That was not to say that Kirsty did not share my values, or was unaware of them, and I think she demonstrated this clearly later in life. What was important, though, was that she had come to them through making her own decisions.

In other ways, though, Kirsty was a happy and normal child, taking great pleasure, for example, in a Barbie doll that Joan sent one day from New York, where she and her partner Gerry were then working. The large parcel contained the doll, some Barbie clothes and a Barbie bedroom suite. Kirsty loved changing Barbie's clothes – though this was the only doll she was ever interested in. Years later, when her own children were little, she used the same doll for the fairy at the top of her Christmas tree. I still put Barbie up there on my own tree now.

Hamish often lost out on my attention, of course, although I tried to do my best for him. One could simply never be sure that Kirsty would have a good day. I had naturally pinned my hopes on the forecast that Kirsty's asthma would clear up by the time she was seven, but it would be another three years before it at last began to ease. Hamish and I had our own happy times, though. He had made a number of friends who often came over and they were always very nice to Kirsty. It wasn't long before he had his own special girlfriend. She was very interested in tennis and Hamish, who had never shown any interest in the sport, went with her to Wimbledon to watch the tournament.

Ewan continued to come for lunch every Sunday, for the most part remaining a weekly visitor. Our lifestyles had become very different. While he was happy enough to talk about his own work, he found it difficult to relate to his children on their everyday level and didn't always understand the seriousness of Kirsty's condition. He once even suggested – meaning it quite kindly, I'm sure – that I should take the children on a camping holiday. True, he and I had taken Hamish camping as a youngster and enjoyed it – but now? A one-parent family with an asthmatic child? Even with Hamish's help, I would still have to drive, supervise the erection of the tent, cook the meals and clear up, always keeping an eye on Kirsty's health. It didn't sound much of a holiday to me.

I went with Kirsty on a long weekend visit to Clymping, near Bognor Regis. We stayed at a hotel near the beach which had been recommended to me. It was a listed building with beautiful old furniture and was also a popular haunt of minor celebrities. Kirsty had fish for dinner, but when it arrived, whole, with its beady eye and its tail still attached, she looked at it with some disgust. I had always had problems trying to get her to eat, so in some desperation I said to her, 'That looks lovely.'

'It might be all right,' she replied, 'but I think it's an exaggeration to call it *lovely*.'

Later that evening she struck up an unlikely friendship with the minor film star (and former beauty queen) Anne Heywood, who was staying there with her husband and little boy. One evening she swept into the dining room in a white fur coat with her poodle on a lead.

'Hello, Kirsty,' she said.

'Hello, Anne,' Kirsty replied. 'Look, your dog's got a flea on its back.'

After a few weeks without a crisis, I began to feel reasonably optimistic about Kirsty's health, so I decided to throw a party with my friends from the theatre – the first such party since my break-up with Ewan. We all looked forward to it. Meanwhile Kirsty was full of excitement about a forthcoming school fundraising day. There were to be stalls, races for children and adults and, best of all, horse rides! The horses duly arrived and were led into an adjoining field, where the children spent a lot of time stroking and feeding them.

When Kirsty returned from school that Friday afternoon she

was unwell. She had a bad night, no appetite and couldn't keep fluids down. I tried tapping her back gently to ease her breathing, but soon realised that she was too poorly even for that. On the Saturday I rang the doctor's surgery and was put through to his locum who told me to dress her in two coats and send her out to play. I looked at the small, hunched figure in the bed who couldn't even sit up properly. Somehow we got through another day – with a little help from Horatio.

By Sunday evening I knew I couldn't afford to wait much longer for medical help. I rang back again and my new doctor answered. He was unwilling to come out, but when he heard the details he reluctantly agreed to visit and gave Kirsty an injection.

'Everything will be all right now,' he assured me. 'She'll get a good night's sleep.'

'But if she isn't any better?', I asked.

'It will be all right... well, if it isn't, ring me at the surgery at 9am.'

His visit seemed to have been terribly quick – or was that my imagination? Was I being overly anxious? Everything told me that they were all wrong. And she *wasn't* better. Everything was *not* all right. In fact, she was much worse. The vomiting went on and she began hallucinating. On Monday morning I rang the doctor at his surgery on the stroke of 9am.

'She'll have to go to hospital,' he now said. 'She'll be dehydrated by now. Come and get a note to take with you. I'll call the ambulance.'

'But I'm alone with her, and she's hallucinating!' I managed to reply. 'I can't possibly leave her alone in this condition. She's only a little girl.'

'I'm afraid you'll have to,' came the answer.

In desperation I rang my neighbour, Margaret Spurring, who, thank God, happened to be in. She was also a registered nurse and she rushed to the surgery where she was told, 'You can't disturb the doctor, he has a patient.'

'If you won't go in now and get the note,' she replied, 'I'll walk right in myself.' The shocked receptionist got the note and brought it back.

Over two hours later we were still waiting for the ambulance. I was now at my wits' end and, clutching at straws, so I rang my previous doctor, my friend Arron Rapoport. He was in his surgery some five miles away.

He gave me the number of the ambulance and I called to hear the driver saying, 'We're looking for a very sick child, it's an emergency call and we can't find the bloody house! We've been looking for two hours.' I cut in and gave him my correct address. The ambulance arrived at the same time as Arron, who had left his surgery to take Kirsty to hospital himself.

At the hospital, the woman doctor blamed the ambulance men for the delay as they arrived and we were rushed through into a small consulting room. I was left alone with Kirsty for a moment but when she started twitching I shouted for the doctor, who rushed back. I was asked to wait outside while they set up a drip and did whatever else they had to do. I noticed a couple standing some distance away. The woman came up to me and told me how marvellous the hospital was and how sure she was that my child would be all right. I turned away from her – she didn't know, and I was not ready for platitudes. It was churlish of me: she had meant her words kindly and I soon regretted my behaviour.

Memory plays strange tricks: my conversation with this stranger is the last thing I remember of that awful Monday morning. But Kirsty recovered, of course, and soon returned home. When Mr Norman, our marvellous consultant, heard of our terrible experience, he made special arrangements for me to prevent anything like it happening again. I was given his private number at the clinic and he promised to dispatch an ambulance from the hospital immediately; Kirsty would always be admitted to Great Ormond Street Hospital without delay.

Of course, the planned party had to be cancelled, but when one of the guests, Harry H Corbett – the younger star of *Steptoe & Son* – heard that Kirsty was home, he said he would like to see her. He arrived carrying a small umbrella as a present and told her that he had been 'fighting off Cowboys and Indians' as he drove down our unadopted and very bumpy Beech Way. This endeared him to Kirsty.

My neighbour, Dr Richard Spurring, whose wife Margaret had been so helpful, now became our new GP. His family had moved into Beech Way a short time after us and they had three children, who all played with Kirsty. On one occasion she was invited to sleep over at their house. In the morning she was suffering from such severe asthma that I had to take her bicycle over so she could sit on it while I wheeled her back. As we came down our driveway it started to rain and Kirsty said, 'Mummy, you have no idea what it is like – I wish I was dead.'

I had never before heard her express herself so negatively and I felt the tears welling in my eyes. I promised her that these attacks, painful as they were, would clear up. Dr Spurring recommended a inhaler to be used hourly. At night, when we were both very tired, I could not remember whether she had used it or not and would try and keep her mind occupied with stories or chatting until another hour was up.

Things slowly seemed to improve. Kirsty attended the school for physically handicapped children fairly regularly. Joan asked me to do some choreographic work in the theatre and suggested that we should both work with children in connection with her Fun Palace – an educational project that was to be built on derelict land in Eltham (though this never materialised). I also gave some movement classes at Hamish's request for him and a few of his friends who were interested and for this we hired a local hall. Hamish was a good mover and enjoyed dancing. Lisa Ullman, Laban's colleague and godmother with Joan to both my children, also visited.

On one of my birthdays, Hamish gave me a sketchbook and some drawing pencils; Kirsty bought me a pair of Wellington boots and a trowel! I even found time to make a small pond in the garden, line it and put some brickwork around it. It was on the slope so it took me some time to work out the mechanics of the problem – at least until I borrowed a spirit level.

Visiting a neighbour one day in 1968, Kirsty suddenly arrived to call me back. 'A lady is on the telephone,' she said, 'asking for Mrs MacColl.' The 'lady' had telephoned from the hospital: it was urgent. I flew down the drive to my house and picked up the phone.

'Are you Mrs MacColl? Do you have a son called Hamish? Can you get to the hospital right away?' She wouldn't tell me what was wrong.

'Is he badly, badly hurt?'

'No, come quickly.'

I braced myself, and dared to ask, 'Is he dead?'

All she would say was, 'Just come immediately.'

I called to Kirsty and told her to bring something to keep her occupied in the car: Hamish had met with a 'slight accident', I told her, and we were going to Croydon Hospital. (This was where the little boy had died, two years before, when Kirsty was there.) I kept my voice as calm and quiet as possible. She asked no questions but came straight away with a few books. Arriving at the hospital, I briefly left Kirsty in the car to find Hamish.

I was taken to a small room adjoining the ward. A matron

came in and told me as gently as possible that Hamish had met with a serious accident. Part of his right hand had been blown away. *But how has this happened?* They needed to know when he had his last meal before they could operate. I tried to think, but... *I don't know: this is so important, but I just can't help them...* He was out at lunchtime with his friends, I told them – and then I was suddenly aware of him through the open door. *Maybe they can't give him morphine until they know?* Yes, I could see him, but I was not allowed to stay... I looked at my handsome son, and once again experienced that same terrible feeling of helplessness and utter desolation. First Kirsty and now Hamish... *Why?*

The matron eased me back to the small room. Someone brought a cup of tea. I could use the phone to ring my husband, she said. I remembered from somewhere that Ewan had a singing engagement in the East Midlands; I left a message for him. I also remembered that I was expecting guests for dinner, and that the oven was still on. Mechanically I made the calls. I rang Denise – she said she'd go and turn it off – and asked Judy to pick Kirsty up and take her home – poor Kirsty! I had almost forgotten her waiting outside in the car. I went out to her and tried to tell her, in a calm, matter-of-fact voice, that it was a little bit worse than we had thought but that Hamish would still be okay and that I had to stay on and wait for the doctor, so Judy would be coming to collect her.

Kirsty was very sensible and calm, asking a few questions – but I think she knew there was more to it than I had let on. I kissed her and returned to the small room. Denise had by now arrived with, among other things, a small half-bottle and so we sat together through the night, drinking occasional cups of tea laced with brandy. It had no effect: I was still very cold and shaking inside. I looked at my hands. Funny, they didn't shake at all. In the morning I was told that there was nothing to be done but wait and in the meantime I should try and get some rest.

At last, the surgeon told me they were transferring Hamish to a training hospital in East London. He needed treatment in a compression chamber, which I understood would force his blood to circulate and so prevent gangrene. The journey was a nightmare. Attached to various tubes, Hamish lay propped up on a special bed in the ambulance for the long trip, but we travelled at a snail's pace, lights flashing. Every bump in the road, every stop for the lights, brought a moan. On arrival, I found the compression chamber quite frightening – a vast cylindrical tank in which the patient was incarcerated for long periods on end. Hamish never complained.

After a period of treatment, he was moved to East Grinstead where he underwent further surgery. The specialist had every hope of saving the thumb, even though the fingers had gone, explaining to me that the thumb's role was more important than that of the fingers. I drove down to see him in intensive care, and it was only then that I at last found out how the accident had happened.

Hamish and a group of his friends had been conducting an experiment, mixing weedkiller and sugar and pushing it into an iron pipe. It had failed to go off and so he went to have another look at it as it blew up. There was some good news: the thumb had been saved. I later heard that Joan had, with characteristic selflessness (and impracticality), offered to donate her own hand as a replacement.

Three weeks later, Joan and her partner Gerry Raffles helped us celebrate Hamish's 18th birthday with him. As part of his convalescence, Hamish and his friend Rob went with their two girlfriends on a camping trip to Italy. On their return, Joan suggested that Hamish should have a vocational guidance test: it might help to clarify his ideas on a future career. Among other things, I learnt from these tests that Hamish was also a very gifted individual.

Meanwhile Dr Spurring made an appointment for Kirsty to attend the Wellcome Clinic, hoping that we might discover what was causing her allergic reactions. It turned out that my suspicions were correct, and that the worst culprit was the dander from cats, followed by dogs and other furry animals, including horses. Before she could begin a year's course of weekly injections, we had reluctantly to say goodbye to Solomon II and our labrador Anya and find them good homes.

Kirsty's interest in pets then stretched to rather more exotic beasts. A chameleon, a gecko and an American grass snake all joined our family. We also provided a home to some stick insects (who persisted in leaving their habitat and climbing the curtains). 'Fred' the gecko lived with us for many years, eventually dying of old age, I think, despite my best ministrations. The main problem with the chameleon and snake was their food: the former was choosy about his maggots, and the latter lived on a weekly diet of one suitably-sized goldfish. It was Ewan's job to procure these from a pet shop near where he lived. After several visits, over a period of weeks, the lady assistant cheerfully asked after the 'lovely collection of fish' we must by now be enjoying. When Ewan explained *why* we were buying so many fish, she refused to sell him any more.

One day I looked out of my kitchen window and saw the local children gathered round an old tea chest in the garden, peering over its top with nervous excitement. Curious, I went out to join them to see a snake hissing and threshing about at the bottom of the tea chest. There was that age-old fear and fascination of snakes. They asked me to get Kirsty, which I did. She looked at the snake's markings carefully and then explained that it was an adder and would only attack if threatened. You could tell it was an adder, she said, by the patterns on its back, and with that she tipped the chest over and the snake escaped into our garden. Although we lived surrounded by woodland and often went into the woods, this was the first time that the children had seen an adder; it was also the first time that Kirsty had seen one. She must have read up on snakes because she explained things in great detail.

When Kirsty was about ten years old, she read an article in the local paper about a nearby resident who bred butterflies. This interested her so much that she wrote to him, and this resulted in a invitation to visit him. He had turned one room into a butterfly house – full of light, warm and sunny – where we saw the most exotic and beautiful butterflies, of all colours and all shapes and sizes. This kind man was so impressed by Kirsty's interest that he invited her back, on one occasion giving her a chrysalis to take home and look after. It sat on a cloth, with a small flowerpot over it, and we set it down on the carpet near the radiator for warmth. And waited...

Late one night, I saw the flowerpot move very slightly. Mesmerised, I watched and saw it move again. Rather squeamishly, I took the flowerpot partly off and saw that the chrysalis had started to change its form and I called Kirsty, who was thrilled, especially when it eventually turned into a beautiful butterfly. By this time, Beech Way was becoming something of a menagerie. I had to deal with a break-out by American grass snakes from their vivarium (I found them later in Hamish's bedroom in a ringbound folder on his desk), relocate stick insects from the top of my curtains to the jam jars where they belonged, supervise the chameleon's exclusive diet of live maggots and tend to the eggs in the laundry room sink, which rather successfully turned into baby trout needing running water. (Apparently we did better than the science lab at school who had supplied the eggs in the first place.) I was more at home with the tropical fish that Hamish introduced us to.

Meanwhile we had all decided that Kirsty might be well enough to attend a normal primary school for three days a week, remaining at her special school for the other two days. She therefore arrived in the summer term, just in time to take the end-of-term exams – and still managed to come near the top. Her first-term report was glowing and I congratulated her on the science comment, which simply said 'Good'.

She replied in a rather dismissive tone, 'You know, and I know, it doesn't mean a thing.' On one of her days back at the special school the nurse rang me to express concern that Kirsty had lost weight. The general consensus seemed to be, however, that she was happy at the new school and provision was made for her to attend the primary school full time.

Arrangements were also made at this time for Hamish to take his A Levels at Croydon College, but in the event this did not work out very well since they could not help anyone, they claimed, who could not keep up with note-taking, which Hamish of course struggled with after his accident. So in the end he took up Lisa Ullman's offer to spend some time at her Art of Movement Studio before finally deciding to train as a doctor of Chinese medicine.

One evening towards the end of 1968, I got a call from my mother Norrie, by then in her late seventies. She seemed a little distressed and tearfully begged me to come over to her flat in Croydon. This behaviour was so unlike her that I left the children and drove over immediately. When I arrived, she was in bed and appeared to be asleep. I managed to wake her. It seems she had had 'a turn' and, realising the door was on the chain, she had crawled over to it and struggled for a long time to remove it before phoning me. I called her doctor – our friend Arron Rapoport – and he told me she had had a stroke, though the prognosis did not seem to be too serious.

I returned to Beech Way to collect Kirsty and a suitcase of clothes and we both moved into my mother's flat while Hamish had a friend to keep him company at home. After a few days the invalid was sitting up and taking a keen interest in everything.

Meanwhile, Kirsty attended school daily and was appearing in a school musical. My brother Pip came down from Nettleham in Lincolnshire, staying overnight. He and Arron sat chatting to each other one evening over a glass of whisky. Arron said to my mother that it was better if she didn't have any spirits just yet. She laughed and told me she considered it most unfair – after all, it was *her* whisky they were drinking!

The nurse visited every day and we all expected her to make a full recovery. We began to make plans as to who would do what for Christmas. Her pastry was always better than mine, so the mince pies were her responsibility. She looked pleased and said she was going to hold a party. In great spirits at overcoming this final 'hiccup' of the year, Kirsty and I went out to buy a pair of school shoes. On our return, a little later than expected owing to the Christmas crowds, however, my mother had lapsed into a coma. It was obvious she had been up and pottering. From then on it was only a question of time. She woke up once and smiled when I told her I loved her. 'You love me too, don't you?' I said. She nodded.

I was alone with her when she died. There was nothing more I could do, so after Arron had certified her death, I slipped away to the school to see the last ten minutes of the Christmas musical, having promised Kirsty I would try to put in an appearance. I didn't tell her immediately that her granny had died: I felt she had achieved so much, being able to attend regularly enough to be part of a school production and I didn't want to spoil the occasion. My mother's funeral took place immediately before Christmas. It was a very sad season for me, of course. She had become a great support to us and things were improving as Kirsty was able to lead a more normal life.

Chapter Four

Tomorrow Never Comes

1969-1976

'It hurts me to breathe.'

<small>KIRSTY MACCOLL TO JEAN MACCOLL, 1969</small>

K irsty was able to do more at school in the early part of
1969. She was continuing with the weekly injections
which seemed to be stabilising her condition and she was full
time. She joined the school choir and took up the violin. She also
went swimming once a week, which she loved, although she
wasn't strong enough to race.

At home, she listened to all sorts of music. I would often listen
and pass the odd comment if I particularly liked something but
generally left her to do her own thing. I had my own music.

Andy Williams had a show once a week on television during
which he would usually sing a few songs. Kirsty was ready for
this: she would take her violin out of its case and stand in front
of the television set, bow poised to accompany him. While she
was no Yehudi Menuhin, I was amazed that having learned the
violin for such a short time she was able to accompany him

without any sheet music. It was around this time that she and a few friends wrote a short sketch for their class, for which Kirsty composed her own song and lyrics, as well as taking on an acting role.

Kirsty got through the winter quite well, though she still had her off-days. I heard from Helen Dunlop, an American friend of mine from my Theatre Workshop days, that she would be coming over to visit and hoped to be touring Ireland. As Kirsty and I had enjoyed our first trip to Ireland very much, I suggested the three of us explore the Ring of Kerry. The plan was agreed.

When we arrived in Cork, Kirsty had the slightest intermittent cough. Determined to take no chances, I thought she should see a doctor before we travelled any further. He said her lungs were clear and there was no problem. Feeling rather foolish at having wasted some time, I agreed we should set off on the final leg of our journey. Driving through this most beautiful part of Ireland we decided to eat at a restaurant as it was by now growing dark and our hotel was only about another half an hour's drive away. After we had ordered our food, Kirsty ran off to play until it was ready. In a very short time, however, she was back again, crying (which was very unusual in itself) as she explained, 'It hurts me to breathe.'

We cancelled the meal and drove straight to the hotel. Once there, I asked the proprietor to send for a doctor and we went to our rooms. Some hours later, I heard slow, dragging footsteps shuffling along the corridor outside our room. I opened the door to see a comparatively elderly man walking towards us. If this was our doctor, he didn't inspire much confidence! After a brief examination, he told me Kirsty had pleurisy, an often painful inflammation around the lung. He brought out a small bottle from his pocket and said I should mix the powder with water, asking me if she was allergic to penicillin. I said I didn't know, as she had never had it before.

'Never mind, dear,' he said, 'she's in the hands of the angels now' – which I didn't find reassuring at all. Asking how much water I should add to the penicillin, and whether or not it should be sterilised, he told me to just use the tap in the washbasin. It all seemed a long way from the NHS.

Thankfully, Kirsty was soon feeling much better, but still had to stay in bed until her temperature returned to normal. I encouraged Helen to go on various day trips in this part of Ireland which she had wanted to do for many years. Now Kirsty was on the mend and a very cheerful convalescent, she soon ran out of books and I said I would leave her for a couple of hours to explore the area and see what I could find to keep her occupied.

This was my first time out on my own since the night we had arrived. I drove round Bantry Bay for several miles and eventually came across a small hamlet. No shop was in sight and I began to think I would return empty-handed. As I slowly drove by each cottage, though, I saw one had a larger window than the others, and stopping in front of it I saw it had an extraordinary mixture of unrelated items for sale: part of a bridle, a piece of scrap leather, a fishing rod, some boot polish – and there in the corner, shining like a jewel in my imagination, was the answer to my prayers: a brand new alto melodica, the keyboard instrument played by blowing through a mouthpiece, in a red case. I was absolutely thrilled, and immediately went into the shop and bought it, grateful that it was still in its original cellophane wrapping. I returned to the hotel and Kirsty in triumph.

The melodica came with simple instructions and a little book of tunes (which she didn't need). Kirsty was delighted, and leaving her to practise I went down to the bar where most of the locals congregated. Before long we heard a series of well-known tunes coming from above – our bedroom, of course. The recital went on for some time and the locals listened approvingly, saying how glad they were that the little visitor was on the mend. As I went back up to check on Kirsty, I saw a strange lady coming out. She said she and Kirsty had been having a chat. As a music teacher, she was amazed to learn that Kirsty had only had the melodica for an hour or two. When Kirsty finally joined the company in the bar already she seemed to be surrounded by fans who appreciated her prowess on the instrument. Wishing to show his admiration, the hotelier asked if she'd like him to demonstrate to her how to pull pints. She accepted graciously.

On our first stroll outside the hotel together, we came across a young girl, about the same age as Kirsty, who had flaming red hair. She volunteered the information that she and all her brothers and sisters played the violin. I was rather taken aback at this, imagining the terrible noise that a whole family of violinists might make. As we got to a large, barn-like structure, the young girl said suddenly, 'That's where I live.'

A red-haired woman had just come out of the door and waved to us as she came to greet us. She invited us in for coffee. I learned that her husband was Austrian and had in fact been a professional violinist. They had met, and married, in Holland after the war, and then decided to try their luck in America. Somehow they had only got as far as the west coast of Ireland. The local people had been very supportive, though and given them the barn which they had slowly refurbished, turning it into a proper home. There seemed to be a large number of children, most of whom were employed locally in small jobs. The woman told me that she had been a violin teacher in Holland and had therefore, at one time or another, taught all her children to play. When I asked her what her husband did now, she said he had to take care of his hands, could do no manual work and although she believed he practised daily, he was 'resting' at the moment. Looking around this huge room, I realised that she had a great deal to do looking after nine or ten children, catering for them and finding time to give them violin lessons. Privately, I thought her husband was something of a liability. We said our farewells and hoped to meet again.

On the return journey we stopped at a rather beautiful guest house outside Cork. On our first visit to Ireland Kirsty had enjoyed the fresh salmon, but we had been warned on this visit to stay away it, since the fish were infected and a number of people had been taken seriously ill. That evening, though, the proprietress told me she had been given the most beautiful salmon, which she would be serving on the menu that night. She laughed at the warnings and said, 'This one looks beautiful.'

Choosing the *hors d'oeuvres*, and before I could stop her, Kirsty asked the waitress for salmon. When the dishes were put in front of us I told Kirsty about the warning and swapped her dish with mine. I broke the fish up on my plate and covered it with the rest of the salad. It looked perfectly good, and I did wonder if I was being over-cautious. I tried a little mouthful no bigger than the size of a sixpence and left the rest. That night, I developed a very high temperature and a raging headache. I needed a doctor but hadn't got the strength to go to Helen's room and ask for help.

I remember tossing and turning and talking in my sleep, and then becoming aware of a calm little voice saying, 'Don't worry, Mum, you'll soon be all right,' and my head being bathed with a cold flannel. I went to the bathroom and was terribly sick.

By morning I felt better. I had Kirsty to thank for her presence of mind. When we went down to breakfast, Kirsty and Helen had toast; I couldn't touch a thing. I suddenly became aware that we were the only people in the room – nobody else was having breakfast...

Once the summer holiday was over, I considered the various options open to me. There is no doubt that, despite occasional recurrences, Kirsty's asthma had eased considerably following the year's course of injections and the sad parting from our cat and dog.

Ideally, I would have returned to the theatre and the East 15 Acting School, but the journey was too far and the times were incompatible with Kirsty's primary school routine. So I decided instead to train as a teacher at nearby Coloma College. I would have a full-time job and as well as this share the same holidays as Kirsty. I was able to direct a musical at Kirsty's own school as part of my training, a production of a fairy tale called *The Woodcutter's Son*, resplendent with castles and dragons – and Kirsty as the queen.

At weekends I even dared to take her to an occasional horse-riding lesson in Godstone, provided she did not risk exacerbating her asthma by helping to clean out the stables. She showed promise and enjoyed being in the open air; in fact, she was quite fearless. As soon as the lesson was over we would rush into the car and, whatever the weather, open all the windows and drive home. All her clothing would then go through the washing machine and she would wash her hair and have a bath to avert any allergic reactions. She gained an initial certificate for riding proficiency, which she added to her bronze and silver swimming certificates. I don't know if Kirsty valued these very much, but they gave me a great deal of pleasure since each one represented another significant step on the way of her improving health.

Things didn't always go according to plan, though. On one occasion, after Kirsty had gone camping with her class, I got a phone call late on the first night to say that she had had another asthma attack: they were very sorry, but could I come and collect her? Kirsty recovered within a day or two, and was philosophical about the experience – and so was I. All I wanted was for her to have every opportunity to try out anything that interested her without anyone making value judgements. I always felt that whatever you tried to do, even if you gave it up at some point, it still counted as a valuable learning experience.

Kirsty had never sung at home because she had never had the breath, but now with increasing health she would hum the odd tune. As I don't sing, she found her own way. Ewan had no input on her musical development – he was more likely to tell her the names of all the wild flowers than of the songs he himself sang. And as she was now at last more often to be found outside in the garden than in bed, Ewan and I agreed that he should bring round his two sons by Peggy, Neill and Calum. The boys were made very welcome and the children got on well enough with each other.

Hamish had meanwhile been pursuing his career and had formed a strong relationship with Marian, a Croydon girl three years his senior, who was then working in the City of London. She became a frequent visitor to our house and both Kirsty and I liked her very much, and were very happy for them. Even so, it was quite a surprise to hear one day in 1971 that they were engaged to be married. I was worried that Hamish was too young, now just 21, but they were confident about their future and I was happy for them. Marian invited Kirsty to be bridesmaid and Hamish asked his friend David Rapoport – my old friend Wolf's son – to be his best man. Marian's father had just retired and was planning to live on Bryher in the Scillies. So, prior to the wedding, constant trips were made with Hamish's help transferring furniture from Croydon to their new home.

The wedding was arranged to take place on Bryher, a few days after Marian's parents had settled into their new home.

Invitations had been sent out to family and friends, including Ewan and Peggy, Joan Littlewood and Lisa Ullman, and everything seemed to be ready for the big day. Kirsty and I followed Marian and Hamish, staying at a hotel on St Mary's, the main island. This was going to be our summer holiday.

Marian's mother invited us to come over and see their new cottage and talk over the wedding plans. Kirsty and I had not been to the Scillies before and found them very attractive, Bryher and Tresco in particular. The cottage was attractively situated facing Tresco, with a channel of water and a beautiful sandy beach below. As we had to get back to the hotel for our evening meal we said our farewells and made arrangements to meet the following day.

I noticed there had been a very slight shower before we left. Back at our hotel on St Mary's we were having dinner and watching the sailing boats. We noticed a speed boat racing across to Bryher and after about 20 minutes we saw it return. The hotel manager came to our table and told me that there was a telephone call for me. I went to the phone and it was Hamish. 'Mum, I'm all right,' he said. He knew that ever since the hospital had phoned about his accident, I had always been very nervous about such calls, so I think he was trying to reassure me. 'I'm all right,' he repeated, 'but Marian's father is dead.'

Since we had only left him an hour or so earlier, this was a terrible blow. He had seemed so healthy and was full of plans for the future. As Hamish explained, Marian's mother had made tea and asked Marian to tell her father it was ready. She had gone out into the garden to find him lying on the ground holding a pair of secateurs. He had been going to trim some bushes, had cut a live wire by mistake and been electrocuted. It was decided to go ahead with the wedding, without the guests.

David Rapoport arrived the following day, and Marian was

given away by a friend of the family, a retired sea captain, in place of her father. On the day of the wedding Kirsty and I went by boat to Bryher and joined the wedding party of local people. After the ceremony we walked through the churchyard on the way to the nearby cottage, pausing only for Marian to lay her bouquet of flowers on her father's open grave. Somehow, we all supported each other and got through the simple wedding breakfast before waving the young couple off as they took the helicopter to the mainland.

•　•　•

Kirsty could have gone either to Croydon High School, a single-sex, traditional academic, secondary school, or a newly built, forward-looking comprehensive. It was the second of these, Monk's Hill, that was her school of choice. It had a new art department and a drama hall with a large stage which augured well for the artistic side of her education. Pupils were streamed according to their ability. Years later, when we talked about this choice, I suggested she might have enjoyed a more academic education, but Kirsty disagreed. She felt she was able to mix with anybody, she said, and it's true that she had only been at the school for a week before she developed a real South London accent.

Kirsty was in the top grade for all her subjects. She continued to play the violin for the school orchestra, but her real love was the oboe and now she had the chance to learn it properly. I don't know why she chose the oboe above any other instrument. It might simply have been because she listened to a lot of music and liked the sound of it, but it was very much her own choice – though I wasn't entirely happy about it, given her struggle with asthma.

When her oboe teacher had to stop teaching for personal reasons, Ewan suggested she might like to learn the classical guitar. I remember driving over to her guitar teacher's place one evening through snow and rain and then sitting outside in the car in the dark, covered by a blanket, with a thermos and a book, waiting for the lesson to end. Her teacher was keen for Kirsty to enter a competition, but she was very nervous of performing in public, and so after one or two attempts he decided they should play duets together: this would give her confidence, he thought, and the two of them did indeed do very well.

Kirsty and I were also now able to spend time enjoying each other's company during the weekends and holidays, free from the constant anxiety over her health. One day we were shopping in a Croydon department store when we came across a grand display of the latest wigs, in different styles and many colours. Kirsty and I were mesmerised when a woman promoting the event came up to me, holding a gruesome black wig, and asked if she could help me.

'No, thank you,' I replied. Then, pointing to Kirsty some distance away, I said, 'but my daughter has always wanted to be a blonde.' Before poor Kirsty knew what was happening, the enthusiastic assistant had descended on her with a range of blonde wigs. The first one seemed to be a 'Dolly Parton'. Kirsty looked at me as I struggled not to laugh, then started to giggle herself. Not to be put off, the woman quickly exchanged it for a 'Veronica Lake' before we could extricate ourselves and head off for a pizza next door.

We also often went up to London to shop for the latest fashions. At this age, in her early teens, she was beginning to be able to wear what she considered fashionable clothes and we particularly enjoyed going around the new Biba shop. She experimented with make-up, but it was always very tastefully done.

Once she wanted to buy some boots. I was unable to go and suggested she could go alone, telling her to be careful, to ring

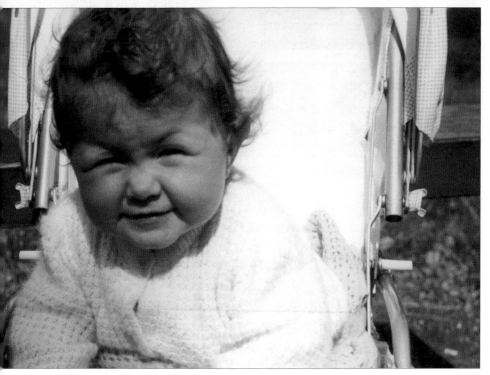

above left: My son Hamish and me, in August 1959. I was eight months pregnant with Kirsty, and Hamish is nine years old.

above right: I used to take Kirsty to Regent's Park when she was little.

below: My beloved Kirsty, nearly nine months old and full of curiosity.

When we lived in Croydon, our great friends and neighbours were the Rapoports. Tosh (and younger sister Julie) and David were willing baby-sitters. They adored Kirsty and we spent much time in their company.

Above left: Tosh Rapoport with Kirsty, for whom she would babysit.

Above right: I love this picture of Hamish's best friend David Rapoport helping Kirsty to put on her shoe.

Below: Kirsty on her bicycle in the garden of her granny's house.

above left: Kirsty's first school photograph, aged four. The headteacher admitted to me one day, 'I'm not sure she likes our games!'

above right: Kirsty, independent and enthusiastic, planned her day at the zoo and was quite self-reliant. 'Don't worry. I've a lot to do. I'll see you later,' she said.

below left: Kirsty at primary school.

below right: I had had to cancel a party because of Kirsty's ill health. Harry H Corbett, *Steptoe & Son*, said he would come and see her anyway. They became good friends.

Above: Kirsty with her father, playwright and folk-singer Ewan MacColl, at Selsdon in 1968.

Below: Kirsty was asked to have her photo taken for *Jackie* magazine. We decided to enliven the event and not take them too seriously.

coming a young woman.

ove left: Another shot taken for *Jackie*.

ove right: While proud that Kirsty was invited to do
modelling job, I was overcome with the giggles –
bably because this was not really our scene.

ow left: A picture I always wanted to take. A glorious
ny afternoon and Kirsty's russet-coloured hair framed
inst a backdrop of autumnal leaves… Beautiful.

ow right: We found photo booths irresistible!

Kirsty posing on her home turf in Croydon; in those days she was singing as Mandy Doubt in the punk band the Drug Addix.

iconic Stiff Records promo shot for Kirsty's 7" single 'They Don't Know', released in
e 1979.

Above: Kirsty signed f[or]
Polydor in 1981. She h[ad]
a hit with 'There's A G[uy]
Works Down The Chi[ps]
Shop Swears He's Elvi[s]'
from her acclaimed
debut album *Desperate*
Character.

Left: Adrian Edmonds[on]
featured in the video f[or]
Kirsty's 1983 Stiff rele[ase]
'Terry'.

me if she was going to be late and be sensible about speaking to strangers on her own. She laughed and said, 'But you speak to everybody!'

The mission was accomplished very satisfactorily, and she arrived back home with a beaming smile and a pair of new boots. She later boasted to her girlfriends, whose parents did not allow them to travel alone, that *her* mother wasn't like that. I was quite pleased about this, though I must confess I had had more than a few misgivings that I had not expressed at the time.

I felt able to take Kirsty off to Paris for a short visit. She dressed very smartly in a black trouser suit with a black peaked cap and her friends expressed their approval of her taste in clothes. I thought this was a good opportunity for her to practise her French. We travelled by boat and train and visited the Eiffel Tower, the Louvre, and then Sacré Coeur and Montmartre, where we wandered round the artists' quarter. I explained to Kirsty that this was one of the areas where my father had taken such inspiration from the artists he had seen working there. We had enjoyed ourselves so much that we rested for a while in an outdoor restaurant and she ordered us a citron pressé. As we walked down the steep steps on our way back to the hotel, I was surprised to see the lights going out behind us. I had no idea it was so late.

The following day I took Kirsty to Parc Monceau and told her a story. This was where her grandmother had taken a small boy called Philippe Liewer to meet her young man – my father. That little boy was the son of friends whom she had known before the First World War – she had in fact helped them move from Paris to the country when it was feared the Germans would overrun Paris – and she had been asked to teach their son English. He grew up to be a leading figure in the *maquis*, the French Resistance Movement, and was parachuted into England

and back again into France on a number of occasions. This was particularly brave of him because he was Jewish, and he managed to help his sister and her children keep one step ahead of the Gestapo. Even so, his sister's husband was taken from his bed one night and shot.

One of his assistants was Violette Szabo, whose famous story was told in the film with Virginia McKenna called *Carve Her Name with Pride*. I told Kirsty that her Uncle Pip was named after Philippe Liewer, and that after the Second World War his sister and their children had come to stay with us in Lincoln. I once took his niece Dominique on a trip to the Isle of Man where I was touring with Theatre Workshop. Philippe later wrote to us, saying that he wanted to come and visit. Sadly, though, he died of a heart attack, brought on by the stress of his wartime experiences, shortly before he was due to arrive. During our visit Kirsty and I took the Métro to Neuilly on the outskirts of Paris, which was the last address I had had for Dominique, though we didn't succeed in finding her.

Later, Kirsty went on a school day-trip to France, and on the way back on the ferry, there was a rather flashy American car, which all the kids looked at with interest. The driver was the successful songwriter Jimmy Webb. He started to chat to the youngsters that swarmed around him – including Kirsty, who mentioned that her dad was the singer Ewan MacColl. Unfortunately, he didn't believe her, and thought she was just showing off... Poor Kirsty!

Although there had always been boys to play with, Kirsty was now reaching adolescence and taking a keener interest in them. She was quickly a popular young woman. I recently received an email from someone in Germany who had travelled at 13 with his class to visit Kirsty's school in Selsdon. The visit was part cultural and part educational. He remembered sitting in the drama hall in the audience when a line of children walked onto the stage to sing. They were led by the most beautiful girl he had ever seen, with glorious red hair – Kirsty, of course. After the performance the German visitors were taken to the homes of the performers for tea. While I was in the kitchen preparing the tea, he and Kirsty had exchanged their first kiss. He went back home to Germany determined to leave school there and then and to return to Selsdon. He was when he wrote the father of a teenage girl, but retained very clear memories of that visit.

At around that same time, Kirsty was offered the choice of classes in either metalwork or cookery. I advised her to do metalwork and she thought this was a good idea. When she joined the metalwork class, the boys all booed her, claiming this was 'men's work' and that she wouldn't be able to cope. About a month later I asked her how the class was going. She gave a quiet smile and said, 'The boys are coming to me for help now.' I was the proud owner of a folding stool and a bracelet, the result of Kirsty's initial efforts.

At this period in her life she was never without a Saturday job. She helped at the local hairdresser's salon and washed up in the kitchens of the golf club, where I would pick her up so that she had time to come home and have a bath and wash the smell of grease out of her hair before going out with her friends. Later on, she worked for *Good Housekeeping*, clearing away and washing up after the various recipes had been photographed for the magazine. When I suggested that Kirsty should open a bank account, she told me she had already done it.

One summer holiday in the early 1970s, Kirsty and I travelled down to the Hartland Quay Hotel in Devon, an isolated spot overlooking the sea about two miles from the village of Hartland. Kirsty soon became friends with all the young people of the village and we went back for the next two years.

The following Christmas we were all invited to stay at my brother's house at Nettleham in Lincolnshire. Arriving in the evening, we were looking forward to helping with the preparations over the next few days. Kirsty's job was to decorate the tree. In the early hours of the following morning, though, I was awakened by Kirsty having a severe asthma attack.

My brother had a Labrador dog and because we had not visited him for some time, I had hoped that Kirsty would not be affected. On later visits she would sleep in my car in Pip's large garage, a designated dog-free area, with the seat folded back and the windows open. This time, however, and as a safeguard we went to the local doctor.

'You know what to do, don't you?' he asked.

'Go home?' I replied and he agreed, adding that I was more understanding than a couple he had spoken to recently. When he told them their child was allergic to their dogs and that they should get rid of them, their reply had been, 'Do you know of a good boarding school?'

The doctor gave Kirsty an injection. With some embarrassment I had to explain the situation to my brother, having stayed barely 24 hours. Kirsty's asthma improved on the journey back and she was quite clear by the time we arrived home. We all spent that Christmas with Dr Wolf Rapoport and family – Tosh, Judy and David.

Kirsty had an excellent English teacher and as a result she was encouraged to take her English Literature and Language exams at 14, two years earlier than rest of her form. When this teacher left, her successor failed to live up to her magic touch and Kirsty would get terribly frustrated when the class got disruptive. She enjoyed learning and couldn't bear for time to be wasted. She must have said something one day about the lesson because the teacher replied, 'If you think you could do better you can take the next class!' - and, by all accounts, she did!

As far as I can make out, taking these exams early left a gap in her timetable, and for the next two years she was allowed to spend the time in her form teacher's office. Her teacher trusted her to use the time well and she didn't betray that trust. It has often been said, and it may well be true, that it was then that she began to write her first lyrics.

She also appeared in two school productions, *Charley's Aunt* and - already a classic - her own godmother Joan Littlewood's *Oh What a Lovely War*, in which she sang 'I'll Make a Man of You'. When it came to her other GCSE exams, Kirsty said she wasn't going to bring much work home to revise: the school had already wasted too much of her time already. I could see that she was preparing to leave school altogether after the exams. Before she did, she told the headmaster that she thought the work could be done in half the time. (She clearly hadn't changed her opinion since writing about 'The School That I'd Like'!) I think he did genuinely seek her opinion and she was never anything but direct and honest.

For someone who enjoyed learning so much, and who worked so well, I thought that to leave school early would be a catastrophe, and I tried to influence her by telling her how greatly I had enjoyed being in the sixth forms at my own school, where I had been able to follow my interests in art, English and French and had also been able to organise dance recitals throughout the school. However, at the back of my mind I always remembered that I had quietly directed my activities towards my own future goal in life - dance - without interference from anyone else.

I began to recognise in my daughter the same determination to forge her own career and follow her own star. But - such was my ignorance – I was a little worried that the pop scene seemed full of young people who could neither sing nor play their instruments very well. Ewan always implied that he didn't mind what she did as long as she was the best at it, but then Hamish, Kirsty and I were always well aware of Ewan's three approved forms of music – folk, jazz and classical.

Whenever Kirsty had free time as she grew up, it was spent playing records in the 'snug'. This was a small office off the lounge which contained one of those old radiograms. She was interested in Hamish's record collection. I would occasionally be introduced to some song, singer or band that Hamish or Kirsty thought was good. We were all great fans of The Everly Brothers, and later The Beach Boys and I also know Kirsty enjoyed one of my records, *Viva! The Music of Mexico* by Percy Faith and his orchestra. One of our favourites was 'Cuanto le Gusta'. My own tastes at this time were more likely to include Borodin's *Prince Igor*, which I loved (not the musical *Kismet* which seemed to me very weak compared with the original), but I do remember that Freddie and the Dreamers was also a favourite of mine – I just loved his antics.

Eventually, with some persuasion from me, Kirsty moved to a sixth-form college and opted to do four subjects at A-level, one of these being Art. During the first term there, Kirsty also attended Goldsmiths College for one evening a week, learning the intricacies and techniques of recording music. I knew nothing about this subject but was pleased for her and, since I had to run her there and back, I enrolled in Russian again. It was soon obvious, however, that Kirsty's heart did not lie in her school work, so I arranged for her to take her A-level in Art a year early and go on to Art College. She thought some of her fellow art students were lacking in motivation and just wasting time – exactly the same frustration she had expressed about her school. Kirsty herself never wasted time: I have always felt she was making up for the lost years and now that her health was restored she was a girl in a hurry. She soon came into her element, and began to socialise and make new friends among the musicians and local bands she met.

GLR radio interview, June 1992

Tracey MacLeod: The next song is by Bob Marley, who wouldn't spring naturally to people's minds as a songwriter first and foremost.

Kirsty MacColl: Well, I don't know why, because all his stuff has proved that it just goes on and on and on, and he's had so many covers of various tracks and I can't see that's ever going to change. I think he was one of the most important songwriters around in the 1970s really. Certainly for me, while I was growing up, and was 16 or 17, the *Bob Marley Live* album was fantastic. Everywhere I went, I heard it – my own particular Summer of Love, I always think of Bob Marley and the Wailers. He was also one of the people I noticed that could present something that was essentially a political theme in a way that was so beautifully musical and so catchy that it crossed over to people who would automatically say, if they knew they were listening to something political, 'Oh, I don't want to hear that, I just want to be entertained.' I think that's a great art, really, if you can cross over into the mainstream with stuff that has a message.

TM: If Bob Marley had lived, what sort of music do you think he'd have been playing now? Do you think he'd be collaborating with someone like Prince?

KM: No.

> **TM:** You don't think he was a collaborator by nature?
>
> **KM:** I just think he was more into living out his lifestyle and getting his message over than kind of showbiz really.
>
> **TM:** The complete spiritual opposite of Prince?
>
> **KM:** Probably, yeah. (*laughs*)

When Kirsty was 16 and her striking beauty beginning to appear, she was asked to do some modelling for a clothes shop in nearby Caterham. The two owners were putting on a small evening show for charity at a school in Purley on the outskirts of Croydon. It was arranged that I should come and see the show, which would take about an hour, and then run Kirsty home afterwards. It had been an extremely busy week for me and I was very tired when I arrived near the school, but also more than happy in the knowledge that I had a week's holiday in front of me and I was looking forward to seeing Kirsty in her new role. I was also delighted that our circumstances had so changed that she could now feel able to enjoy the various opportunities and activities that came her way.

When I looked at the leaflet she had given me, however, I realised that I was extremely early. Having had no lunch, I was feeling quite hungry but after a quick walk I soon discovered that all the local shops had closed; the only place open seemed to be the pub on the corner. I ordered a double vodka to celebrate a pleasant evening ahead and a well-earned holiday. When the barman brought me my drink, I asked him what sandwiches or other bar food there were on offer – only to be told that didn't serve food, not even crisps, and all I could buy was a tiny shrink-wrapped cellophane packet of some sort of nibbles. (This was the 1970s!) So I snaffled them up in the first couple of minutes, and then eked out the vodka until it was time to go.

Walking across the road to the school, where the doors were at last now opening, I saw a crowd milling around outside waiting for friends before being ushered inside to take their seats. Some of them had had the foresight them in advance. I made for the first vacant seat, halfway down the length of the hall. I had a strange feeling of being some sort of alien among people who had known each other for years. A gentleman came onto the stage and was greeted with applause – he was obviously very well known – before explaining that the two owners of the dress shop, both of whom he mentioned by their first names, would be giving a running commentary on the dresses being shown that night. He also recited the names of the young models: the only name I recognised was 'Kirsty MacColl'.

I was now feeling extremely happy. The first model walked down the steps onto the stage and we all watched with interest. Then Kirsty appeared, standing at the top of the steps on a sort of balcony. Whether it was her professionalism, the way she turned – first one way, then another – or whether it was the pride of a mother seeing her grown-up daughter on stage that made me start laughing, I am not sure. It was more likely something to do with a double vodka on an empty stomach. But as she came down the steps, Kirsty caught my eye and, seeing me happily laughing, she flashed a brief smile before returning to her professional pose. She was wearing a simple A-line summer dress made of a filmy cotton with a floral design, knee-length with an extra fullness in the skirt. She had a soft straw hat to match with a wide brim, and swung a light-weight handbag from her arm. I quietly giggled my appreciation, and as Kirsty swept around the stage before exiting, she again caught my gaze, smiled at me and became the professional model yet again.

I was grateful for the cup of tea – and the two biscuits – that came with my ticket at half time and I was back to my normal self by the time Kirsty and I met up afterwards. When I tried to explain the cause of my hilarity, she just smiled. She also said she'd been asked to model again, but didn't think she would: once was enough.

Kirsty always knew her mind. One day, at around the same time, when she was taking the first tentative steps of her musical career, she told me she was going off to sing somewhere with a friend. I'm afraid to say I didn't take much notice and on her return casually asked how she had got on. It turns out that – much to my surprise and pride – some promoters who were looking for a possible Eurovision Song Contest singer had expressed interest in Kirsty's talents. She was having none of it, though, telling them in no uncertain terms, 'I'm sorry, but I'm not a family entertainer.' And on a later occasion, Kirsty returned from a visit to Ewan looking extremely annoyed. It was not in her nature to tell tales, but it appears she had been asked to sing on a folk record that Peggy Seeger was then making which included female relatives. At this age, in her later teens, Kirsty did not want to offend her father, but she had no wish whatsoever to take part in the recording.

When she was younger, Kirsty had once gone over to join the boys, Hamish, Calum and Neill, who were playing music together. She had offered suggestions, all of which were ignored, and Hamish told her to go home. She came back frustrated and upset, and told me the problem. Once again I encouraged her not to worry and to believe her turn would come. Her ideas were far more mature than people gave her credit for – she was forever fighting her age and apparent lack of experience.

The attitudes of most of the male musicians she encountered in those early years were patronising: she was required to be a pretty singer and nothing else. Kirsty always seems to have known what she *didn't* want to be: not a model, not an art student, not a family entertainer. Despite these early setbacks, though, she also knew what she *did* want to make of her life. Her original and dedicated approach to her music led from her leaving school at 16 to signing her first record deal just two years later.

Chapter Five

London Girls

1977-1984

'Singing is the only thing I want to do.'
KIRSTY MACCOLL TO JEAN MACCOLL, 1981

To celebrate Kirsty's 21st birthday in 1980, I gave her my mother Norrie's diamond ring. She was absolutely thrilled with it and suggested that it might deter any unwelcome advances! Now she certainly seemed ready to fight her own battles and had discovered from very early on the fickle nature of the music business. She had been busy with her full-time career since the age of 18, making many friends and, I'm sure, falling in and out of love. Like any teenager, she was more likely to confide in her intimate friends than in her mother and her lyrics often reflected the ups and downs of her life.

When Kirsty first left home and with Hamish having already flown the nest, I had decided to study for three years for an Open University degree, partly because I knew I would miss having Kirsty around at home. With a view to eventually returning to my own career, I also started giving Sunday classes at the newly opened Pineapple Dance Studio in Covent Garden for actors and dancers. I needn't have worried about being lonely, though, as I was still directing plays and only found the time for my studying at very unsociable hours.

After completing my degree, I returned to freelancing, directing a Molière play for drama students and choreographing for young people at the Theatre Royal in Stratford. Kirsty and I still found time to meet up and chat about what we were doing. On one occasion we met at Selfridges, to celebrate our different successes. She looked radiantly lovely and so happy and confident that I remember saying to her, 'You do look nice.'

'So do you,' she replied appreciatively. We walked around the store, eventually coming across a counter selling cheap costume jewellery. On the spur of the moment we egged each other on to buy ourselves a 'diamond' ring each for 30p and, giggling like little girls, we popped them on and marched out, flashing our fingers like stars. She then took me to a restaurant where the waiters presented each of us with a red rose – it was Kirsty's treat and she was obviously well-known. (Later on in her career she also took me to Langham's, where she had worked the same effect.) In the short time between my gift to Kirsty of her grandmother's diamond ring and our 30p extravagance in Selfridges, she had come a long way in her career. In a way, we had both graduated.

After leaving art college in 1978, Kirsty joined all-male band The Drug Addix as their vocalist, performing under the name Mandy Doubt. I knew nothing about the world she was entering but had every confidence in her, feeling sure that she knew what she was doing. I just hoped it wouldn't be too tough. She was making her own way and all I could do was support her to the hilt. After all, she was taking after me.

I dropped her off at a venue in Putney in the early days and she asked if I would like to come in and see the band. Realising that this was a rare privilege afforded to few, I accepted. The steps down were steep and uneven and the cellar itself was very dark indeed. There seemed to be a lot of junk around - though it could have been musical equipment, it was hard to see. The boys in the band were busy tuning up and balancing their instruments and I sat quietly in the dark for a long while until I had to go to another appointment - and left without actually hearing them play.

The atmosphere reminded me of my old Theatre Workshop days. The theatre at Stratford, London E15, had been absolutely dire in the early days, and yet we had all succeeded in making magic in such unpromising surroundings.

In the end, I was only ever to hear The Drug Addix play once. I had to pick up Mandy Doubt from the Swan and Sugar Loaf pub in Croydon after a gig. As I stood in the bar waiting, a man standing next to me nodded to the thunderous noise going on above our heads. 'Bloody racket, isn't it?' he said. I was torn between agreeing with him and declaring an interest by standing up for my daughter's contribution - though the noise was so loud, I'm not sure he would have believed me if I had. I defy anyone to have been able to sing through it.

It was at this time that the Irish promoter Frank Murray remembers first meeting Kirsty at Camden's Electric Ballroom. Kirsty came to him to be paid and they sat and chatted for a while. 'She seemed like a very nice person with a great sense of humour,' he recalled - a quality she probably needed after the release that year, on Chiswick Records, of the Drug Addix's one and only EP. 'She always had a smile and a chuckle when I saw her,' remembers her accountant Ronnie Harris, whose lifelong friendship with Kirsty began when she was contemplating a deal with Dave Robinson of Stiff Records, who had asked her in for a solo audition on the back of some Drug Addix demos. According to Ronnie, Dave Robinson, had promised her a 'few thousand'. She then had a chuckle because a 'few' could of course be any number from £2,000 or more. And knowing Robbo as she did, she probably thought it could only be the £2,000. I always think of Kirsty when anybody ever mentions the word 'few' in respect of money. Kirsty always considered herself lucky to have the gift that she had... and it was a privilege to have known her.

When Kirsty signed her record deal with Stiff, she did not have the stereotypical wide-eyed ingénue's gratitude, but carefully studied the contract, asking questions to make sure that she exactly understood the terms of her position.

She had had to come up with a new song for the Stiff audition pronto, so she wrote 'They Don't Know', which became her first single in June 1979. I remember encouraging everyone to go out and buy it, and it certainly received a lot of airplay on the radio. 'Kirsty's musical career began on the same day as mine in June 1978,' remembers Billy Bragg,

when Chiswick Records simultaneously released 3 EPs as part of their Suburban Rock'n'Roll series, among them my punk band Rift Raft and Croydon's answer to the Velvet Underground, Drug Addix. Me and my mates returned to obscurity but Kirsty was spotted by Stiff Records who signed her as a solo artist. I bought her first single, 'They Don't Know' and admired her ability to sound like the Shangri-Las. As a singer, she was a one-woman all-girl vocal group and in a previous era would have made a tidy living writing songs for Phil Spector's stable of artists.

Unfortunately, Billy Bragg's admiration for 'They Don't Know' wasn't shared more widely since a distribution strike halted its success before it could fulfil its chart potential – though Tracey Ullman later reached the Top 10 with her 1983 version. The bad luck continued with Kirsty's next single, 'You Caught Me Out', which she co-wrote and recorded with members of The Boomtown Rats. After frustrating delays, it was eventually permanently shelved. Feeling that it hadn't been promoted sufficiently, Kirsty left Stiff, eventually signing up with Polydor, and it was with this label that her big break came.

It was around this time that Jools Holland first met Kirsty, and was immediately impressed by her:

We first met, I think, in 1979, 1980, something like that, maybe a little bit earlier than that, but that was the first time we spent some time together and she came over to the flat I had in Blackheath. We were going to try and write some songs. I think she'd been on some of the same shows Squeeze had been on.

The flat was on the top floor of this Victorian building, and she said, 'What are we going to write then?' We fiddled around trying to write something, and then I remember there was a song that I'd written with Chris Difford called 'All Fingers and Thumbs', a sort of a honky-tonk song, it was just on a little demo. To get warmed up she said, 'I'll sing that,' and it was amazing, because it completely transformed the song and made it sound real authentic. It was like a country and western hillbilly sort of song, that's what it was, but the way she sang it – it transformed it from being this bloke, me, singing it in this South East London flat, and it suddenly sounded like... you could see great American roads stretching out over these dusty landscapes and little wooden shacks and it was all about drifters and people who were all fingers and thumbs.

It was the first time then that I realised what a difference getting someone to sing a song makes. I learned then from her doing that what could be done – made me realise what a great thing it was. It also made me realise what a fantastic voice she had. There we were, talking about writing songs, but really she could write brilliant songs anyway, and when she sang songs which were naturally in her mode – and it's not everyone whose natural mode is to sing in a country and western, swing, boogie-woogie style, but that was her style, she could do that, that was great – she could really make them come alive, you know. She didn't think of her own voice being a particularly powerful thing, but she was wrong: it really was amazing. It brought life to a piece of music that didn't have life before. She wasn't confident perhaps of her voice, but it *was* great.

After doing that, she had some songs and they sounded great and she heard some other demos that I'd done. I remember after that, after we'd worked out how to put down this song and she put the vocal on it, we went down to the quiet local pub with my brothers, I think – so many people they didn't all fit in the car. There was something like ten people in a Ford Escort, absurdly overloaded and she was sat underneath about four people in the front seat, her face completely squashed against the window. I remember her looking through this crowd of bodies saying, 'Well, thanks for a lovely night out, I'm really enjoying it' – and I also realised then what great company she was. So we went to the pub and she was very upright as a personality, she lit up. She had that thing, which some people do, where if you were having a conversation with her she'd be saying some things that were amusing and she'd somehow make it so that whatever you were saying would be amusing as well, which then in turn had a cyclical effect, or whatever, which makes *you* be even more amusing, which makes *her* more amusing... and she had the ability to do that. I saw her do that a few times. After that I became an admirer: I thought she was really great.

GLR radio interview, June, 1992

Tracey MacLeod: We're going to talk about songwriting. How hard was it for you to pick out five or six great songwriters from your collection?

Kirsty MacColl: Well, there are certain people I think of as being the most important. They created the sort of stuff I grew up listening to and made an impression on me.

TM: What's your idea of the perfect song? Do you go for lyrics, structure, or sound?

KM: Well, it depends. If you're writing it's one thing, if you're listening it's an overall impression that it leaves you with - if it makes you feel good or it makes you feel something, it's done its job.

TM: When you looked at your five songs, did you notice if the songs had anything in common with each other?

KM: Well, they're not all in the same bag, but I think there's a certain peculiar Englishness about at least a couple of them...

In early 1981 the promoter Frank Murray got in touch with Kirsty again through a mutual friend at Stiff, Annie Holloway (about whom Kirsty later wrote her beautiful song 'Annie'). 'Annie wanted me to listen to a tape Kirsty recorded,' recalls Frank, and later, when I listened to it, one track stood out: it was 'There's a Guy Works Down the Chip Shop Swears He's Elvis'. I knew she had a hit there. We eventually met again and she asked me to become her manager. She was already signed to Polydor Records at the time and was about to release a single, 'Keep Your Hands Off My Baby'. This got some airplay and reintroduced Kirsty to radio. We then released 'Chip Shop' in May 1981, which became a big hit. It should have been a No. 1, but Polydor blew it. They had no marketing plan, and I think the record peaked at No. 5.

The actor-musician Carl Chase recalls meeting Kirsty in this period, when he was starring in London in an early tribute show by Ken Campbell, *Hank Williams: The Show He Never Gave*. They were introduced one night after the performance, he remembers:

She was 21 at the time and had just had a hit record with a song called 'There's a Guy Works Down the Chip Shop Swears He's Elvis'. Kirsty was a very shy, sweet, young girl who told me that she had really enjoyed my show, which was very nice of her. The head of Acuff-Rose music publishers, Tony Peters, happened to be there as well. So it was suggested that Kirsty and I recorded a duet together. The song was called 'We Can't Go On Like This', written by Liverpool musician Roger Tomlin. It never was released, but I still have the demo and the fond memory of how far ahead of me Kirsty was in the recording studio. Remember, I had been a cab driver only three months earlier and was a babe in toyland when it came to theatre and the big bad world of recording. Although only six years older than my eldest daughter at that time, Kirsty had an ease about her in the recording studio and took only one take to my three before we finally finished the track. Kirsty was an incredible singer and a real down-to-earth person, and for the short time I spent with her I felt she was my friend in scary old London town.

Kirsty's collaborator on 'Chip Shop' was musician and friend Philip Rambow. The song was a witty, rocking number pointing the finger at lying scoundrels everywhere, a theme she would return to with relish throughout her song-writing life. Philip recalls those early days:

[Kirsty] was the guest of my friend and former PR, Glen Colson. He introduced her as a newly-signed to Stiff Records singer-songwriter and suggested that perhaps we could write songs together. Kirsty liked that idea. I was older and had had some success, but had never co-written before. We were all struck at how beautiful she was – how open and exuberant. Glen always had impeccable taste in the artists he worked with so there was no question that this young girl had talent and a bright future.

The job of the artist is to make the obvious, obvious. Some people used to be confused by Kirsty's lack of marketable image. Perhaps it's because instead of seeing herself as any one of the many talents she possessed – singer, songwriter, guitarist, backing singer, arranger – she was an artist who incorporated all the talent at her disposal into the projects that came her way with equal enthusiasm. She was also ambitious as a person and reflected all elements of human experience with equal honesty and openness. This makes it hard for media people to deal with – they prefer a one-dimensional product that can be easily identified by the general public. Kirsty was an artist whose medium was (mostly) music.

Like many great artists, her drive and motivation may have partly come from personal loss and/or family hardship. All her friends knew that she would have liked to have had more recognition from Ewan for her work, and one way would have been for him to have supported her at one of her gigs.

She had really high standards in all aspects of her life and expected the same from friends and colleagues. She was a tireless worker when it came to making music and a prodigious party person when the work was done. She was never anything about half measures: if the glass was empty it had to filled up again – to the brim.

She was generous to her co-writers, always insisting on a 50/50 split even if she only used your riff. She would do all the lyrics and the melody, but say that the riff was the inspiration and so that merited half the song. Her instructions to me were given in a typically straightforward way: 'Just whack a guitar riff on any old bit of tape. Don't do any fancy demos or other instrumentation and for God's sake don't hum along with the riff – it will put me right off!'

I'm not sure Philip is exactly right about Kirsty's attitude towards working with her father. Steve Lillywhite remembers a later occasion when Ewan visited the couple. 'We took him up to the studio to listen to her songs and lyrics. He asked for the music to be turned down a bit and for copies of the lyrics.' Steve recalls that Ewan's manner was not that of a proud and indulgent parent who would like whatever his child had done but displayed, on the contrary, a very professional approach, following the words and listening to the music. At the end, he looked up and said simply, 'Fantastic.' But on the other hand, as Kirsty's brother Hamish puts it, 'Dad had always despised pop music':

In his eyes it was against his political beliefs, it had no history that he could see – I mean it was not an art form that had been honed over several hundred years – and was therefore not credible. It is also true that he was immensely competitive and so he was jealous of the acclaim and the money pop stars received. I could not think of him and Kirsty working together. Kirsty ridiculed folk-music as the 'beard-and-sandals brigade' – with her it was definitely a matter of style, not a particular political viewpoint. Folk singers appeared to her to be socially inept people who lacked any *fashion* sense and I mean that in every sense of the word, not just clothes. They were 'out of touch'. The Pogues were different – 'punk folk rock' – and they refused to be bound by traditional purists of any kind. In later life, though, Kirsty's taste in music grew much broader and she enjoyed listening to Bulgarian women's choirs and Mexican folk bands. I doubt she saw these as folk music, although they were.

No, Kirsty thought working together with Dad would be ridiculous. Dad made a series of prize-winning shows for radio – *The Radio Ballads*. They were groundbreaking, won the Italia prize a few times... but there was one, I think the last one, about young people, that was so wide of the mark it was embarrassing. How someone who had once been young himself could be so far out of touch is beyond me. The songs and music could have been written by Kurt Weill and Brecht. I remember when I was about 13 being encouraged by my dad to go to a study group at the

Communist Party of Great Britain Marxist-Leninist. They were reading and discussing the Communist Manifesto. There was a group of about eight and someone from the Party leading the discussion. We started reading out loud, taking turns, and I realised that there was only one working-class person there, a woman and she was asking some very telling questions. Why did we have to learn a new language to appreciate this book? The Manifesto had been written in the middle of the 19th century, then translated from German to English, and remained unchanged. It was largely incomprehensible to me, let alone the average working-class man or woman. In other words, the process was elitist and egotistical from the beginning. I left after two sessions, cured of any Communist sympathies. The fact that my dad was taken in by all this (and I mean by the politics, not the injustices) just shows me he was the usual romantic looking for the universal panacea. He decided it was Communism but he could just as well have decided it was God, or Mammon.

Speaking as Kirsty and Hamish's mother, I can well understand their feelings. My parents were Conservatives, my grandfather a Socialist. I remember, at the end of the War, when he was living with us after his home had been severely damaged by bombing raids, he refused a lift in the car on principle when my parents were going to vote. He proudly walked to cast his own vote for the opposition. Travelling widely and mixing with people before joining Theatre Workshop had probably made me more of a Socialist, and I certainly learned much more about politics in later years without becoming a Communist. Things I could not accept, I would argue about. As Kirsty once said to me rather proudly, 'You had a mind of your own.'

Ewan's background was very different. The only surviving

child of Scots parents, he was brought up in Salford. His father was a working man, a trade unionist and a Communist. Life in the 1920s and 30s was very hard and always harder for the poor. His father was unable to earn when on strike, so his mother Betsy worked to support the family. As much as he admired his father, the young boy would have liked a greater show of affection. This background moulded Ewan's character.

In later years, George Bernard Shaw (himself an early enthusiast for Communist Russia) was to say in a newspaper interview that there were only two playwrights of genius in the country: Ewan MacColl and himself. Ewan had moved on as an artist but his politics had not. And, running through everything, as Hamish says, was his romanticism. Ewan's 'weapons' were his songs and plays.

Hamish, unlike Kirsty, often sang with Ewan, who often told me how much he admired his son's voice. Hamish wrote a few folk songs himself, but found it much harder to write lyrics in the modern style because of Ewan's dismissive attitude towards all things pop. I determined that Kirsty, from a very early age, would grow up finding things out for herself and go her own way. The only time I nearly slipped up was when she wanted to leave school at 16 and we reached a compromise. I swiftly realised how wrong I had been and gave my support to the performing career she had set her determined mind on.

Jools Holland remembers that determination well, from a recording session with Kirsty he produced in 1981:

Anyway, she rang and she had a deal with one of the labels – Frank Murray was then her manager – to cut five songs, which was quite common, I think, in those days. I don't know if it still is, but the record company would give you the money to do five tracks. Anyway, we went into a studio in St John's Wood in 1981. She wanted me to produce them, that was the thing.

She also said, 'I've got all these and I know who I want to play on them, I know what I want, but I just need someone to pull it all together - do you want to come and do it? We've only got a week to do five things, do you think that's possible?' The way that I'd always worked before, we'd go in and really steam in at it without stopping, so I said, 'Yes.' I mean, it is quite ambitious, but we did - I've got a list somewhere of what they were. On the front of one of my diaries is the sticker from the tape box from that session.

She liked lots of people around the studio, she wanted to have lots of fun which was cool. I was much more serious - 'Are we going to get this song right? Is the drum track sounding good?' - and in fact I learned from her that the way to do it is to have fun while you're doing it. If you're not enjoying doing it, then it's normally not working very well. So when I go in the studio now it's fast and fun, that's what I like to have.

So we cut these different songs, and she was great. There were quite a few people around the studio and when she came to do her vocal, I knew she was slightly apprehensive, which was daft because her vocals were great. In fact - another thing I learnt from her - she said the best thing is when I just sing and don't think about it, and sing live. Of course, they were the best ones, the ones we kept mostly.

People will do that, then they'll redo the vocals - it was normally her first take, which is the same with a lot of the people that I know that are really great like, say, BB King or Van Morrison, who I've worked with since. That's how they work - it's the first take. Duke Ellington used to do that. That was true of her, too, which I think also says something about what she was about as a musician. She was like those artists, there is something spontaneous about them - the same way as her conversation was. You couldn't ask her to repeat the thing because it was in the moment, and it was the same in her vocals.

Anyway at one point, she was going to redo the vocals because in those days that was how you did a record: you did the rough vocal then you did the 'proper' vocal – but now I know that's a lot of nonsense: it was the first one that was the right one. So she did this and she wanted to redo the vocal but there were a lot of people in the studio – friends and stuff. There were some great people and some odd people, some annoying – like anybody, she had some friends who were really fantastic and some who you couldn't work out what they were for but it didn't matter, they were just all there. But when it came to doing the vocal everyone was sitting around in the control room having cups of tea and chatting, so I quietly went out and I got the engineer to mute the sound so nobody could hear us, and I said to her, 'Do you want me to get rid of everybody for you to do the vocal?' and she said, 'Who?'

She actually hadn't noticed that there were about thirty people in the studio.

But although Kirsty managed to focus her concentration even in a crowded recording studio, live gigs presented a different challenge, as Frank Murray remembers from her 1981 tour of various rural ballrooms in Ireland:

It was on this tour we discovered that Kirsty was very nervous about performing live. On the first night Kirsty got through the set so fast I had to ask Gavin Povey, the piano player, to sing a few numbers. She finished so quick we still had 45 minutes left to play. Needless to say, the promoter was none too happy. We were short-changed on a couple of gigs so it was not a great experience. On the plus side, we enjoyed ourselves thoroughly – we did laugh a lot, there's no doubt we saw the funny side of things. Kirsty had a great sense of humour and the guys in the band were incredible. The band were Gavin Povey, John Dillon, Andrew Bodnar and Lu Edmonds. Kirsty did two TV shows which she enjoyed despite her nervousness.

'I think she felt basically insecure in the public eye,' remembers Pete Glenister, Kirsty's later collaborator and friend, 'she just felt really on the spot':

In Ireland she had a really loud band who didn't really listen. Kirsty's really a roots player – I'd never call her 'folky', but the roots music of Britain, songs that really made you listen. It was about the words; she was in the best tradition of English song with Ray Davies – that school of songwriting – whereas when she went out on her first tour, everyone was trying to be punky. I know the keyboard player was Gavin Povey. I think Billy Bragg was there – it was like the Stiff bunch.

'She didn't really suit punk rock,' agreed Bono, 'she was much too savvy for that kind of angst.' At the same time he counted Kirsty's creativity among the greats of her generation: 'I'd put her up with Morrissey and people like that, and across the road from Shane MacGowan – that calibre of songwriter.'

Billy Bragg certainly remembers Kirsty's contrasting attitudes towards the public stage and the private studio. 'A notoriously shy live artist,' he wrote, 'it was those of us who had seen her perform, albeit in the studio, who were in awe of her abilities as a singer and songwriter.'

I remember this period of her early touring career very clearly. I had had a postcard from one of the band while Kirsty was in Ireland which said she was feeling a lot better now – and had stopped throwing up! I was still concerned that I hadn't realised how nervous she felt about performing. On her return she told me how badly she had suffered and when I realised that this was a serious problem I suggested to her eventually that perhaps she should think about trying something else. Her eyes filled with tears as she said, 'Singing is the only thing I want to do.' In that case, I suggested, she should take her time over it. It was obvious, however, that at the same time she had enjoyed both working with the band and singing for radio.

The 1981 tour had been arranged to promote her first album, *Desperate Character*, put out by Polydor in June, which featured a collection of snappy Kirsty songs along with a few covers of 1960s numbers that were thought insufficiently commercial to release as singles. Kirsty had been very excited by the new songs she had written. Much as she had enjoyed 'Chip Shop', she felt that she had moved on. She played the record through to me when it came out and was bitterly disappointed when it didn't do better in the charts.

After returning from the Irish tour in late 1981, Kirsty and the band recorded and released a Brian Wilson song, 'You Still Believe in Me'.

'Again, this got some radio play,' remembers Frank Murray, 'but bombed. About a year later she performed with Matchbox at The Venue in London. She only sang three songs but she was still very nervous.' Much later, when she was interviewed on TV, Kirsty was quite open about her stage fright, explaining that she was excruciatingly shy and found the whole process of performance terrifying:

'People expected a kind of bravado that I didn't have,' she

said. 'If you're nervous you can't breathe, and if you can't breathe you can't sing.' After a childhood so overshadowed by asthma, that was quite something to say.

'Her harmonies were her trademark,' Jools Holland recently told me, during a long, affectionate and reflective interview I did with him.

The other thing about musicians is it's important they sound like themselves. So it's like, if I could copy Art Tatum exactly on piano, there'd be no point. The great thing about Kirsty is that there was nothing bland about her, and her voice was very distinctive. Not only did it bring life to songs, the way she did harmonies there was a specific way – the same way that if you hear a Beach Boys record you know it's them. She used to do harmonies with herself – she did that on some of those demos we did. She used to worry about them, and ask 'Do you think we should just get back-up vocals in?', and I would say 'No, what you do is great – it sounds so distinctive.' Partly it was the mixing of her voice and also the particular modal harmonics that she used.

When you heard her on the radio, you knew it was her straight away, whatever she was singing. With her harmonies, it was like times a hundred. It was like Ray Charles said: 'They can like my music or not like my music, as long as they know I was telling the truth.' It was the same thing with Kirsty. She also had her own sound which is about the most important thing you can have. There are some musicians who are the most fantastic virtuoso players so they can make any sounds, and copy people – but it's not the same as sounding like yourself.

GLR radio interview, June 1992

Tracey MacLeod: The first one is The Beach Boys. Why did you pick this one?

Kirsty MacColl: Well, I covered this song about ten years ago, and it did absolutely nothing. I just thought it was a really nice song. It's off *Pet Sounds*, and that's one of the most important albums, I think, if you're getting into song writing. Structurally it's so different to anything else that was around at the same time. The song's called 'You Still Believe in Me', and it's just very gentle and romantic.

TM: The thing that record has in common with your own work is that multi-tracked harmony technique. Did they use different techniques to what you do?

KM: Well, for a start there was loads of them, so they'd have had to sing in unison anyway, because they didn't have multi-tracking like you do nowadays. It was a completely different way of recording. I don't think you can get that sound now because the sort of equipment people use is too expensive to get that cheap sound, you know.

TM: You believe that lyrics should be able to stand alone without the context of the song. Does that hold true of The Beach Boys, do you think?

KM: Not in a lot of cases, but the songs of theirs that turned me on were the older stuff that was masterminded by Brian Wilson. When he split, it all went rapidly downhill. Lyrically they're not one of the bands I look up to and think they write the best lyrics – but I don't think you're going to beat the production of *Pet Sounds*.

Shortly after the release of 'You Still Believe in Me' and apparently deaf to its lyrics ('I know perfectly well I'm not where I should be, I've been very aware you've been patient with me...'), Polydor dropped her.

'Kirsty didn't like rejection,' comments Dave Robinson. 'The first time she left Stiff it was her own decision, so Polydor dropping her had a bad effect on her. She wasn't able to entirely swallow that and she drifted for a while at that point.' Polydor's decision left the five tracks Kirsty had recorded with Jools Holland, as he explained, unreleased:

Anyway, the five tracks for whatever record company it was – they never picked up on them. Rather daft, record companies are, often. The same thing happened to Squeeze. Somebody in the record company says, 'Let's pay for these five tracks' and the person who asked for them gets sacked or whatever. They were fantastic, those tracks, they were really great. I've got them somewhere. 'Shutting the Doors' was one, which we worked out and put on that record recently. ['Shutting the Doors' was remixed and released on Jools Holland's 2003 album *Jack O the Green*.] It's a shame they weren't picked up, but I've seen that – it's not uncommon. She was quite tough, she just decided to move on to the next thing, you know. The music comes through in the end, though, which is why I was pleased to put 'Shutting the Doors' out, because it meant it reached other people, and they could hear it.

Chapter Six

All I Ever Wanted

1982-1984

'It's a funny old world for London girls.'

<small>KIRSTY MACCOLL, 'LONDON GIRLS', 1983</small>

In 1982, after completing my degree, I was invited to Switzerland to direct a Laban movement course in Zurich. I was asked to stay five weeks. During this time I lent Kirsty my car, as she had just passed her test. Hamish wrote that she was rushing around like a 'busy bee', but driving safely. By the time I came home, Kirsty had moved into her own ground-floor flat near Holland Park. It was pleasantly situated, had its own front garden and was certainly a great improvement on the one she had been renting. I was able to supply her with many of the usual necessities – towels, sheets, kitchen equipment, the usual stuff – until she could choose her own. The flat had only one bedroom, which meant there was very little room for storage and clothes. Hamish came to the rescue, though, and offered to build a mezzanine floor with steps leading up to it. When it was finished, Kirsty was thrilled. Hamish is the only member of our family (and, I think, Steve's) who is any good at DIY. Her bed went upstairs leaving plenty of room for storage space below. I would often drive up to town on a Sunday and join her and a few of her friends for lunch at the restaurant at the top of the road.

Although my own days as a performer were over and Theatre Workshop no longer existed as a company, our work was still in demand. I was now choreographing a musical at the Central Library Theatre in Manchester. It was like old times as I knew the theatre, and many of the actors working there, very well. That Christmas, Hamish and Kirsty stayed over with me and we were joined by four of my students – three Japanese and one New Zealander. We had great fun improvising stories and accompanying ourselves with percussion instruments. I still have the tape we made.

By now, Hamish had qualified as a doctor of Chinese medicine, and was working as an acupuncturist and also teaching T'ai Chi and other forms of martial art. From time to time he also sang in public with his father. We were all of us forging creative ways through life and all had the greatest respect for each other's work.

Later on, Kirsty and an American friend of hers were invited by Joan Littlewood to Paris where she was then living. (Her partner Gerry had died in 1975.) They took a few days out and Joan introduced them to her friends and generally wined and dined them – including a night with Joan and her friend Baron Rothschild (she once wrote a book on his wines). When Joan rang me to tell me they were coming home the next day, she told me these 'two young birds' – Kirsty and her friend – had had a great time.

In the spring of 1982, Sheila Hancock invited me to join the Royal Shakespeare Company as their movement trainer and choreographer. Sheila had briefly been a member of Theatre Workshop, and was a great admirer of the productions, so when she was asked to direct *A Midsummer Night's Dream* she thought of me. Her production ran in parallel with *Romeo and Juliet*, directed (with the same cast) by John Caird, and after rehearsals in London the company was scheduled to tour both plays, with Sheila in charge, until the summer, when it would return to Stratford-upon-Avon for the tourist season.

The large bus duly bumped its way up part of the unadopted road, the cast spilled out and I welcomed them to my garden, explaining what I had in store for them. They were to pair off in twos: one of each couple would be blindfolded, and after settling on a pre-arranged sound, the blindfolded person would try to establish contact with their partner. This the assembled company took in their stride – it seemed a doddle. I took them through my own woods to the deeper thickets beyond my garden. Blindfolds were then put on, and the partners scattered around, moving some distance away before making their agreed sound. It was surprising how these town-dwellers responded to this very different environment. Many of us were in hysterics as we stood watching. Confronted by Shakespeare's 'thorny brambles and embracing bushes', members of the group angrily tried to force a way through rather than circumnavigating these natural hazards, despite the many minor injuries they were sustaining.

The hide-and-seek exercise then saw us roaming over a greater expanse. I think it was here that Robert Eddison, an experienced and accomplished actor, well into his seventies at the time, lost us, only to reappear at Beech Way much later, long after the rest of us had left the wood. We collapsed on the grass bordering the woodland, nursing our insect bites and bloodied scratches, but all of us aware that the afternoon had been a valuable experience. The lunacy of Theatre Workshop's improvisations, when cowboys and Indians had battled it out to the finish, was not dead. A new generation of thespians was prepared to continue the tradition, with mad battles of their own in hostile woodland. I rather think Will Shakespeare would have been proud of them; it certainly helped the movement of the actors in the production.

And at the very least, Peter Quince (as played by Robert Eddison) could speak with feeling in the *Dream* when he declared, 'Here's a marvellous convenient place for our rehearsal. This green plot shall be our stage, this hawthorn brake our tiring-house...'

My RSC contract required me to stay with the company during their first week of touring. As one of these venues happened to be Lincoln, my home town, I was delighted and enjoyed the opportunity to stay with my brother Pip and his family. Kirsty also promised to come up to see one of the performances. After our asthma-curtailed Christmas trip a few years before, the arrangement had always been for Kirsty to sleep in my car, with the windows open, in my brother's large garage whenever we visited. This time she would motor up to a health farm booked by the record company some 20 miles away and drive over to see us before the performance. As it turned out, this decision may have saved her life.

Early in the morning I awoke to cries of 'Fire!' from my sister-in-law and her frantic calls for Pip: he seemed to be missing. Sitting up in a daze, I noticed that my pillow was brown, but white where my head had been. The smoke was overpowering as I rushed to the bathroom and soaked a towel in water. Quickly wrapping it around my head, I opened the door into the hall. It was impossible to see anything. I thought my brother might be in the garage so, after feeling it for heat, I opened the door and went in. The fumes were suddenly much worse and I knew that no one could have lasted more than minute or two in there. I knelt down to feel the concrete around the cars in case

Pip was lying unconscious and, after making my escape, I was greatly relieved to see him coming back from a neighbour's, having called the fire brigade. The fire had actually started in the garage and it was almost two years before the house was habitable again. I dread to think what might have happened if anyone had been sleeping there.

That evening, after the performance, the local council invited the company to a buffet supper celebration. Since the rest of my clothes had been ruined by the smoke of the fire, I only had my training kit to wear: not the most glamorous costume in town. I thought entering the reception with Daniel Day Lewis might take some attention away from me. In fact, the man on the door took one look at me, in some surprise, and then told me that this was a reception just for the Royal Shakespeare Company. Dan replied very politely that I was their choreographer.

Earlier in the day I had been telling Kirsty about the company, and said how much I had enjoyed working with Dan and that he didn't seem to have a girlfriend... Now, as Kirsty caught up with us, I introduced her to him. She gave a nice smile and after saying, 'Hello,' joked, 'I can find my own boyfriends, Mum!'

And very soon afterwards, she did.

That was Kirsty, all over.

● ● ●

Meanwhile, though, Kirsty was successfully pushing through the brambles of her own career, as Frank Murray again remembers:

I went down to Dingwalls one night to see Jools Holland and the Millionaires. I knew Jools from his time with Squeeze, and I asked him if he would be interested in working with Kirsty. Jools agreed and brought Pino Palladino, and I think he also brought Johnny Turnbull. I got

Hans Zimmer to play some Fairlight [synthesiser] on a couple of the tracks. Dave Jordan produced some tracks – I had worked with Dave in The Specials. These recordings formed the bulk of the songs for her second album. Polydor rejected them as not being commercial enough. In 1983 I signed Kirsty to Stiff Records and they duly released 'Terry'. This was a minor hit, and we had Adrian Edmondson direct the video.

Mark Nevin, a friend and fellow musician, remembers playing on the sessions:

She asked me to play guitar on some new songs that she was recording at the tiny, and slightly strange-smelling Pathway Studios in Islington. Two of the songs, 'You Broke My Heart in 17 Places' and 'Terry', went on to be covered by Tracey Ullman. Kirsty was very tough, but also very vulnerable, like a child. We then went our separate ways, and it was not until 1989 that our paths crossed again.

As Jools Holland told me, that's exactly how paths and ways tend to go in the business in which Kirsty was now beginning to find her feet:

In music, what happens is that you have great long periods where you don't see people for a long time, and then you'll see them again and it's like no time has passed, which is quite nice. So Kirsty and I used to bump into one another when we were both doing festivals. After that, I bumped into her from time to time, and she was always one of those people I was so relieved to see. You know with some people, you see them in the corner of an airport, lift your newspaper up and hope they aren't going to say, 'Hello'? 'Oh hello, how are you, haven't seen you for a bit. How lovely...' With Kirsty it was the exact opposite. It was her all over – you'd put your newspaper down and run over.

Kirsty's lyrics were always very honest. She had no time for what she thought were the rather overblown ballads that men wrote for, to, and about women, crying over their lost loves – no, she always felt that women should play a more positive role, and were not the helpless maidens portrayed by male songwriters. 'If there was one legacy that Kirsty had,' wrote the music journalist Colin Irwin, 'it would be the value she put on lyrics: the compassion she had for people, and bringing the characters to life.' None of which is to say, of course, that the female voices Kirsty sang about didn't get hurt when a relationship failed – of course they did; but they pick themselves up, and get on with life. As she sang in 'Terry', 'Anyway it doesn't matter now, 'Cos I have met somebody new...' And there was always Kirsty's endless gift for laughter, as the full title of 'You Broke My Heart in 17 Places (Shepherds Bush Was Only One)' so marvellously shows. 'To this day,' remembers Frank Murray, 'I can still hear the sound of Kirsty's laughter.'

Following her return to the Stiff label in 1983, and the release of 'Terry' that October, I heard from Hamish that Kirsty had indeed met 'somebody new', someone of whom he obviously approved. That special someone turned out to be Steve Lillywhite, who had been producing Simple Minds when Kirsty came in to do some backing vocals. It was a busy and exciting time, both professionally and personally. As Frank Murray remembers, Kirsty had been introduced to and inspired by the music of Billy Bragg:

She had gone out for dinner with Andy McDonald, who had signed Billy to his label. Andy gave Kirsty a copy of Billy's 'Milkman of Human Kindness' album [*Life's a Riot with Spy vs Spy*]. Kirsty loved it. She called me and insisted I come round and listen to it. The songs were great and we listened to it over and over. Kirsty made up her mind she would try and do a cover of 'A New England'. Around this time also, I introduced Kirsty to Simple Minds through a friend of mine, Frankie Gallagher, who was working with them. He invited us down to the Town House Studios where they were recording. Kirsty stayed in contact with them after that and did some backing vocals. It was during a recording with them that she first met Steve Lillywhite. Kirsty started dating Steve and consequently, when the time came to record 'A New England', Steve was on board as producer. Kirsty had started a creative relationship with Pete Glenister also, by now, and Pete's guitars are beautiful on this track.

Pete Glenister himself remembers first meeting Kirsty in Paris at around this time, when he was playing on an album by the Abba singer Frida Lyngstad, *Shine*, which Steve was producing. 'Kirsty and Steve had just got together,' recalls Pete:

I think Steve had just done a Simple Minds record, and she was a huge Simple Minds fan, so she'd come with him to Paris. She was effectively vetting the songs for the record. It was one of those recording sessions like in the old days when a bunch of musicians would get taken somewhere and you'd be holed up in a hotel and wouldn't be required all the time. It doesn't happen like that any more – they get wheeled in, they play and they leave. We were in Paris for about a month, so Kirsty and I used to look around and go to cafés, the opera and shops. We always used to shop on tour. All over America we'd go to malls, and she would tell me what I should buy for [my wife] Ingrid. She was responsible for a lot of credit card bills... she would *bully* me into buying things! Steve said, 'When we go back, we're going to make a record. Come down and play on it.'

So that's when we started playing together, on 'A New England'. That was the first of her records I played on – me and Simon Climie, who was the keyboard player. When we came back [in 1984], he and I started to work with Steve on the record, programming stuff – it was all done with programmed drums; Steve had just bought a Fairlight. Then Kirsty became pregnant with Jamie while we were recording that.

'When I first met her in late 1983,' remembers Billy Bragg,

Tracey Ullman was riding high in the charts with her version of 'They Don't Know'. Those penny-pinchers at Stiff had Tracey sing over Kirsty's original backing track and when Ms Ullman couldn't quite reach the high notes, they kept Kirsty's vocal. It is unmistakably she who sings the high 'bay-bee' that begins the third verse. Kirsty had come to see me because she wanted to record a version of my song 'A New England' which duly appeared in 1984 and marked the arrival of a new pop sensibility in her work. She had recently married whizz-kid producer Steve Lillywhite and together they fashioned a huge chart hit out of my spartan original. Kirsty lifted me out of the indie ghetto and into the Top Ten. My debut album *Life's a Riot* went gold as a result.

Over the New Year 1983 to 1984 Steve was working with Big Country in Glasgow for a live TV broadcast. Kirsty was there too for the celebrations, and on the first stroke of midnight she called me to wish me a Happy New Year. She sounded very happy and I could hear the jollifications going on in the background. Then a little later the phone rang a second time. To my surprise, it was Kirsty again: 'He's asked me to marry him!' On the last stroke of midnight, Steve had proposed to her. It seemed to me that the last chime was still echoing out as she told me the exciting news. I was delighted and sent my love.

After I put the phone down, I found myself thinking back to an early New Year's Eve when she had been a child of just eight years old. She had stayed up then to watch the New Year in on television. Then she had said she had a special surprise for me and turned on her radio. A programme was just starting, which I think was called *Night Ride*, on the new Radio 1. The presenter began with a letter from a listener which he read out. I sat intrigued and unsuspecting, and then heard the words: 'I am Kirsty MacColl and I live at...' giving our full address, and continuing, 'I have a dog and a cat and I live with my mum, Jean MacColl, and my brother Hamish and I listen to your programme regularly and would like you to play something for my mother.' Whether or not Kirsty chose the tune I don't know, nor do I now remember what it was – but I did wonder what sort of mother other listeners would think me for allowing an eight-year-old to listen to a programme that came on the air after midnight! Even so, I thanked her, feeling rather stunned. I had absolutely no idea that she had been listening to this programme. And now, just a few short years later, Kirsty's own songs were being played on the radio.

Sometime after the news of their engagement, Steve's mother Marie invited me to go over and meet the family at their home in Egham in Surrey. As it so happened, I was taking a Laban movement class nearby and Marie kindly offered to pick me up in her car. Saying a hurried farewell, I gathered up the drum I used to beat out rhythms during exercises and had no time to change out of my training kit as I rushed towards her waiting car. Marie looked beautifully smart as she prepared to welcome her new relative and I did wonder what she would think of this strange woman who was Kirsty's mother. She was very friendly, though, and took me home and offered me a gin and tonic. I felt I needed it. Then she and her husband took me out to dinner before I caught the train back home. Despite our very different lifestyles and interests we got on very well indeed and were of course both very happy for the young couple.

We all met at my house to make arrangements for the wedding. It was decided that the church would be the beautiful St Leonard's in Chelsham, just two miles or so away from the Selsdon home where Kirsty had grown up. The date was set for 18 August 1984. Since Steve and Kirsty were away working together most of the time, as mother of the bride I was left in charge of the wedding arrangements. I was so used to directing plays that I was more than happy to take this in my stride. Kirsty had chosen her own wedding dress and was very eager for me to come and see it. I thought it was lovely, made of an ecru silk with a tight off-the-shoulder bodice, large puffed sleeves and a very full skirt. As she was going away to work with Steve she asked me to sort out the bridesmaids' costumes, giving me a totally free hand. I spent a lot of time at John Lewis's looking at materials and patterns before making a decision.

The two bridesmaids were her close friend from her days at Stiff Records, Annie Holloway, and her stepsister Kitty MacColl. I had a list of people that Kirsty and Steve wanted me to invite, along with their telephone numbers. Several of the people from the pop music world were unknown to me, but many later became my friends. I'd heard of Holly from the band Frankie Goes To Hollywood, and, of course, Frida from Abba, and I also knew of Bono from U2. At times I felt like a director whose cast, while very willing to come together for the one performance, were equally difficult to pin down to a specific date. So many of them had complicated touring schedules of their own. I also had to arrange for those travelling from a distance to stay at the hotel. Luckily the Selsdon Park Hotel was only a few minutes from our house and was also the venue for the reception.

As for the menu, Kirsty had expressed a preference for one of her favourite meals, Christmas dinner with all the trimmings, and she also loved Baked Alaska – but she soon realised this was not suitable in what turned out to be an August heatwave.

Come the day, the whole Lillywhite clan would be there, as well as my family, the Newloves and the MacColls and Lisa Ullman and Joan Littlewood, both of them godmothers to Hamish and Kirsty – and appropriately representative of both my work and Ewan's. Also invited was Kirsty's old music teacher from her school, who kindly volunteered to play the organ. While travelling around London, Kirsty had noticed a pink Cadillac parked in front of some commercial premises, and bold as brass had asked the owner if she could hire it for her wedding. This was the first time he'd been asked such a thing, but he was happy to oblige and his son even acted as chauffeur. He also dressed in pink!

On the morning of the wedding it was all go. I went to and from the church with the order of service which had to be handed out and liaised with the vicar, the volunteer organist and the visitors, sweating gently in the church as they waited for the bride. Of course, it is her traditional prerogative to be late but in Kirsty's case this was partly because she had her hairdresser friend working on her, a duty that had got progressively slower with each glass of champagne she was handed.

At last I was told that they were finally ready and went back to my place in the church to wait. Kirsty told me later that all the neighbours along Beech Way stood at their gates to wish her well as the party set out and that when the car turned out onto the main road at a stately pace, everybody had started waving. This was an unexpected pleasure for her, and she delightedly waved back. (My ever-faithful neighbour Margaret Spurring told me later that after Kirsty had driven off, our front door was left wide open and she had gone across and locked everything up for me.) The last people to arrive were Hamish and his partner: their ancient car had broken down on the motorway and they had been given a lift by a sympathetic motorist.

At long last, the Reverend Christopher Wheatcroft told us the bride had arrived, and the organist began to fill the church with music. For this I was very glad, since the fluttering candles were by now getting very low. Kirsty looked radiantly happy as she came in on the arm of Ewan, who was dressed in the full and (to him) enormously uncomfortable rig of a morning suit with a grey top hat. Since this was the first time he had ever been required to dress in such a fashion, I did wonder whether he thought he was playing a role in a Theatre Workshop production.

When Steve joined her, Kirsty winked at him and the service began. The church was packed with family, friends and colleagues of the couple. The curate had meanwhile briefed the congregation about putting their hearts into the singing, adding that 'Some of you can sing very well,' as he glanced over at the guests from the music industry we had put in the choir stall. During the service Bono spoke briefly on faith, hope and love – 'and the greatest of these is love.'

When the ceremony was over, and they were pronounced man

and wife, Steve grinned and gave a little victory salute which drew smiles from those around the church. After signing the registers, the couple walked out into the sunshine, followed by the congregation, to where the photographer was organising the group pictures. The pink Cadillac awaited the newly married couple and, amid clouds of confetti, they headed off to the reception followed by their guests. Among these were my old architect Eric Mayne and his wife June, who stayed the night with me at Coombe Cottage. He said later that he approved of the house he had designed, praising its warm and embracing atmosphere.

I wasn't sure whether the Selsdon Park Hotel had arranged for any special flowers to decorate the dining room, so I had asked two friends, Tom Field and Rodi Okorodudu, to collect some flowers that had been saved at the back of the church and to take them in the car to the hotel. What I didn't know was that these flowers had been put in large vases filled with water and the men could hardly lift them. Instead of taking them out of the water, for some reason they staggered out with the two heavy containers and dragged them slopping into the car.

Ewan wasn't well enough to come to the reception, so my brother stepped in and gave a speech. Steve Brown, Steve's best man, did likewise. In the evening there was dancing, and I remember Holly Johnson partnering me – he later told Kirsty that I had more energy than he did! What time did Kirsty and Steve leave, and where did they go? I simply have no idea. I myself left quite late, taking Eric and June home with me. In the morning I rang my brother, who said that the hotel staff seemed to be in a state of some confusion. He had ordered breakfast for two in his room, he told me, but fresh ones had been arriving at regular intervals – he had just received number five. When I went over to sort everything out, I heard that the partying had gone on most of the night: some of the staff on duty had joined in the celebrations, so almost everyone next morning was rather hungover and lacking sleep. It was a good 'review' of one of my more successful productions!

It seemed like only yesterday I had given Kirsty my mother's ring for her 21st birthday and now she was on her honeymoon, wearing her own wedding ring – and one slightly superior to the 30p diamonds we had flashed in Selfridges. Both in her musical career and in her personal life, she had come of age.

Chapter Seven

Manhattan Moon

1985-1988

'...You were pretty, queen of New York city'
SHANE McGOWAN AND JEM FINER, 'FAIRYTALE OF NEW YORK', 1987

Ewan celebrated his 70th birthday on 25 January 1985 – he shared the date with Robbie Burns – and the occasion was marked in some style by a special jubilee concert at the Royal Festival Hall in London. It was the height of the Miners' Strike, and Arthur Scargill and other NUM members were among the audience. It was a full house, and Kirsty, very heavily pregnant, together with Steve and myself, were there to lend Ewan our support. On stage accompanying him were Peggy, Neill and Calum, while Hamish, also on stage, sang with his father. Pregnant as she was, Kirsty was also enjoying the first flush of her own musical fame: her cover of Billy Bragg's 'A New England' had become a big hit. Frank Murray, her manager at the time, explains: 'When we released "A New England" [in December 1984] Kirsty was pregnant with her first son Jamie. This posed a problem with the BBC at the time. The producer did not think pregnant women should appear on *Top of the Pops*, so I think Kirsty just got one live appearance – after that they would show the video.

Thankfully, things have changed and being pregnant is no longer seen as an impediment to appearing on TV, but Kirsty did have to fight for her *Top of The Pops* appearances.'

Ewan's first grandchild, Jamie Patrick MacColl Lillywhite, was born at The Portland Hospital in London, on 20 February 1985. Steve rang me to say that they both wanted me to be the first to see their new son. I rushed up to town, but such was Kirsty's newfound fame that a journalist beat me to it and managed to get a photograph of her holding Jamie for his paper. After his departure, other members of the press were banished; Kirsty needed some privacy with Steve and the family. Her room was full of flowers from friends, the record companies and other well-wishers. I came away delighted, a very proud grandmother indeed, and returned home to phone Hamish and the rest of my family and Kirsty's many friends.

Frank Murray heard the news of Jamie's birth while on tour with the Irish band The Pogues, which he had also started to manage:

I got a call one night from my wife to say Kirsty had given birth to a baby boy, Jamie. At the time I was sitting in a hotel bar with Shane [MacGowan] and Spider [Stacy], so we ordered up some champagne and celebrated Jamie's arrival. Soon after, Kirsty asked me to be a godfather to Jamie, which I proudly accepted. I returned the compliment a couple of years later on the birth of my son Aran and Kirsty gladly accepted the role of godmother.

It was now obvious that Kirsty's flat wouldn't be large enough for a family. Steve had to return to work with The Rolling Stones in New York to produce their album *Dirty Work*, leaving Kirsty to look for suitable accommodation. She decided to live in Ealing, a pleasant, leafy part of London and, very importantly, near to Heathrow. Kirsty took me, along with baby Jamie, to see a house in Mount Park Road. It was an old double-fronted Victorian house on three floors, and seemed just right for their needs, having two spare bedrooms that could be turned into a soundproof studio with their own set of steps leading up from outside. Kirsty 'wanted to be a mum and was proud of it,' as her friend and accountant Ronnie Harris remembers and 'her children were her one priority'. But at the same time she 'was always aware of her talent and never wanted to give it up, and consequently, when the right time approached, she continued to make wonderful records, with wonderful people.' The new house promised to fulfil both these needs. There was a large garden with great potential and the house itself was conveniently situated. Over the next few months the stairs and floors were taken up as the whole house was rewired.

Meanwhile, Kirsty had written and recorded her follow-up single. 'He's on the Beach', a warm and vibrant song about a friend of hers who had suddenly decided to emigrate to Australia ('And I don't blame him'), was released in June 1985, but failed to repeat the success of 'A New England'. So by that summer, and with Steve away, Kirsty was ready to take ten days off. She invited me to accompany her, along with her friends Jenny and Annie. I'm sure Kirsty was missing Steve, but she had a professional attitude to work and knew that separation from him was, at times, simply inevitable. In any case I know she expected that, when the time came for her to travel as part of her own career, Steve would be there to look after the children.

And so the four of us – Kirsty, Annie, Jenny and I – as well as baby Jamie, now aged about four months, all flew into Corsica that June. We discovered when we picked up our rental car that our hotel was on the other side of the island from the airport. Although both Annie and I offered to drive, Kirsty would not hear of it. It was a winding mountainous road with sheer drops and the new mother was not risking her baby with anyone but herself at the wheel. She drove through the heat of the day and asked me if I would mind having the baby in my room so she could catch up on her sleep. I was happy to take him and offered to have him in my room for the whole of the holiday. I think Kirsty was pleased with the arrangement – she trusted me. I, on the other hand, like many grandmothers must do, felt rather overwhelmed by the great responsibility.

We had a relaxing time together. The hotel garden ended at a small beach and I was even introduced to windsurfing, at which I persevered daily with everyone's encouragement. When it was time to come home, we managed to get a flight from an airfield near the hotel – though the runway was actually more like a long road with a mountain at the end. I had never seen such a small airport and the plane itself was correspondingly tiny, with facing seats along the fuselage like in a bus.

• • •

In early September 1985 I got a call from Kirsty. She and Jamie were in New York with Steve, who was still producing The Rolling Stones, and the two of them were going to the recording studios every day. The young woman looking after Jamie had some family problems, and Kirsty wondered if I could come out and look after Jamie. I was free, and excited at the prospect of my first transatlantic flight.

After landing in JFK airport, a helicopter had been booked to take us across the Hudson River into Manhattan, which was quite a nerve-racking experience as the helicopter seemed to be a particularly ancient model and even had a hole in the floor through which I watched the brown water skimming beneath us. It seemed to take forever to get to the other side, and when we landed – with the helicopter tail dangling over the edge of the landing ground – I took a cab to the address I had been given in Manhattan. This was a penthouse flat in a very smart area. The doorman said Kirsty had just rung and was coming right over, so I waited with him for a few minutes until she arrived with Jamie. She was very upset not to have been there to greet me, but had simply mistaken the time. For the next week or two, Jamie and I enjoyed a wonderful late summer in New York.

Kirsty and Steve would often return home after all-night recording sessions just as we – baby Jamie and I – were leaving the flat. We would go off every morning, armed with bottles of milk, a few soft toys and a small folding pram. Living in Manhattan, I would walk up to Central Park each day, passing Fifth Avenue and other well known streets. Chatting away to Jamie, who always looked around him with interest, we went to the lake where small boats sailed dangerously close to each other, watched over by their equally small owners. The café had poor coffee but excellent banana cake. After a few days Jamie and I came to know the park very well – so much so that when Americans visiting the Big Apple for the first time asked me for directions I was able to guide them with some competence. After our banana cake, Jamie and I might go on to the children's zoo (not a patch on Regent's Park!).

I had a phone call one evening to say that Tosh Rapoport – my old friend Wolf's daughter, who had now lived in America for many years and was married to an American – wanted me to visit her in hospital. She had just given birth to her first child, Thomas, at the age of 43. It was marvellous to see her and we were able to catch up on all the news. She had come to America as a young gymnast with an interest in dance and I had given her a few classes, but she discovered she was suffering from the symptoms of early onset arthritis and instead managed to get onto a course in business studies at Harvard University, where she met her husband. (She later became one of the most successful businesswomen in the country.) When I visited mother and baby in hospital that day, she told me that Kirsty had also been in to see her – and given her some advice. Tosh was rather amused that the baby she had babysat for all those years ago was now an expert in childcare!

With Steve and Kirsty so busy with work, Jamie and I would occasionally venture further afield, taking a cab to explore other areas. I discovered that Bloomingdale's, the famous department store on 59th Street, was unsuitable for prams (the display stands presented a series of complicated obstacles), and the pram also caused difficulties with the cab drivers. They would blankly look on as I struggled to get my purse out to pay them while holding the baby in one arm and hanging onto the pram with another. In the end I gave them the option of either holding the baby or folding out the pram for me. They were usually so terrified of holding Jamie that they eagerly dealt with the pram, and so I got the entire manoeuvre down to a couple of minutes.

It had been arranged that at the end of my visit the family would all fly home to England together and two days before we left Kirsty asked me if I would sort out the fresh food and other perishables that needed to be disposed of in the flat. I filled three carrier bags, waited until almost midnight and then took them with me in the lift down to the front door, and went round the corner to where I knew a tramp regularly slept on a grating through which hot air rose from the basement of the neighbouring building. I arranged the carrier bags around him as he slept, hoping they would not be stolen overnight and that he might wake up to think Christmas had come to New York early that year. It is strange to reflect that the song by which Kirsty is perhaps best remembered – 'the most popular folk song of the past 30 years', Billy Bragg calls it – would be about the sort of Christmas in New York that sleeping tramp might have expected. It would be another couple of years before 'Fairytale of New York', the Pogues song on which she guested, would be released, but it was soon after our return to London that winter that the foundations of that brilliant collaboration were laid.

In early 1986, Kirsty and her manager, Frank Murray, amicably went their separate business ways. 'She was putting her recording career on hold,' explains Frank, 'and I was becoming more involved with The Pogues. We both went for lunch, and she asked me about the Pogues, what kind of people they were. She hadn't heard much of their music but she had read a lot about them. I told her she would like them. I also told her they had a song that I would love for her to sing on once we got to recording it properly. She said I should call her when it was ready and if she was around she would listen to it. The song was "Fairytale of New York" and in the intervening years fate had it that Steve ended up being the producer of that song. The rest is history.'

Her co-vocalist on the song, Shane MacGowan, later fondly remembered first meeting Kirsty in 1985, just after the release of The Pogues' first album, *Rum, Sodomy and the Lash*, when they were both managed by that 'same "loveable" Irish shyster':

She seemed reserved and shy and said very little, though me and Spider [Stacy] were trying to chat to her in our own drunken, obnoxious way. I first got to know her properly when her husband was trying to produce *If I Should Fall from Grace with God*. We had a long chat down the studio when she was as out of it as I was and it turned out that the shy, red-haired Gaelic beauty was funny, charming, intelligent and a real gas to talk to. But we soon became good friends, and she was soon boosting my ego, hypocritically lecturing me about my excessive drinking while keeping me up all night slugging champagne...

'Fairytale of New York', produced by Steve, was eventually released in November 1987 and became a massive favourite in live concerts. At the same time, the friendships Kirsty forged with the various members of the band's extended family lasted for the rest of her life – and beyond.

'Kirsty and I remained great friends,' says Frank, 'and I was delighted when she came on tour with The Pogues. The pre-show nervousness had gone, and she sang her heart out every night. The Pogues' fans loved her. Her vocal on "Fairytale" has never been matched – a lot of people have tried and will continue to try, but Kirsty reigns supreme.' The song has become a classic of the underdog human spirit and, as Spider Stacy remembered, whenever Kirsty joined the band on stage to do 'Fairytale', 'the audiences absolutely loved her.' The shambling grandeur of its performance – along with her dance with Shane MacGowan – has become famous. Why does the song work so well?

According to Shane, it was something to do with Kirsty's 'particular talent for arranging and harmonising with her own voice while sounding warm and human' – before adding, 'Sorry if I sound like a bloody jazz critic!' Billy Bragg also points to the personal human warmth of Kirsty's performance, and I think I agree with Billy's view: 'She brought something of herself' to that record, he says:

When Shane MacGowan cries into his beer, 'I could have been someone,' Kirsty's quick-as-a-flash response, 'Well, so could anyone!', was very much in keeping with her attitude to life. All of us who sat whingeing in her kitchen about fickle husbands, lovers, record companies, reviews, etc, got the same short shrift. She would laugh, get you another beer and play some fabulous Celina González track, inviting you to dance your cares away.

'As long as there are Christmases,' wrote Carl Chase after Kirsty's death, 'her incredible voice lives on.'

· · ·

Before that stunning success with The Pogues, Kirsty and Steve, after setting up home in the finished house in Ealing, were enjoying the delights of marriage and parenthood – and in due course another collaborative production arrived. Louis Stephen MacColl Lillywhite was born on 3 September 1986, again at The Portland Hospital – though this time Kirsty did not have a hit in the charts and we were left in peace and quiet to enjoy the new addition to the family. I had given Kirsty a very pretty maternity smock that I had used when I was pregnant with her and she wore it when she went into labour. She had her photograph taken in it with Jamie. I was amused – and rather touched – that at this late hour she felt she must wear it.

Jamie had been told to expect a little brother or sister and was most delighted when Louis eventually arrived. Kirsty asked not to be informed of the sex of the baby, but the nurse had ignored or forgotten her request and let slip it was to be another boy. Kirsty always said that if she had had a girl she would called her Atalanta.

Christmas that year was a marvellous occasion, with all of Steve's relatives as well as Hamish and I joining Kirsty and Steve. There were so many of us, in fact, that they had a folding table-top made to accommodate all the diners. Kirsty always enjoyed entertaining and was herself an enthusiastic cook.

She had worked very hard to get the new house organised and by the time we were all gathered there for the festive season, she was beginning to put her stamp on it. She admired the work of the mosaic artist Phil Hardaker very much and one of the first things she commissioned from him was a multi-storey structure that illuminated a corner of the lounge. Joan also gave her a costly ormolu sideboard from her own flat in Blackheath (a reproduction of a famous piece) and a large and very unusually shaped mirror.

Early in the New Year of 1987, when Louis was just a few months old, Kirsty was in need of a break and when she asked if I could look after Louis while she and Steve took Jamie with them for a short holiday in the Caribbean, I was more than happy to oblige. Three-month-old Louis and I had a grand time together. For Kirsty, the first priority was always to find a reliable person to look after the boys.

When she had been on holiday on Formentera with Annie Holloway a few years before – the Spanish holiday she sang about so beautifully in 'Annie', one of my favourite of Kirsty's songs – she had got to know a German girl called Connie, who was then a professional child-carer working with small children. She was highly qualified and obviously loved her job. Kirsty remembered her warmly and now gave Connie a ring to ask her if she might like to come over to England and look after the two boys – and she did.

It was partly thanks to Connie, whose boyfriend lived in West Berlin, that I decided to make my own grand tour in the summer of 1988, after being invited over to Poland by my old friends George and Anna.

In those days one could go to a British Rail ticket office and take time over the planning of one's journey – and this was one heck of a journey. Over a few weeks of such visits I worked out a real itinerary: first of all to Paris, then on to West Berlin; then across the border to East Berlin, and then into Poland, visiting Poznań, Wroclaw, Warsaw, Krakow, before heading back through Czechoslovakia to Vienna, Zurich (to see Laban's grandson Claude Perrotet), then back to Paris again and home. The proposed journey became a source of great interest to Nigel, the manager of the local British Rail ticket office, and we became great pals. I could only afford to do it because of the kindness of the friends and relatives who put me up.

My first stop was Paris where I stayed for a few days with Kirsty and Steve, who were working over there and renting an apartment with the children. Since Connie was now looking after the kids, Kirsty and I had a great time exploring the city together. On my last evening, Steve offered to look after the children himself and we had a meal at an excellent restaurant before taking in a famous café that had been the legendary haunt of artists and writers. Since it was such a beautiful night we decided to walk home rather than take the Métro – only to find Steve's rather anxious face peering through the window at us when we got home, much later than intended. The hours had fled by and Steve had been concerned for us.

The following evening I said my goodbyes and boarded the night-train for West Berlin, having booked a sleeper. The train stopped for an hour before entering West Berlin in the early morning. Connie's boyfriend was there to greet me, as arranged, and took me to his flat where he had arranged for me to stay for the night. He then apologetically left for work, saying he would meet up with me again that evening. I was happy enough to go off exploring on my own, remembering that my last visit to Berlin, with Hamish and Kirsty, had been in 1963. I made a point of revisiting the area where we had stayed and that marvellous hotel with its memorable soufflés. In the intervening 25 years, the hotel had prospered tremendously – all thick carpets now, polished brass and soft lights. In fact it seemed to have prospered rather more than me and, sensing that a meal there would take too much out of my budget, I instead took a bus-tour around the city. Sitting on the top deck, I listened to the American tourists talk with awe about the Berlin Wall as they tried to peer over it to the unknown territory beyond – the Eastern Bloc. 'Tomorrow,' I thought to myself, 'I'll be on the other side.'

That evening I met up again with Connie's boyfriend. He took me round to some friends and neighbours and we had a very sociable evening. The following morning I was taken to the mainline station and put on the train for Poznań. The only other occupant of the compartment was a young woman who had been visiting her father in West Berlin and was now returning to Poland. The train left on time – and then moved at a snail's pace into East Berlin, stopping for a long while at the outskirts of the city, before at last picking up speed until we reached Frankfurt-an-der-Oder.

There our compartment doors were pushed open unceremoniously and a policewoman in a stark grey uniform looked in with an official non-committal expression reminiscent of those worn by the officials I had encountered all those years before. She strode into our compartment and reached forward to the blind, pulling it right down. I wasn't sure whether this was to keep prying eyes out or to conceal what was to happen next. What I did notice – and it was very hard not to – was the large leather gun holster she wore at her hip. My German had not improved since my previous visit, but I wasn't unduly concerned. This time I had all the right documents and it was only myself I had to worry about. After checking my papers, she asked me about my jewellery and a note was taken of my watch and two rings. She also took note of all the currency I was carrying, which seemed to cause her some confusion because I had my various spending money in separate plastic bags for each country on my route. This all took some time, of course, before she indicated she would like to look through my hand luggage. I smilingly opened it for her, knowing full well that there was a much larger case of mine on the rack above me. This she turned her attention to herself at length. She wanted me to lift it down. I gave an apologetic smile and quietly made myself age ten years.

We had reached an impasse: she wasn't going to lift the heavy case down and I seemed incapable of doing so. After a brief moment of indecision, she conceded defeat and instead turned her attention to my fellow traveller, who caused her a good deal less trouble.

When I arrived in Poznań, I managed to pull the case off the rack and struggle on to the platform with it. I looked at the indicator board which had trains going to Warsaw and Moscow and various stations in between. I was on my way.

The last time I had been in Poland, George and Anna's daughter Sybill had been a shy fifteen-year-old. Now she was a married woman with two children of her own and a professor at Wroclaw University. I checked for a local train that would arrive at Wroclaw in mid-afternoon. A young man standing next to me spoke English far better than I did German so we got on famously – but he recommended a different train. I had never been on a local Polish train before. I sat next to a rather inebriated gentleman who was most charming and talked to me very pleasantly, never seeming to notice that I could neither understand nor reply to him. I had been told that the train had a restaurant car and when I enquired where it might be found – 'Restaurant?' I falteringly asked – I was told that the train was about to stop and the restaurant car would be attached. In due course I went to the door, and sure enough, there it was, attached to our compartment. I was now quite hungry, and although the food seemed meagre – some soup with ham in it, and black bread – it was wholesome and filling and reminded me of all the folk tales I had read to the children.

When we eventually arrived at Wroclaw, of course, there was no one to greet me, since I had not told Sybill what time I would arrive. So I now practised the observation skills honed by my Laban training! I noticed that passengers were leaving the platform by one of two routes: the first seemed to involve climbing a lot of stairs and going over a bridge and the second descending even more stairs and going through a crowded tunnel; neither way seemed much fun with my heavy suitcase. I then noticed another exit with what seemed to be an equal number of ascending and descending steps, but the thought of choosing the wrong exit and ending up who knows where stopped me in my tracks. At that moment, however, I saw in the distance a very smart squad of Polish soldiers marching in my direction, led by a sergeant and a young officer.

I politely asked the officer if he could tell me where I might find the taxi rank. He clicked his heels and bowed very courteously and said, certainly, they would take me there. We got some strange looks from the other Polish travellers but our mission was accomplished. The officer then offered to call for a taxi for me, but I thanked him profusely and said I could manage from here. With that they bade me goodbye, and marched off.

What language did we speak? Some English, I suppose, the odd word of German, some French, and very occasionally a Polish word, all the rest accomplished by smiles and gestures and goodwill – I have always met with so much goodwill on my travels. At least I was able to hire the taxi myself, with my few Polish words, and arrived at Sybill's flat feeling very pleased with myself at having made the journey safely and – more or less! – unaided.

Anna told me she had received a phone call from Kirsty who, no doubt remembering our adventures with the authorities the last time we had travelled in Poland, rang up to ask how – and indeed where – her mother was. Anna laughed, and told her I was fine and full of energy. When Kirsty told the story later, she would laugh and say, 'Perhaps my mum needs a sedative.' I think Kirsty had faith in me, and knew that I'd probably get to wherever I wanted to go eventually, but there were always hazards, I suppose, behind the Iron Curtain and she just wanted to know that I had safely arrived. Actually, I think she was rather proud of my adventures: I was catching up with my life.

After two weeks in Poland, including a marvellous trip to Wawel Castle in Krakow, I said goodbye to Sybill and her family and travelled overnight across Czechoslovakia. I would have loved to have revisited Prague and Brno for old times' sake, but tourist hotels were too expensive, so I arrived across the border in Vienna in the early morning. I was immediately struck by the city's enormous comparative wealth. After depositing my luggage at a small hotel in the inner ring, I took myself on a sightseeing trip. At St Stephen's church in the centre of Vienna there was a demonstration protesting against President Waldheim, whose war record was then under scrutiny.

There was certainly no lack of food in Vienna. The restaurants were doing great business and there were small orchestras in the streets which added to a very festive air, after the rather sombre lifestyle of the East Germans. One of the things I always admired so much about the Poles was their sense of humour and their resilience through years and centuries of invasion by neighbouring countries. And now here in Vienna, I once again I found myself walking through the streets of a capital city in the evening, feeling every inch the European. I had two things to do: one was to treat myself to a sample of the world-renowned

Sacher-Torte recommended to me by my mother, who remembered the dish from before the First World War. (It was as good as she said it would be.) The other was to send off a Spanish postcard of a view of Marbella to Nigel at the British Rail office in Croydon, which I had carefully kept with me throughout my trip, along with its Spanish stamp. I didn't know whether it would get there, but I wrote thanking him for his help – but also told him that the itinerary he had helped me work out had gone slightly awry and I had now somehow found myself in Spain...

Leaving Vienna, I headed for my next overnight stop in Zurich, where I met up with old friends and visited my favourite restaurant, before once again taking the sleeper for Paris on the long journey home.

It seems that my Spanish postcard, with its Spanish stamp, postmarked 'Wien', did indeed reach Nigel's British Rail office, where I am happy to say it caused much confusion and amusement.

Chapter Eight

Busy Life

1985-1994

'Cause my friends are people who love me...'
KIRSTY MACCOLL, 'WRONG AGAIN', 2000

In early 1988, Steve found a small villa in Plan de la Tour near St Maxime on the Côte d'Azur and this became a regular holiday home for many years. It was just after Kirsty's great success with 'Fairytale of New York' when they got the place about an hour's drive from Nice and half-an-hour from St-Tropez with its expensive boutiques and fabulous yachts moored in the harbour. Other, less obviously rich, crowds sat at the pavement cafés eyeing the rest of mankind.

Kirsty and I went shopping there in August the following year during a heatwave and I treated her to some thigh-length green suede boots at a knock-down price. After all, who wants such things in a scorching August? She was delighted with them, telling a friend, 'Guess what my mum bought me!' They later appeared in one of her videos. On another visit she bought me a leather jacket.

We never travelled very far during our stays there, mostly just exploring the region and occasionally finding a new restaurant.

The village itself had a number of adequate restaurants only a few minutes from the villa. Steve and Kirsty usually went in the summer when there were breaks in their schedule and, later on, only in the school holidays. I was invited to join them from time to time. We did go one Christmas, but the French don't really 'do' Christmas – it's the New Year that matters more there. It was still extremely hot at midday, but the evenings were cold and we loved sitting around proper log fires. One New Year, Hamish and I joined the family and we all went to one of the village restaurants where the locals had also booked in for a seven-course meal with dancing between courses. I danced with the local butcher while the Italian chef delighted in making sporadic appearances through the evening, wearing a hat that lit up.

When Jamie was about eight, Steve and Kirsty thought the boys were old enough to order their own meals and allowed them to go to the local crêperie with their friends. Steve told Jamie he'd be nearby at a café if they needed anything. When the boys arrived at the crêperie, the owner of the restaurant (who had been forewarned) asked them what they'd like to drink. Jamie wanted Coke, but six-year-old Louis asked for cider. After Louis was persuaded to have a Coke instead, the boys ordered, drank their drinks and Jamie asked for '*l'addition*'. The bill came to more than he had in his purse, but this did not faze him unduly. Thinking on his feet he asked, 'Can I leave my brother with you?' and went off to his dad to get some money to pay Louis's ransom.

Much time was spent at the pool, which was built into the side of a hill up a set of murderous steps. Table tennis was another favourite pastime for visitors. The pool was shared by the local residents in the Mas de Pierre area and from it one had a fantastic panoramic view over the surrounding countryside. It was a marvellous place and Kirsty loved to entertain friends with their children. Her friend the photographer Charlie Dickins fondly remembers one particular visit:

> Kirsty and I were in the South of France staying at Plan de la Tour as we used to do. We would often leave Steve and the kids to their own devices and go off to 'do some photography', as this was the way we used to work, which ensured Kirsty was relaxed. This day we went to visit a Cistercian Abbey and before any shots were done we had a look around. The church was lovely and cool and a welcome escape from the heat outside, and we approached the altar. There was very little sound inside the church, but Kirsty commented on the acoustics being amazing. Being tone-deaf myself I was all too unappreciative of this fact and so to demonstrate Kirsty sang her scales. The beautiful sound she made was strangely otherworldly and I shall never forget it. She drew many gazes of wonder from the other visitors.

One of the photographs of Kirsty that Charlie took on that happy day is on the front cover of this book.

On one occasion, soon after they had bought the villa, and when Steve couldn't get away from work, I accompanied Kirsty and the two boys over to France. On the drive from Nice to Plan de la Tour we passed a forest of mimosas which inspired her song – with French lyrics! – 'La Forêt de Mimosa'. On the same trip we drove out to visit Port Grimaud, the strange and exclusive artificial lagoon city. Returning home that evening, she set up a barbecue and we had an impromptu party with local visitors. During their last holiday together at Plan de la Tour, Kirsty gave Steve a framed photograph of the boys as an anniversary present.

•   •   •

'La Forêt de Mimosa' was one of many new songs that Kirsty began writing and recording towards the end of 1988. They appeared on her hugely successful album *Kite*, released the following April. It was her first new album in four years. 'When I started working with her,' remembers Pete Glenister, 'it was very sporadic between children, but then we started writing more in earnest for *Kite*.'

> I'd been working with Terence Trent D'Arby and she came up to me after one of his gigs in New York, and said 'Remember, you're only on loan and when you come back you're with me.' I remember she was with Steve in New York doing a record with David Byrne and Talking Heads, *Naked*, and I think it was during these sessions that she first fell in love with Latin music. All the musicians who were playing on the record were based in New York.

'Free World', 'Innocence', and the country-inflected 'Don't Come the Cowboy with Me, Sonny Jim!' were all instant classics and *Kite* displayed an extraordinary range of styles and moods, showcasing what Shane MacGowan later described as Kirsty's 'unmistakable, beautiful voice and a unique talent for making great music: she's equally great at writing and performing her own stuff and interpreting other people's songs.' And it was the album's only cover version, of Ray Davies's 'Days', that is perhaps most fondly remembered – both by Kirsty's many fans and by the musicians involved in recording it.

GLR radio interview, June 1992

Tracey MacLeod: The next band, The Kinks, are obviously a different kettle of fish in the lyrics stakes. They write sort of story songs, is that something that attracts you?

Kirsty MacColl: Yes, I think Ray Davies is one of the best songwriters I've ever heard. The stories that he tells are so well done and so simply done. I think it's a real art to do something that's that clever and to make it sound simple. At the end of it you're not thinking, 'Gosh, they were trying really hard' – that's where the art comes in. He writes about things that aren't really fashion fads, in a way that makes his songs stand up: they can be moved forward into the next decade and still be great songs.

TM: Why did you choose 'Lola'?

KM: You don't hear it a lot on the radio, and it's just got everything in the song – it's got this intrigue and mystery and surprise, and the undertones of smouldering sex, of course, which we all like to get in a song now and again.

'My favourite session that I did with her,' remembered Smiths guitarist Johnny Marr,

was 'Days'. I think we played it for about ten hours, and we were getting the feeling for it – it was full on and we were starting to nail it. Then we were finally playing what would be the final take: we were holding our breath when we hit the last chord and after all that work – she'd really put us through it – we just heard silence through our headphones. Then she said, 'About bloody time!'

'Most people tell me that she was a perfectionist,' Jools Holland told me, before fondly retelling Johnny's story (though Jools's version has Kirsty announce 'About bloody time. Now let's go down to the pub!' – which certainly sounds like her). 'She knew when the take was the right take,' continues Jools:

Sometimes it can come quickly and sometimes it can take a long time, but she would never want to have something that wasn't exactly right, it had to have the right feel and I think that's why everybody has such great respect for her. Also, each element in the song has to be good – every track, the vocals, all the elements had to all work together. She would never come into the studio and bellow at people, but she quietly knew exactly what she wanted and would keep doing it until it worked out, which is really the sign of somebody who knows their art, and what they want from it.

She was fortunate because her personality when dealing with lots of people helped – she was very charming, really amusing. There was also a steely determination, a will to get it done. The music had to be right, but when you were working with her you always felt you were having a bit of a laugh, which is a talent in itself. That's not what everybody was doing – what they were doing in fact was making a record.

She wouldn't hesitate to tell people what to do; music was the thing. She was the servant of the song and she would assume everyone else was that too; it didn't matter who you were. When that happens, though, the truth of it is, when musicians are working, if somebody does that and they're not talented and can't cut it, that's not very good – but if they *can* cut it, all everyone else wants is for that to work.

Sometimes she would just throw things in and mix things up because she knew that if you mix things up for a

138

moment then something else comes out of that - like she would change the key for everybody and because everybody is caught off guard that can be good too. She knew a lot of the things that make music work, a great wisdom about music which, for somebody so young when I first met her, was very unusual. The most important thing was knowing what was going to work for her. And I suppose that was why I identified with her, because I felt the same thing.

If recording 'Days' had been hard work, the filming of the video for its release as a single in June 1989 wasn't all plain sailing either, as Pete Glenister, her close friend and writing partner from the time, remembers all too well: 'I'd been up all night with Ingrid, having our first daughter. The next day I had to go out and do this video in Godalming on the river bank. It was April and it was freezing; they were lighting it so it looked like summer. We sat in our summer clothes in this bloody punt going up and down the river all day - it was the coldest day of our lives.'

The video itself was very strange. Kirsty was wearing her wedding dress, I noticed, with a stout pair of Wellington boots on underneath. They did a sort of cartoon sequence and she was wearing a hideous blonde wig. 'I always thought she looked like King Charles II in that,' Pete told me. 'It was just awful... But *Kite* was very well received and a lot of people still say it's her best record.'

'Days' was a big hit, but the depth, wit and maturity of Kirsty's own songwriting was what really made the album special.

'Writing with Kirsty was a very strange process,' recalls Pete:

You didn't sit in a room and try to write a song - at least very rarely would you do that. She would say, 'Do me a little track.' If you had a tune, you'd put the tune down; if you had an idea for a lyric, you'd tell her what it was and she'd go off with it. You might not hear anything for two years. I remember I'd given her one of the tunes which ended up on Kite. She'd said, 'Send me something like The Smiths' – she was a huge Smiths fan.

GLR radio interview, June 1992

Tracey MacLeod: Your next record is by The Smiths.

Kirsty MacColl: I think The Smiths are legendary amongst me and most of my friends. This particular song, 'The Headmaster Ritual', is just so good – the lyrics are fantastic, Morrissey's lyrics are always spectacular in some way. I can never understand people who say, 'I find him really depressing' because I've always found him incredibly witty, and I think they've missed the point. In this song, the delivery is great, and the playing is fantastic, but the lyrics are something else. I think it's probably one of the best songs about being at school that I've ever heard.

Pete says, 'Me, being a bit up my own arse, was a bit offended by this – that she wanted me to write "something like The Smiths". Anyway, I did something quite jangly – she always loved jangly guitars – sent it over, and didn't hear anything. I assumed she'd lost it. But during the recording of *Kite*, this song appeared. I'd long since forgotten about it – it had been years beforehand – and now she'd done this whole thing: "Innocence". It was fantastic. That's what it was like working with Kirsty, anyway – you wouldn't even necessarily meet, just send her a tape in the post or something.

'With most people, you sit in a room and you start groaning at each other. Eventually someone might have an idea for a lyric, or something like that. I'm not being awkward, but other people... Anyway, especially if Kirsty was feeling a bit depressed, a bit blocked, you would just send her a tape. And eventually she got to the point where she said: "I want to do something."

'I think "Free World" was the best thing on it. The tracking for that record was largely done in New York with all those Latin musicians Steve had been working with on the David Byrne records, which was where Kirsty met Angel Fernandez, the trumpet player.'

Kirsty really did 'want to do something' and the success of *Kite* at last secured her some public recognition of the talent, industry and sheer style for which she was already famous behind the scenes. 'I remember, about three in the morning,' wrote Johnny Marr, 'me and Kirsty and Keith Richards sitting around playing Everly Brothers songs':

> She was saying, 'The key's too low, change the key' - so I changed the key, but she said, 'No, no, go down a little bit,' and 'Do it like you were doing it before.' Keith Richards was looking over at me with this hangdog expression, and I thought, 'This is brilliant: she's berating Keith Richards - she's kicking his arse!'

•　　•　　•

When the boys were little they attended the local Montessori school in London and later went to Durston, a local prep school. It was planned that they would eventually go as weekly boarders to Dunhurst, the junior school of Bedales in Hampshire. They went down to the school, stayed a couple of nights and took the entrance examination. Dunhurst said they'd be delighted to have the boys, and recommended that Louis should move up an academic year. Kirsty had had the boys' IQs tested privately, and they were both considered very intelligent.

Steve and Kirsty preferred the liberal atmosphere of Bedales to other suggested schools and going to the functions there became part of the yearly routine. Kirsty loved the role of proud parent – watching her young sons in a production of *Bugsy Malone* (in which Jamie was a singing villain and Louis the smallest member of the gang), for example, or visiting the school on its open days. We were very impressed by the polite and friendly attitude of all the Bedales children. During another school play, Kirsty and I were sitting in the audience, proudly watching Jamie survey his troops from the on-stage balcony. When he was proclaimed King, I turned to Kirsty and whispered, 'You know what that makes you, don't you?' And she beamed and said, 'I'm the Queen Mum!'

●   ●   ●

One evening in 1988, during one of my regular visits to Ealing, Kirsty and I watched a documentary on Ewan's life. It began with a commentary on his early days in agit-prop theatre and went on to describe the formation of the professional Theatre Workshop Company, which he founded with Joan Littlewood. The programme mentioned some of his plays, which Joan had directed. He then seemed to have suffered a severe bout of amnesia – not once mentioning that I had been the choreographer for his plays and that we had two children in the music business. And then the programme abruptly turned to the later period in his life when, having left the theatre, he concentrated on a folk-singing career with Peggy Seeger.

I was slightly shocked by this air-brushing, but Kirsty was absolutely furious – I had never seen her so angry. She felt that

Ewan had behaved extremely shoddily and immediately rang him up to tell him so in no uncertain terms. She had started recording the programme, she told him, for his grandchildren to look at when they were older. She had turned the tape off in disgust. Kirsty was extremely direct and went to the heart of the matter with all guns blazing, accusing her father of being thoroughly self-centred – he had done us all a grave injustice, and he must be made aware of that fact.

I remember hearing the sound of his voice on the telephone in the spaces between Kirsty's tirade, mortified and utterly apologetic. He also rang me with many and profuse apologies. But I really felt that his words were pretty meaningless after the hurt that we – and especially Kirsty – had suffered, so I just said, 'That's all right. Let's leave it at that.' And that is more or less what we did. For all that Ewan's remorse was genuine, I think we both felt he had 'sacrificed us' to his career and image. We were neither of us ones to hold grudges, but though I don't believe the subject was ever mentioned again, something of the hurt remained with us both.

Ewan had been treated for angina over a few years and died in hospital on 22 October 1989 at the age of 74. I'd had a phone message from Kirsty in the afternoon – 'Mum, I think you'd better come. It won't be long now' – and I'd left straight away. The drive should have taken an hour but I got lost in the darkening streets and after being misdirected by a passer-by I had wasted another 20 precious minutes before arriving at the hospital.

Hamish and Kirsty were waiting outside. I rushed over to them. They walked on either side of me to the entrance. 'No need to hurry... It's all over.' An arm went around me.

'When did he die?' I asked.

'About 20 minutes ago... it wouldn't have made any difference.'

'I know, I know...'

My reason told me that they were right and there was nothing I could have done, but reason is never any comfort in grief. I said my own private farewell to Ewan in the silence of the room – but no, that's not really true. I saw a healthy Ewan sleeping and I wanted to wake him up. I wanted Joan to come in and start some almighty argument over artistic policy or the relative merits of French cheeses – they delighted in these dramatic slanging matches and this, if anything, would surely rouse the silent figure into the restless energy of his life. But he lay there still. Over 40 years of memories flooded chaotically into my head and with every sort of emotion. Love. Anger. Joy. Grief. We had experienced it all. And in spite of everything that had happened between us, privately we continued to have the greatest respect for each other's work. The last time we had met, I had showed him a couple of chapters of my autobiography. He had offered advice and encouraged me to go on with the project, though in the event it never materialised. We had reminisced over our Theatre Workshop days and he laughed as I reminded him of a few hilarious moments from the past. I'm glad I made him laugh. I stroked his hand. At least he was free of pain. 'I'm going to celebrate your life, Ewan,' I told him. 'We can be very proud of your two children. Goodbye...'

Hamish, Kirsty and I returned home together, where Steve was waiting for us. Raising a glass to toast Ewan's memory, Steve smiled and said, 'Wherever he is right now, he'll be busy – probably sorting out the trades unions.' Hamish answered quietly and with some feeling, 'I hope not!'

Kirsty's personal relationship with Ewan had never been an easy one, of course, but a number of her friends have told me that she had begun to reappraise her father's music. 'She had latterly been catching up with some of Ewan's Argo recordings,' remembers her friend and collaborator Boz Boorer, who had also worked extensively with Morrissey, 'and was acquiring a belated respect and liking for them'.

'As for her father's legacy,' Billy Bragg later wrote, 'I don't recall her ever recording one of his songs':

Only once was I able to coax her into performing one – she made the exception for a good cause. In the mid-90s we did a benefit for the miners at Tower Colliery in South Wales. She joined me in the encore to sing a moving version of her father's mining song 'Schooldays End'. Later, on the long journey back down the M4 in thick fog, she regaled us with a boozy selection of music hall songs her father had taught her – amongst them her famous rendition of 'Lydia, the Tattooed Lady'. But that night was an exception. Once, when we sat down and pondered whither our recording careers might go in a music business that she once described as 'getting less about music every day', I suggested we make an album of folk songs together. My idea was shot down in flames when, echoing comments her father might have made about pop, she said, 'I fucking *hate* folk music.'

And perhaps she was beginning to reconcile herself to her own roots. On 7 January 2001, she was due to unveil a plaque commemorating her father at the Working Class Movement library in Salford. A mutual friend told me that she intended to take the boys along to introduce them to their grandfather's memory.

In fact, both Kirsty and I did actually go to see another plaque commemorating Ewan in London – though we were not closely involved in the proceedings. We had only recently heard that such a plaque had been laid, at the base of a tree in Russell

Square. We went there together on his birthday, 25 January, in the year 2000 – 15 years after his Festival Hall Concert concert. We joined a small gathering of a few fans, as well as Peggy Seeger and her family. Ewan had been dead for over 10 years and the few people there mostly seemed rather elderly and of his generation – it would have been his 85th birthday, after all. One man had brought a small bottle of whisky to share and someone else a few shortbreads. Neither Kirsty nor I had met any of the fans before and I'm not sure they even knew who we were. After a little while we said our goodbyes and returned to the car.

On the way back, thinking about those elderly fans of Ewan's, I told Kirsty that although growing old is a difficult process, so long as one's mental faculties remain intact, life could still be fun. However, if ever my mind began to deteriorate, I told her, and I went 'gaga', then I would not want to go on. Kirsty smiled and looked across at me. 'Yes, Mum,' she said. 'But how would we know?'

● ● ●

By the time of Ewan's death, I was pursuing my own freelance career, working at various drama colleges and at the Theatre Royal. I had decided to set up my own movement and dance courses when I heard that the Pineapple Studios in Covent Garden had become available. When I hired it for my classes, I had to carry in my own sound system, tapes, drum and dance kit. Parking was virtually impossible, but my equipment was so heavy that I had to take it in the car. One Sunday morning, after arriving with my equipment, I had to leave the car for a moment outside the studios to lug the sound system up the steps. I smiled apologetically at a driver who had just come up behind my car and was tooting furiously.

'I'll just be a minute,' I mouthed.

'I'm taking my children to church!' he shouted out angrily. 'I expect you're a bloody *Guardian* reader!'

Eventually I was hiring the studio three nights a week for warm-ups and choreography, and on Sundays we had a Laban movement class in the morning followed by an actors' class in the afternoon. Returning from our lunch break one Sunday we entered the studio expecting it to be empty and came across a small figure sitting cross-legged in a corner. He said his name was Kamisawa Kazuaki, and explained that he had just arrived from Japan. He wanted to study with me and had found me through the British Council.

We all found his name quite difficult to pronounce, so I asked, 'Do you mind if I call you Kami?'

He smiled and said, 'Please do – Kami means "God".' From then on he was Kami to all of us and became a very important member of our group over the next two or three years.

On Friday nights, I taught a history of the theatre course back at Coombe Cottage. I was enjoying what I was doing more than ever, even if I was earning rather less.

One weekend I invited my old friend Howard Goorney, who had been an actor in Theatre Workshop, to conduct a class. My aim with the group was initially to introduce people to Laban's theory of movement, whether or not they had any other dance training. Over a period of time they became very proficient and their enthusiasm was quite remarkable, enabling me to take them to a more advanced level. The acting class was essential to all those taking the full course whether or not they wished to be actors.

Trevor T Smith was another old friend and colleague who had worked with Joan Littlewood and was now taking a regular part in all my classes. He had been asked to direct a morality play called *The Castle of Perseverance* in a production that combined professional and amateur performers. I was his choreographer, and my students were among those who performed it in a church somewhere near the Kennington Oval. Rosemary Leach gave a marvellous performance as God, I remember. Another of my Japanese students, Satchiko Takamura, also performed in the production. Satchiko had come over to England to study the piano and her family had hopes of her becoming a concert pianist. But she had also had dance training, and I could see that what she really wanted to be was a dancer. So she spent her time practising the piano, taking piano lessons – and also coming to my course at Pineapple as well as spending time with me at Coombe Cottage for one-to-one work. She was a very serious and industrious student and though her parents believed that one could only ever be good at one thing (and had chosen her future career for her as a pianist), Satchiko's great talent as a dancer was obvious. Her solo dance in *The Castle of Perseverance*, to which both Kirsty and Hamish came, was quite wonderful.

Another project that evolved from my classes was a production we eventually took to Altenar in what was then still West Germany. It was a very ambitious work. I had chosen a strong anti-war theme, for which I had designed the choreography (involving around a hundred dancers from all over Europe) and Trevor T Smith composed the music, arranged for two pianos and a choir. Trevor and I worked for the best part of a year on this project, preparing for the event.

In order to keep himself free from other engagements – and to keep his agent sweet – he had been turned down at every acting audition his agent had sent him to. I once asked him how he had managed to do this.

'I always wear this suit,' he replied, 'and it has never failed me yet.' Looking at the suit, I understood his reasoning, since it was a particularly hideous mustard-green tweed that clashed both with his hair and his complexion. Every time he wore it, he said, he was confident of never getting an offer. He still meanwhile needed to earn a living, however, so he played piano in a swanky venue, arriving there each night in his dress suit and cycle clips on an old-fashioned bicycle.

The male lead in the Altenar production was my Japanese student Kami, who brilliantly enacted the part of a sort of anti-Christ figure, and his new wife – the couple were on their honeymoon in Europe – also danced a minor role in the enormous cast. After two separate choirs had turned the work down as too difficult, we finally managed to find a German choir willing to take it on. One of Trevor's friends, who was a concert pianist, also happened to be going to Germany at the same time as us and agreed to play for us. The dancers arrived on a Friday night, most of them staying in youth hostels or bed and breakfast places, some in hotels. They were introduced to the theme and practice of the choreography, and by the following Tuesday morning the whole thing was due to be televised before a live audience.

I then discovered that Claude Perrotet – Laban's grandson – had involved himself in the event, along with the artist and movement teacher Christine Rogge. I also invited another movement teacher, Sam Thornton, with whom I got on very well, to work alongside me. It was my job, then, to co-ordinate this vast number of people into an artistic whole. Things were never quite easy with Claude, though, and when we arrived early on the day someone said they had seen him being taken away in a police car. It seems that, instead of walking up the steep road to the rendezvous, he had decided instead on a more direct ascent – through a number of local residents' back gardens. This had apparently necessitated the negotiation of a series of suburban hedges. German families tend to take pride in the tidiness of their gardens and had been shocked at seeing this evident barbarian clambering over their neatly cut hedges and had called the police. Claude must have acquitted himself well, since the police then personally drove him to the meeting place – or else, and quite possibly, didn't trust him not to make the same mistake twice.

It was hard work, but very exciting, and with the help of both Sam Thornton and Christine Rogge, the event was pronounced a great success. I shall never forget the words of an elderly man in the audience who came up to me afterwards to say, 'You should perform this in every town in Germany.'

We left for home in the afternoon – after a broken date with one of the cast. This was an exceptionally able young male dancer who had worked on the project with enormous enthusiasm. He had told me he would like to talk to me when I had the time, but on that last morning of our stay I discovered that he had left abruptly some time after the celebrations. It was only then that some of the other students told me that he had recently come over the Wall and it was when the photographers had appeared at the very end of the work to take pictures for the local papers that he had decided discretion to be the better part of valour. I was very disappointed to miss our date, since when you find a good dancer who is keen to learn, it is generally a good idea to hang on to him.

•   •   •

Back in London, I was interested to see that Kirsty was setting her mark on the new house. She was with Hamish one day as she looked around her new garden. At the far end was a rather gloomy, overgrown area, with a dilapidated path leading around it. Kirsty wanted a pond put in with some fish. Hamish suggested she should contact a friend of his, Julian Jones, who was an authority on all aspects of water supply, pollution and conservation.

After many meetings, Steve and Kirsty decided that the whole project would make a good subject for a television documentary for the BBC as part of its 'Byline' strand. In *Don't Go Near the Water* – the title came from a song by her beloved Beach Boys, a beautiful cover-version of which she released that year – Kirsty voiced her concerns about the levels of water pollution in Britain and especially the standards of drinking water, tracing the route of her water supply back to its source. The programme, broadcast on BBC 2 in June 1991, was genuinely ahead of its time, as Julian himself remembers:

Kirsty was offered a programme by the BBC and picked water and the aquatic environment because of her long interest in this area. As she had patiently listened to me going on about the serious problems here, as well as solutions (reedbeds, etc), whenever I visited with Hamish, she felt there was something special that we could do for this subject. Steve encouraged Kirsty greatly in the project and kindly picked up the construction bill for what was an extremely ambitious aspect of the programme: the construction of a full reedbed wastewater treatment system, ornamental pond with bridge and 'Flowform' water treatment sculpture (a miniature recirculating waterfall system designed to resemble those in the wilds of nature).

The construction (and the team building the project at times included builders, carpenters and plumbers) took over the garden and garage throughout the winter and because the system was a one-off, it took much longer to build than anticipated, trying Steve and Kirsty's patience greatly. The construction of the system was featured as a theme throughout the programme and was innovative not only in terms of television (a bit like later home and garden makeover programmes) but also in her pioneering of the revolutionary concept of not flushing waste away out of sight, but retaining and treating it on her own property. Prince Charles built a reedbed at Highgrove for this purpose shortly after the programme went out.

During the programme Kirsty went to the outfall of her local water company's sewage works and found from the evidence of pollution in the river that it did not work very well. Kirsty's blunt and frank attitude to pollution problems, complete with specially recorded songs, made for a unique programme. The backing Kirsty brought to an otherwise niche method of waste treatment profoundly affected attitudes in the global environmental movement. The entire board of directors of the Severn Trent water company watched the programme and voted £2 million expenditure on reedbeds for their smaller sewage works. By 2006 they had built over 250 such systems.

The album Kirsty was working on at this time, *Electric Landlady* – originally titled by Kirsty 'Al Green was my Valet' – came out in the same month, June 1991. The sessions, which Steve again produced, were in New York, as Pete Glenister remembers.

She asked me to go to New York. I think she wanted someone with her that she knew, to bring a little bit of London to the session so it wasn't completely Puerto Rican, so I was delighted to go. It was very exciting.

The first session was 'My Affair'. The band were given the chord chart, and struck up and went off like a train – on goes this samba, and off they go! These guys can play! Mark Nevin wrote the song with her, but couldn't make it to New York to do it with her. He rang me the day before, and talked me through this chord change – which was all very expensive chords indeed, not your three-chord rock'n'roll, all these fancy jazz chords which he didn't really know the names of – he'd just worked them out on a guitar. Most guitar players just know where to put the fingers – they don't know what to call it. So I'm struggling through this chord change and they're off like a train!

Basically the band had started and we'd got to the end of the first chorus, but neither Kirsty or I had actually started playing yet because we couldn't figure out where they were at. Latin players all avoid playing down beat, and we both started laughing. The band stopped and realised the drummer had to play 4/4. They're fantastic players, well versed in jazz.

The song was all written and demoed with Mark. It was the only song on the album that was like that, most of the older songs were more straightforward. For the end part, we had Sal Cuevas, this amazing bass player who was actually a famous guy – a prison warder on a prison ship moored off Manhattan, he was semi-professional. He just started doing the bass line. No one's ever played it since – some bass players have got somewhere near it! He was playing what the piano usually plays, and the other guys just joined in, so the vamp at the end is all completely improvised, then they put the horn track to that afterwards. He was the superstar. In Latin bands the bass player is the superstar. He sat at the front – like, 'I'm definitely the coolest one in this room' – and just ran all this stuff off. He was brilliant.

GLR radio interview, June 1992

Tracey MacLeod: Do you think to be interested in a song you have to be interested in the songwriter?

Kirsty MacColl: I don't know about that, but the stuff I usually like the most is performed by the writer. I tend to be less interested in people that just do other people's songs. I'm not terribly interested in hearing women singing songs that have been written by men for a woman to sing. They're supposed to be presenting an image of how a woman feels and I don't know any women who are so wimpy as all these male songwriters seem to make out, you know. I think it's just more interesting hearing people who have got something to say. I must say I'm not a big fan of the more introspective – or impressionistic, I should say – female singer-songwriter, with grand piano and lots of trailing veils... I can't stand pianos anyway...

TM: What, you never work with a piano?

KM: Well, not if I can help it – not if I've got a guitar in my hand.

TM: Are you interested in experimenting with structure in your songwriting?

KM: It's quite hard to break out of a standard structure and you get used to how it works, but that's what you're trying to do all the time – break your own barriers and say, 'OK, I've never done anything like this before, let's see if it works' and try to extend yourself in that way.

TM: What about 'Walking down Madison' [1991]? That's quite a different-sounding song for you. I was wondering if it was written as a conventional song – and then you worked on it in the studio and gave it a different sort of production?

KM: Well, I think all the singles that I've had out have been radically different from each other, really, and that's just one of them. I'd written the lyrics originally for that one about three years before Johnny Marr came up with the music. He sent me a cassette of an idea he had for some music which ended up being 'Madison'. I thought it went really well with the lyrics that I'd remembered writing down. I knew what sort of feel I wanted because it was a really New York kind of song – a very kind of urban thing. That lent itself to the sort of 'rap' part, and to the funky feel of it. It would have sounded bizarre as a country and western song, you know – it wouldn't have worked, I don't think.

Chapter Nine

Dancing in Limbo

1993-1994

*'I'm an autumn girl on the endless
search for summer.'*

KIRSTY MACCOLL, 'AUTUMNGIRLSOUP', 2000

My 70th birthday was on 15 May 1993, and Kirsty arranged a big party at her house for the occasion. I drove over from Coombe Cottage in the early afternoon with the intention of giving a helping hand. It was a beautifully warm and sunny day, and Kirsty told me to relax and sit in the garden. She and Steve were just about to go and do some shopping. I was a little surprised that nothing seemed to have been done in the catering line and offered to make some sandwiches, but all help was refused. So I sat in the sun and waited for their return.

An hour or so later, Kirsty and Steve came back laden with carrier bags. They appeared quite relaxed. The guests were expected from 7pm. and I changed, still not having seen any food anywhere. Although I had the greatest of trust in Kirsty, I did wonder if she was not a little too laidback about the food arrangements, but I was soon too occupied in meeting the many guests to concern myself about them. Steve was pouring out drinks and the party spirit was well and truly underway.

Joan was there with her great friends Victor Spinetti, Philip Hedley, the director of the Theatre Royal, and Lionel Bart. The actor Richard Wilson also came as one of Kirsty's guests. They had both been part of a group of artists who were invited to travel to the Palestinian settlements in Israel to view the conditions. Brenda, my great friend and assistant for all my productions, was also there with her husband, Rodi Okorodudu. My dance students were also there, happily mixing with members of The Pogues and other musicians and singers, as well as some tone-deaf friends.

A noise outside the house brought Kirsty in to tell me there were some other guests at the door. Would I let them in myself? As I did so, the sound of bagpipes suddenly swirled up from the street and I was amazed to see a bagpiper turning into the house. With him came a girl who played her clarinet for us later.

That lone piper was very much a Kirsty gesture. On one of Jools Holland's *Hootenanny* New Year's Eve shows she performed the Cole Porter song 'Miss Otis Regrets', originally recorded by her with The Pogues in 1990 as part of the AIDS awareness project *Red Hot + Blue*. Jools remembered it was played 'with all of the bagpipes':

> She is the embodiment of that thing which is in folk music, in country music, that the music isn't quite perfect – and that's what makes it perfect. It's hard to explain that, but you get the spirit and the feeling of the music playing really well, but it's the fact that there's a rough edge to it that makes it come alive. She was a person who was very good at identifying that. In the 1980s there were a lot of drum machines and so on, being 'perfect', and she was the opposite to all of that. Her records were truly perfect because they were the opposite of all that.

She also had a fantastic costume, I remember. She was very pleased with her costume – I remember her beaming face coming out of the dressing room. The song is quite gloomy, really, but she said, 'I think it's the very thing to cheer people up on New Year's Eve, don't you?' And it was fantastic, it was a show-stealing thing, it really was. Also, that was the first year we were suddenly more popular than BBC 1, which was unheard of! In a way, that was her thing. She'd come along and knock things into popularity, she had that charm about her.

Anyway, we had huge numbers of people seeing that and I said to her later, 'That was the first time the ratings have gone mad for the show.' With our normal show it's not about the ratings, but with that show it suddenly became a huge thing. She said, 'Oh, if I'd known that, I'd have done something different! You didn't tell me people were going to be watching. I thought that because it was you, nobody was going to be watching!'

Kirsty's ability to 'knock things into popularity' extended to people, too, and her great talent for throwing parties. As the bagpiper and clarinettist at my party were being suitably refreshed and the swell of guests spread through the five downstairs rooms, people kept coming into the lounge to say how wonderful the food was – and I thought I'd better go and see what I was missing. It was generously laid out in the dining room and conservatory and the spread was magnificent: different home-made pastas, sausages and mash, marinated lamb chops, various salads and all sorts of delicacies for both vegetarians and carnivores filled the tables. A delicious smell of cooking drifted in from the kitchen as the party went on. I remember the mixture of admiration and appreciation with which Victor told me that new hot dishes were still being placed on the table. Kirsty spent much of the evening in the kitchen, with friends coming and going as she beavered away, but still found time to chat. Steve meanwhile kept the glasses filled. It was only when the cheese and biscuits, and trifle, had been brought out that we all at last sat down and listened to the musicians. Spider Stacy of The Pogues took out his tin whistle; someone played the piano; guitars were brought out.

'Her parties were just fantastic,' remembers her close friend Fuzz Boniface. 'She was a great cook – a bon viveur of every description, really, just brilliant fun. They usually ended up with a jukebox being pumped up and everyone dancing for their lives.' Billy Bragg was also a frequent guest at Kirsty's legendary parties. Their shared success with 'A New England', he wrote, 'also had the effect of gaining me entrance to her community of friends who gathered at her large suburban house to drink, eat and listen to great music':

She knew so many people, not just in the music industry. There was always someone there who seemed totally out of place but who was a dear friend of the hostess. Once, someone came dashing up to tell me he had just met Bob Hoskins. 'Look, look! Here he comes now,' trilled the star-struck guest, and we all turned round to see that 'Bob Hoskins' was in fact Lionel Bart! Another time I arrived just too late to hear her and Brian Kennedy sing folk songs to Joan Littlewood...

Gradually our guests started to drift away, and we said goodbye to the last at about two in the morning. I had had a quite wonderful birthday – and the buffet had been superb. So much for my offer to make some sandwiches!

• • •

A few months before that marvellous birthday party I had made an appointment with an eye consultant because I felt there was something slightly wrong with my left eye. It turned out to be macular degeneration and nothing could be done about it. It would get worse, I was told, and the other eye could be affected; it may come on slowly or quickly. I returned home with the dawning realisation that living where I did was not ideal. Since there was no public transport, I needed my car to get anywhere, but there would come a time when I could no longer drive. I also had an acre of garden which I would not be able to maintain. Kirsty and Hamish said they would support me in whatever decision I chose to make.

After talking it over with Kirsty, I decided to start looking for properties in the Ealing area, where I would have more opportunity to see my grandchildren and to help out whenever I was needed. I had been living at Coombe Cottage for getting on for 30 years. Now I looked around the house and wondered just where to start. There was also a large shed packed with garden equipment and other things that had accumulated over the years. I started to sort out a few things as I put the house on the market with a local estate agent and waited for a buyer. It was now April and a good time for likely buyers to be looking at properties in the area.

It was interesting to see the different reactions of the prospective buyers when they saw the house. There were one or two who completely ignored the view and only wanted to know whether there was an en suite bathroom. They were not the sort of people I would want to buy the house. Some were concerned about the bumpy, 'unadopted' road – which simply meant that the residents maintained and repaired the road themselves. And still others thought it was a little isolated –

though of course its 'isolation' was something most of the residents of Beech Way treasured. After such a lacklustre response, I also decided to advertise in a newspaper, and that same afternoon I had a call from an architect who wanted to come over immediately to view the property and its location. He brought his family with him and they at once fell in love with the place and wanted to buy it. He didn't even have a survey done. I told him that I was looking for a new place myself, and that this would probably take a few weeks. In the end it was five months before I finally moved out.

It was strange to think of myself moving to Ealing and living in a 'proper' street, as opposed to the place that Jamie and Louis so loved. I had given them their first camping experience when they were about three and four years old. Pitching the tent on my back lawn, they couldn't wait for the midnight feast – at 10pm. I loved the view of woodland and sky with not a house in sight from my windows, feeding foxes and badgers, the glorious sunsets, the frosty autumn dawns and silent snowfalls and learning to recognise the spoors of wild creatures.

I remembered again watching Kirsty from my kitchen window as she played next to a young fox cub, each oblivious to the other, and that glorious moment of innocent surprise when they saw each other for the first time. And the time Kirsty politely told another fox to wait – he had come early for some lunch – as she busied herself making him lemon curd sandwiches, which she then threw down for him. I once saw a fox carefully inspecting my two rather pathetic raspberry bushes and then very delicately tilting his head, baring his teeth and picking a single raspberry so gently and with such precision before moving off that I was astounded.

It would be a terrible wrench to say goodbye to this place, this plot of land I had found, against all the odds and on which

I had built such a marvellous home. I knew I would never find another place like it in London – but the pull of family was strong and I had to remind myself that without a car I would indeed be isolated and that as I got older I would never be able to keep an acre of garden under control.

One hindrance to my plans was Laban's grandson Claude Perrotet, whom Lisa Ullman had invited to study at her studio following his death. Claude's grandmother was Suzanne Perrotet, who as a young girl had Claude's father Andre. After completing his course at the studio, Claude had returned to Switzerland, where he now ran regular dance courses himself. I went there many times, but this time, in the summer of 1993, I initially refused his invitation because of all the complications and upheaval of moving house. Claude, however, became more than a little belligerent: what sort of excuse was moving house, he asked; 'You British make such heavy work of it!' It seemed that he had absolutely depended on me, and so I reluctantly agreed to go, at the beginning of September, to work with his senior students for a week. I then had to come back and clear out 30 years of possessions in the next four weeks. Needless to say, he was not my favourite person at this time...

There was also a final and rather severe last-minute problem. After keeping the buyer waiting for five months – he as keen to buy as I was reluctant to sell – I had eventually agreed to sign away my home to him. And then, the day before I was due to move, the solicitor rang with some bad news: it seems the flat I was buying was not as stated in the specifications. This was a bad blow to my plans, but Kirsty and Steve invited me to stay with them while I resumed my flat-hunting.

Contingency plans had to be put into action immediately. They had also asked me to go to Australia (via Los Angeles) with them and the boys in December – so I had to find something quickly. Instead of being delivered to the new address, the furniture went into storage.

I stood in the empty room, light and airy, with its windows wide open to the warm sun, though it was already October. Outside, the car was packed to the brim with things I would need in my temporary bedroom at Kirsty and Steve's. As I stood with the vacuum cleaner, trying to memorise every last detail of the view, there was suddenly an impatient banging at the door that announced the arrival of the new owners, eager to take over. I wished them well, and made my way along Beech Way to my neighbours Richard and Margaret, who had invited me to lunch before my departure for Ealing.

After taking dear old Solomon to a cattery, I arrived like a refugee at Mount Park Road, where I was given a very warm welcome. I'm sure Kirsty understood the turmoil of my feelings but I was determined to make the most of my new life and immediately set to work over the next two weeks in search of a beautiful garden – with flat attached!

It was at this time that I heard from my old friend Brenda that she had suddenly been taken ill and after a couple of days in hospital was now at home, though still not feeling well. Her family rang me the next day to say she was back in hospital and semi-conscious. She had smiled, they said, though her eyes had remained shut, when they told her I was coming to visit. I went to Epsom Hospital the next day with a book of poetry which she loved. I talked to her and read a few poems. I hoped she could hear them. She died the next day. After attending her funeral, I returned to flat-hunting, determined to make the most of my opportunities.

Then, just before we were due to set off for Australia, I found my garden (and flat). When the trees were in leaf, the surrounding houses wouldn't be seen. It needed a lot doing to it but it was south-facing, with eucalyptus and fruit trees. I had

...other, more understated, Stiff promo shot from the early 1980s.

© *Davide Levine*

Above: Kirsty and Steve's wedding day, 18 August 1984. Family, friends, colleagues, musicians and producers all gathered together at the reception at Selsdon Park Hotel

Below: Kirsty and Steve on the bonnet of their wedding car, with Frida from ABBA a U2's Bono flanked by Paul Rutherford and Holly Johnson from Frankie Goes to Hollywood in the back.

ove left: Kirsty and Steve proudly showing off their newborn son Jamie, born in ›ruary 1985.

ove right: Kirsty wearing my floral maternity dress, with Jamie, while awaiting the minent arrival of son number two, Louis, in September 1986.

low: My much-loved grandsons, the apple of Kirsty's eye.

Above left: One night in New York in 1985, while Steve worked at producing the Rolli
Stones, Ronnie Wood drew this skilful sketch of Kirsty.

Above right: Kirsty 'n' Keith Richards.

Below left: Steve also produced U2's first three studio albums; this Polaroid of Bono a
Kirsty was taken while he was in town to hook up with Keith Richards on the track
'Silver and Gold'.

Below right: Kirsty and Steve enjoying themselves.

ove: With Billy Bragg, whose song 'A New England' Kirsty covered in 1985, her
sion reaching Number 7 in the UK single charts that year.   © *Charles Dickins*

low: On stage in 1988 with The Pogues, singing perhaps her greatest collaboration,
: 1987 hit 'Fairytale of New York', during a tour which helped her to overcome her
ge fright.

Above: Kirsty and co on the set of the video for 'Days' in April 1989, with Pete Glenister. Kirsty wore a huge blonde wig, her wedding dress, and muddy welly boots underneath!

Below: Kirsty with Pete, her close friend and writing partner.

Above: My beautiful daughter and me. It's funny – we were often pictured like this, with my arm thrown protectively round her.

Below: Kirsty with her father, shortly before he died in 1989.

Kirsty's ability to create wonderfully layered harmonies meant she was much in deman as a backing singer. She sang backing vocals on a number of The Smiths' songs, and collaborated with both Morrissey (*above*) and guitarist Johnny Marr (*below*), with who she co-wrote her 1991 hit 'Walking Down Madison'.

© *Charles Dick*

work to do here. Three of the rooms opened onto the patio. I made an offer, but had still heard nothing back by the time I left with Steve and the boys for Los Angeles, the first stage of our trip. Kirsty was coming several days later with Steve's mother, Marie, who each had various work and social commitments to complete before leaving. On arrival, we booked in at the LA Hilton. My room was superb. I lay on the floral bedspread and pressed a remote-control button. Silently, the huge floral curtains glided open. At the touch of another button, the net curtains opened to reveal the hills in front of my window, and the magical letters 'Hollywood' spelled out before me. To be honest, I would have liked to have been able to spend more time in the bathroom, with its dressing table crammed with flasks and packets of various skin potions, nail polish and bath oils.

We met an American friend of Steve's whose boyfriend was English. He told me he was in real estate. I ventured to suggest that this was perhaps not the safest business to be in, given that the San Andreas fault line threatened one day to cause widespread destruction to Los Angeles. He replied, quite seriously, that he had chosen his property very carefully, well away from the danger points. I wondered how he could tell!

Steve also took us to Disney World. The boys thoroughly enjoyed it and even I was pleasantly surprised: it was commercial and sugary at times, of course, but I had to admit that some of the rides were quite fun. But my appreciation of LA culture suffered a blow on the drive back when it proved virtually impossible to buy almost any sort of notepad or notebook to keep some kind of record of the holiday. We must have stopped at at least three stationer's shops, all to no avail. Perhaps Americans don't keep diaries? Kirsty and Marie flew in the next day and we all went out to celebrate with Kirsty's childhood friend Alison, who was now married to Jay Boberg, an American in the music business.

Two days later we embarked on the last leg of our journey. To our surprise, we lost a whole day on the flight, expecting to arrive on 23 December, only to find that it was already Christmas Eve in Sydney, where Hamish was waiting for us. He had found rented accommodation for all of us and bought some basic groceries. The house was in a cul-de-sac overlooking the beach, with a view across Sydney to the bush beyond. After sorting ourselves out, Steve and Kirsty rang friends who arranged for us to have Christmas lunch at a well-known restaurant by the harbour. There was a huge choice of menus: the usual turkey and roast potatoes with all the trimmings, followed by Christmas pudding, ice cream and trifle; or roast goose, lamb and beef, lobster, prawns, mussels, as well as a range of recognisable fish and some other, to me very strange, oddities. It's strange to reflect how frequently descriptions of Christmases – and Christmas dinners – appear in these pages. That Christmas lunch in Sydney, with the doors to the veranda wide open to the beach beyond and the temperature well into the 90s, with my lovely family all around me, was certainly among the very happiest I ever spent.

In the next few days we did Sydney, visiting the zoo and Woomera Park (famous for its *Skippy* television series), as well as some friends who lived just outside the city. Both Kirsty and I had work to do, though, Kirsty going off to do a radio interview, and I – after borrowing her elegant jacket – to a book launch for my first Laban book with Century Press.

Kirsty and Steve had a lot of friends to catch up with – not least Terry, whose emigration, 'going away... twelve thousand miles to Sydney Bay', had featured in Kirsty's 1985 song, 'He's on the Beach': 'And he says it's brilliant there... And sunshine everywhere'. We certainly agreed, and I took the boys swimming daily. Marie also enjoyed the swimming, but after suffering a bad stomach upset from the mussels at the restaurant, she also became very homesick: I don't think she had ever been away from home before at Christmas. And so after a phone call or two, it was agreed that she would be happier going home earlier.

Steve and Kirsty also accepted an invitation to visit their old friends the Thompson Twins – Tom Bailey and Alannah Currie – who had moved with their family to New Zealand a year or so before. They had been regular visitors in Ealing and the children were near-contemporaries and friends. On their return, our family all said they had preferred New Zealand over Australia, in large part because there were far fewer poisonous or stinging insects and general creepie-crawlies – though I'm not sure Kirsty would have been all that daunted, after all the expertise in such creatures she had gathered as a child.

Since Hamish was doing his own thing, I took myself off for an adventure of my own. I took a flight to Noosa, in Cairns in Queensland, where I swam daily and took bus trips through the countryside, surprised that the bush looked so green, almost like Surrey in parts – though the sudden descent of darkness at 6pm, despite the summer season, always took me by surprise.

Soon after we had all returned to Sydney after our various excursions, I became aware of some grey smoke rising up above the bay in the area of Woomera Park. By evening it had spread and was thick and black. The next morning flames could be seen intermittently and the fire had spread further around the outskirts of Sydney itself. The sun was now partly obscured. The friends we had visited were now due, though they arrived more like refugees than guests, with their dog and a suitcase full of photographs and their passports in case their house had been destroyed by the time they returned.

The fire crept behind us by the second evening, but was still on the periphery of the city. We could smell it in the air and could see the black ash sprinkling the neighbouring streets and beach. Perhaps we were naive, but we never felt personally threatened since we could always, we thought, escape onto the beach if necessary.

On one of our last days in Australia, we all went out on a tourist pirate ship in Sydney Bay, where six-year-old Louis was promoted to captain and had to wear the appropriate three-cornered hat. On our return, Terry came over with sausages of all kinds and took charge of a splendid barbecue in the glass-sided conservatory overlooking the beach – the perfect end to a perfect holiday down under.

This time we were only passing through Los Angeles, which had just suffered an earthquake, and we didn't see the damage, which was apparently severe in some areas. I thought about the Englishman in real estate I had met and wondered how his portfolio of properties had fared.

Of course, the ground was moving under all our feet that year in one way or another. On my return home, I learned that my offer on the Ealing flat and garden had been accepted and in early 1994 I moved into my new home, along with my cat Solomon III, who lived out the rest of his long life in comfort there.

But it also became clear to me that a faultline had opened up in Kirsty's marriage. I sensed that things weren't going too well, though her humour was always there, and her pride in her sons unstinting. As she sang in the title song to her 1994 album, 'It's sink or swim in these Titanic days'.

Chapter Ten

Last Day of Summer

1995-1999

'I know an island where the people are kind...'
KIRSTY MACCOLL, 'MAMBO DE LA LUNA', 2000

One sunny day in April 2006, I sat down on a bench in my garden. I noticed two butterflies circling one another as they fluttered over the pond and then a dragonfly flew within inches of my face to alight on the marsh marigolds. I was relieved to see glimpses of red, black and gold moving under the reeds, fearful that the herons might have taken all the fish over the winter. The sun was warm on my back and it seemed that spring had arrived overnight, bringing everything back to life.

With the sun on the water came the memories. One of my last of Kirsty was of her in khaki shorts, standing thigh-deep in the middle of the pond, looking so beautiful, strong and healthy as she planted waterlilies and other plants taken from her own garden pond. She explained the qualities of each of the plants, passing on her own experience to me – a mere novice where pond cultivation was concerned. Baskets of special soil made of hessian were carefully laid in place and held down with pebbles. Her attempts to catch a few of her own fish had not been very successful, so we had gone to a garden centre and selected some small koi and goldfish.

I remembered with such pleasure how happy I had felt seeing her that day, so full of life and confidence, so successful in the latest phase of her brilliant musical career and so proud of her two young sons – as proud of them as I was of her. I suddenly felt that my face was wet with tears. For the same sun that now streamed down into my garden had, only a few days before, shone on the waters off Havana, where Kirsty's ashes had been scattered. I thought of the flying fish we had seen from our boat on that sad journey, and the image of that same creature on the sunny cover art of what had become her final album.

Tropical Brainstorm was her most successful record and represented a brilliant re-flowering of her musical creativity, her passionate vitality and her personal love – now all so brutally cut short, with never a sign or gesture or simple acknowledgement of remorse from those responsible.

Kirsty had earned her success with *Tropical Brainstorm*, the culmination of years of hard, dedicated work, including a painful period of personal re-adjustment, through which her cheerful personality had rarely wavered. Her death, at the height of her powers and at the beginning of an exciting new period in her life still seems altogether too cruel. This book is part of my attempt to come to terms with that fact.

I'll never know quite how, following the slow and sad collapse of her marriage to Steve, she managed to run a band, go on tour and organise her career in those years, at the same time as having the boys at home every weekend and in the holidays. We all tried to lend a hand, of course, but as Hamish remembers, there were good times and bad times: 'Kirsty had to carry the burden of running things which didn't always go easily. At one point Kirsty had to deal with a cancelled tour which involved paying out a huge sum to musicians who had been signed up. She was uncomplaining about such problems as her philosophy was to get on with life.'

Arriving home in England after my Australian holiday, by spring 1994 I was ready and willing to move into the London flat I had briefly viewed and made an offer on before the trip. When my friend Sybill came over from Poland to stay, she had to share the floor with me – that part of the floor, that is, that was clear of the mountain of books stretching from the windows to the opposite wall. I bought a bed, bookshelves went up and Kirsty helped me plan a new kitchen with an oven like hers. I had been staying at Kirsty's while she was on tour, so my furniture was all in storage, and Solomon had been staying in a cattery because of the risk to Kirsty's asthma.

I was getting phone calls and letters from Austria, Holland, Switzerland and Germany. (I had set up my first summer holiday courses in England in response to my first book, *Laban for Actors and Dancers*, which had come out the previous year to very favourable reviews.) Many of my students contacted me at my new Ealing address, saying they wanted to come for a week's summer school. When I replied that I was still sleeping on the floor in the new flat and awaiting furniture, they encouraged me to find a suitable venue in the area and it was because of their enthusiasm that I eventually found the proper premises to run a course. I hired a hall just up the road, found somewhere to stay for everyone and one day in July they all arrived.

In the old days, before Kirsty was born, Ewan had taught my dancers to sing and some of the men even went on to record with him. I now thought it would be a good idea to include singing as part of what I was now calling a theatre course. I asked Sheila Hancock, with whom I'd worked in 1982, if she knew of anybody who could take over this role of singing coach and she recommended John Dalby, a singer, actor and composer. John lived nearby, was a great asset to the course and in time became a very dear friend. Over the next five years John and I shared the summer school, which for three years was held at Bedales in the summer holidays and for two years after that in Ealing.

It was after the first two or three courses that I decided to have singing lessons myself with John. I have to say I showed no particular aptitude for singing but being the mother of two singers I thought I would have a go. In retrospect I was surprisingly shy about it, I suppose because I was starting so late in life, but Kirsty had always been supportive. She said I was too tentative. Being shy about my singing, though, made it difficult to breathe properly and breath control is a key element of dance technique. I persevered and John, despite his quips, was a very good teacher. My friend Denise remembers that I plucked up the courage to sing along with the others at one of Kirsty's great parties at Mount Park Road, while Kirsty looked on, smiling encouragingly.

Of course, Kirsty herself knew all about the nerve it takes to sing in public – Billy Bragg called her a 'notoriously shy' live performer – so the long American tour she and her band embarked on in March 1995 must have been daunting. 'She was going through a bad patch at the time,' her friend and guitarist Pete Glenister told me, 'because that's when she'd split up with Steve and nothing seemed to go right. But she got happy on the tour because she was away from everything, and it was a really nice bunch of people who got on really well – [her manager] Brigette Barr, the crew, Dave Ruffy, Glyn Wood the tour manager and all of us on the bus.' As things turned out, it was just as well they got on: not only were the gigs relatively few and far between – Kirsty once told me that the USA was like a Polo mint: nothing in the middle – but there were also a few problems with accommodation, as Pete remembers:

The first two dates after we arrived were in Atlanta, where we were in the worst hotel I've ever stayed in. I remember arriving at the motel, right next to a ten-lane urban freeway. There were brushed nylon sheets, far too much air freshener and the place was full of hookers and pimps. There was a pool out front which was full of broken furniture. It was just the arsehole of the universe – the worst place. I didn't even want to lie down on the bed. My shower was a pipe across the top of the cubicle with a broken head on the end. The guy at reception gave me the key to the room next to mine and told me to unscrew the showerhead from there. It kind of worked then. In the end we left after the second gig rather than have to stay another night and drove overnight to the next one.

Brigette Barr was her manager at the time – she was great, and Kirsty loved her. It was the first time Kirsty felt she had a manager who was a soulmate. Brigette was a fan. She worked for Peter Asher Management. The record company would give you a manager and Peter Asher was the biggest name on the West Coast so she became Kirsty's manager. Brigette's remit was that whatever happened we were going to break even, not lose money – so if you did a big gig you got a nice hotel, a small gig... you know. We stayed in some really dodgy places. It was actually a very happy tour – but definitely the worst hotel I've ever stayed in on any tour.

The problem was going from Minneapolis to the West Coast finding gigs that she could do, because there's this gaping hole in the Midwest. We always used to play in Boulder, Colorado. That tour it was packed, a really good night. I remember driving all the way down there. There was this weird club that had this bunch of tables you could stand at and some sitting tables all unlit at the back of this cavernous club. There was a little dance floor in front of the stage, which was lit a little bit, then the stage. But the whole place was very dark. It was a great gig and at the end we got a genuine encore. We went back on and the first thing Kirsty said was, 'Right, I'm not playing another note until I can see your faces. Come out, come out, wherever you are!'

She was feeling confident that they all would – I'm not sure I was. But then they did all come out, very sheepishly, into the light. It wasn't a particularly young audience, though. In fact, as they slowly appeared, Kirsty said to us, 'Look at them! They're like the living dead!', and it was like that. We started again with 'Chip Shop', and Kirsty was really pleased. There were a lot of people down the front who we could now see were having a great time. That was a nice tour; I really got to know Kirsty during that tour, more than I'd ever done before.

GLR radio interview, June 1992

Tracey MacLeod: Kirsty, you've got a couple of gigs coming up.

Kirsty MacColl: Yes, I've got a great band – Mark Nevin, Dave Ruffy, Gary Tibbs, Jamie West-Oram – and we've been out and about doing various places and we're hot to trot now.

TM: You're enjoying live performance a bit more now?

KM: I am, I'm the rock'n'roll bitch from hell now – it's all change!

Kirsty had also continued to record, though not at first for any specific new project. 'Caroline' and a cover of Lou Reed's 'Perfect Day' (a duet with Evan Dando), appeared on her retrospective collection *Galore* – though it is perhaps another song from the same period, the haunting and beautiful 'I Am Afraid', that best reflects her outlook at this time. (It wasn't released until Nigel Reeve's 2005 *Croydon to Cuba* compilation for EMI.) Boz Boorer was involved with all these sessions and with Kirsty's cover of the traditional ballad 'Butcher Boy'.

'Spider [Stacy] was in the midst of his drinking days,' Boz recalls, 'and had to be coerced into playing the whistle melody [on 'Butcher Boy'] over and over and they eventually stitched his contribution together from nine or so separate takes.' At one point, Boz himself had offered to play whistle on the track himself, but Kirsty was adamant: 'I want Spider!'

Kirsty was also commissioned to write some instrumental theme music for a prospective Carlton TV series, from Kirsty's point of view rather aptly titled 'Picking up the Pieces'. She worked with Boz again on this side-project. 'Kirsty asked them,' he remembers, 'which of her songs was their favourite':

When they replied that they liked 'Don't Come the Cowboy', Kirsty asked if they wanted a country song for their theme. They said, 'No.' So she asked if they wanted a harmony vocal theme of the sort she specialised in. They said, 'No.'

'So... what sort of thing *do* you want?' asked Kirsty.

'Erm... something with a northern soul vibe to it.'

She told me she thought of replying, 'So why the hell do you want *me* to do it?' – before thinking of the money and saying yes. This was one of the very few occasions that Kirsty *didn't* speak her mind. She could always achieve the impossible – like getting me to dance! Anyway, she called me up, and we worked it out.

Galore was released in March 1995, and 'after that', as Pete Glenister remembers,

> There was a real pause for breath for Kirsty. A 'greatest hits' package draws a line under your career and it's hard to get going again. She found it really hard – she was very down at this time, and we were talking on the phone and talked about writing some things.

Billy Bragg has a different take on *Galore*'s release:

> When the 1995 collection of her best songs, *Galore*, was being prepared, Kirsty MacColl contacted various friends within her musical community and asked them to write tributes to her for the sleeve notes. In a way this was more fitting than using press cuttings because she never got the credit she deserved for her talents... Words of praise duly poured in from the likes of Bono, Morrissey and Shane MacGowan. She thanked us all in the CD booklet for making it possible for her to 'revel in the glory' of reading her obituaries 'without the inconvenience of actually dying.' In a dark twist reminiscent of one of her own songs, when her real obituaries appeared in the week before Christmas, it was from these sleeve notes that almost all of the quotes were taken.

The cover art of *Galore* included a famous photograph of Kirsty wearing a Castro cap, lighting a Cuban cigar from a flaming dollar bill. But her interest in the island of Cuba ran deeper than a photo opportunity and represented a lifelong commitment to its people. When Billy Bragg suggested to Kirsty that they might record an album of folk songs together, the idea, he says, 'was shot down in flames... She had a better idea, anyway.' That idea had first sown a seed in her imagination as far back as her 1991 *Electric Landlady* album, for which, as Billy remembers,

> she had recorded a track in a New York club with a bunch of Cuban musicians. 'My Affair' was the first hint of her growing obsession with music from Latin America. A year later, she travelled to Cuba for the first time, and fell in love with the place and its people. Always willing to back up her politically charged lyrics with action, she became a stalwart supporter of the Cuba Solidarity Campaign and made numerous trips to the island throughout the 1990s.

Kirsty made her first trip to Cuba on her own, but later on she took her two boys with her. She used to pack great bundles of clothing into her own luggage to give to the people there on her trips, especially children's shoes (as Boz and Lyn Boorer remember) since they were so expensive to buy there, and kids grow out of them so quickly – with the result that Cuban children often went barefoot. She mobilised her friends in the same cause and instilled in her own children the same noble aims. Louis was particularly intrigued, I remember, by children begging for chocolate. And when, just a few short years later, I had to ask the boys where they wanted Kirsty's ashes laid to rest, it was Cuba that they both immediately thought of.

'During these years,' wrote Billy Bragg, 'Cuba revitalised her. She learnt Spanish and, travelling to Brazil, became fluent in Portuguese.' And there was always the music.

'She played with me a couple of times,' Jools Holland told me, 'she played a guitar, the piano a couple of times as well. She would just doodle and work out harmonies where the notes were. She would be working out where a harmony might be and then she would play the guitar':

It was also very like her, I think, to learn classical guitar. She was very open-minded. So later, when she suddenly had this huge interest in Cuban music, a whole other world had opened up. I think that again illustrates a really artistic mind open to new ideas and to be excited by the input of all that new stuff.

She did however introduce me to Boz [Boorer] – she just knew so many people that were really good musicians, she could have set up an agency! In fact, if I was after a certain type of musician to do something, I would always trust her judgement.

Kirsty took the time to study Spanish at the University of the Third Age in Ealing, where she was a very motivated student, not only of the language itself but also of the entire culture. Her tutor suggested that she should go on to take a degree in the subject but, as she told me, while she was very flattered, she had to turn the idea down since she already had a career. And her ambitions were also slightly different to the average student: as Jools put it, 'I know exactly what would have been happening: she would be learning Spanish so she could tell them jokes.'

She certainly used impressively fluent colloquial Spanish when ordering in restaurants during a holiday I spent with her and the boys in Spain in 1997. She had a friend with a house near Malaga and invited me along for company as she was still then on her own. We all flew out to Malaga and hired a car for a short break – swimming in the pool, reading books and going out for meals. Kirsty did all the driving. It was always fun going shopping with her and she bought me a watch from a Moroccan tout when we visited the market. When I turned on the television the next morning, the bulletins were dominated by the terrible news that Princess Diana had been killed in a car crash in Paris. Like so many other people, we followed the bulletins through the day, and we were all shocked by the news – a young mother killed so pointlessly in a needless accident.

•   •   •

Kirsty loved the modest and quiet private holidays she spent with her boys during those difficult years, which provided some much-needed relief from the pressures of her career. Sometimes I would join her, and at other times her friends would, or her brother Hamish, who was by then living in Stroud, where he was busy teaching Chi Kung after a long career as a practitioner of Chinese medicine:'I started studying at the Liu Academy in 1973 – martial arts and Ch'an (Zen) Buddhist and Taoist philosophy':

This was the time of Bruce Lee and the *Kung Fu* TV series. Our teacher, Liu Hsiu-chi, was a charismatic and intelligent man. He was keen to open a clinic of Chinese medicine and within a year he'd found a suitable premises and persuaded many of his students, me included, to sign up for a course. I quickly found that I had a particular talent for it and although all the students got to work in the clinic, I found myself working there most of the time, helping with everything from massage to moxibustion, from note-taking, via acupuncture-needling and tapping to the teaching of exercises. It was a very exciting time for me, as I broadened my skills by the use of meditation and exercise. By the time I was conducting consultations myself, I was able to sense the physical state of a patient, which manifested itself as a shared sense of their own pain or discomfort, and its location, within my own body.

The clinic was very successful, but after a couple of years I fell ill myself with a complaint that none of these traditional treatments could ease. Master Liu could do nothing, and an operation became necessary. Shortly before this, I happened to meet a colleague from the Spiritualist Association of Great Britain, who told me that the reason that I was unwell was that my natural healing ability was coming into conflict with the system I had been taught. Although I didn't know what to make of this, years later I can say he was probably right – but at the time the idea of giving up something that was plainly valuable, and in which I'd invested so many years of study – and so many years of my life – seemed unthinkable. Anyway, after my op I returned briefly to the clinic but found that I'd lost heart, and instead decided to treat patients in their own homes.

While this proved successful, however, I felt perpetually ill and began to dread each new day. It took another year for me to realise that I would either have to stop or it would kill me.

Hamish's friend Julian Jones (who had designed Kirsty's reedbeds) lived near Hamish's home in Stroud and another of his friends, Matthew Wallis, eventually married Sonja, the last of Kirsty's succession of nannies, a brown-eyed and bubbly Australian whom we all adored. We were a very tight-knit family unit in those years, and in a roundabout sort of way, we all of us played a small part in introducing Kirsty to James – the great love and blessing of her final years.

In 1998, an American friend of mine, Hope Hardcastle, heard that my grandson Louis wanted to play sax. Her husband had recently died and there was a very good alto saxophone going begging in her cellar. Louis telephoned her in advance and arranged to go and see it with Steve. When they both arrived, Hope was astonished to see that Louis was only a boy – then just ten or eleven years old – but she took to him immediately and Louis started to play saxophone at school.

There was a a young music teacher at Bedales called James Knight, who also played sax and was an inspiration to Louis. He eventually persuaded Kirsty to go to hear his teacher play.

Kirsty invited James to join her and a group of friends for an evening out later in 1999. Nobody else could make it – James still doesn't think Kirsty had set this up – so they found themselves on their own for the evening. Boz Boorer later told me that when James came on the scene, he, Dave Ruffy and her other friends took it upon themselves to 'look after' Kirsty and made sure James knew he 'had them to deal with if he messed her around'. But after a while (and over a few beers), they concluded he was 'all right'.

Kirsty's friend Lyn Boorer – Boz's wife – remembers this as a very happy time. 'My relationship with Kirsty,' she told me, 'even though we were both musicians and she encouraged me so much to play, was a relationship of just being girlfriends and mothers and sharing the ins and outs of basic family life.'

One night in late 1999, Boz and I were playing one of our regular gigs at the 12 Bar Club down in Soho. We were playing with a guy from Nashville Tennessee named Sonny George. Kirsty had met Sonny with us at her home in Ealing at one of her legendary parties. She liked the way Sonny sang, with his strong, low Southern drawl. I think she was accompanied by James on this particular evening. The night was great and a lot of the crowd were thrilled to see Kirsty down the front of this tiny little venue, dancing her heart out to this obscure guy's music and really enjoying the gig.

After the show, when the punters had left, in usual tradition the band were offered a drink from the bar when all was quiet and emptying out. Kirsty was in our company and was offered a nice big glass of red wine, which she accepted and was enjoying very much, when she needed to visit the lady's room. While she was away from the bar, though, somehow the barmaid removed this lovely glass of wine without telling anyone or asking whose it was.

Now we have a little problem! Kirsty comes back to join us all and her drink is gone. So she asks the barmaid – who snaps at her that the glass was left unattended, and that the bar is closed and she can't have a new drink. She starts telling Kirsty that she has to leave the club – she wasn't in the band, she says, and can't demand another drink. The barmaid is furious now and starts moaning and groaning. Anyway, she goes and gets the bar manager and starts telling him about this red-headed troublemaker... When this little guy – the bar manager – came over, ready to chuck Kirsty out, he nearly had a fit when he saw who she was – 'Oh my God! I can't believe it's Kirsty MacColl! You are one of my *favourite* singers' – and proceeded to pour her another lovely big glass of red wine.

James himself remembers the many gigs, 'ranging from Latin to rockabilly to rap and back again' that he and Kirsty went to during their early days together. But of the 'hundreds of things' he remembers about Kirsty and the time they spent together, he told me,

I think one of my favourite memories is writing the song 'Good For Me' together. Of course, we didn't know then that it would be Kirsty's last song. I had done a little demo of it and Kirsty had put some lyrics to it. We spent a day recording it at home with Richard Mainwaring at the desk. Seeing Kirsty playing guitar again was great and when it came to singing it she wouldn't let me sit in the control room. In fact I wasn't allowed to even see the lyrics. A couple of hours passed and I went in to have a listen and was, as anyone would be, amazed. It's something that I will always treasure: a love song for me from Kirsty – and such a beautiful one at that. One of the greatest things was singing the outro backing vocals with Kirsty. She obviously really loved me because it's not something she ever did. That's not to say it didn't have to be perfect! Just standing next to her doing massive harmonies and her holding my hand (musically and literally) is something I'll never, ever forget. I still find it difficult to listen to that song. I think I always will.

For Kirsty, friendship, music and love always went together – but the music still had to be perfect. 'She was a very straight talker,' remembered Dave, talking in conversation with Pete Glenister, 'and really intelligent. That's why she didn't suffer fools – it wasn't because she thought she was better than you. And she really loved her music.'

'She really lived for it, didn't she?' agreed Pete. 'Especially on tour, when her compilation tapes would go on *every* night. When she was into something, you really knew about it.' It was with Dave and Pete, her long-term musical collaborators, that Kirsty had meanwhile been working on a set of new songs with a dramatic new sound, inspired by the 'new world' of Latin American music she was now exploring:

Pete Glenister: Kirsty was listening to loads of Cuban records, and one day she said, 'How are we going to do something as good as that?' So we started looking at techniques. She had a great record collection – quite old: 1940s, 50s, early 60s Latin music. So we decided we could sample some music, chop it up, and see what we come up with. We spent a day doing that, then we did a bunch of programming, adding some bass, drums and percussion, and we gave her a track. And again, it was one of those things where another few months later, Kirsty played us this thing – it was 'Mambo de la Luna'. We just put a few more bits and pieces on it and that was the song. So we said, 'Right, we know what we're doing now: a funny kind of Latin thing of our own making.' And she said, 'Let's do some more like that.'

We spent another day and took another sample, this time of a Willie Bobo track and that became 'In These Shoes?' I spent one day on the backing track; she came over the next day with the whole thing. Then she got talking to Kevin Nixon and he decided he was going to manage her. I was actually really excited about this. We felt sure we really had something with just those two tracks and Kevin then set up a structure with Kirsty.

She paid the two of us, me and Dave, to work on that project. It was Monday to Friday, 11am until 6 or 7pm. It never turned into one of those 'up all night' affairs. It was at my studio in Bermondsey – which she hated. Getting to Bermondsey from Ealing is not the best journey in the world. She used to arrive usually about lunchtime and then moan at me for being in Bermondsey. Then we'd get going. It was a wonderful time.

Dave Ruffy: That set the way I still work. I had a little annexe with a drum booth, with two studios working together. Sometimes it would be really nerve-racking trying to get all the parts –It was like a workshop – you'd be doing non-stop work, you weren't doing the same thing all the time. It was really exciting.

I remember being at Boz Boorer's studio and it was fairly early on. She was doing a film theme, 'Picking up the Pieces', at Boz's studio. She came in. Now, I knew she'd been on a date the night before, so I just said, 'How was your date?'

'Shit,' she said, 'but I've written a song about it.' And that was 'England 2 Colombia 0'.

Pete Glenister: Although musically it was all going really well, personally she was in bits at the time - I'd say her absolute lowest time. If you listen to that song, you'll hear that we kept most of the vocal from the demo. You can hear she's nearly crying.

Chapter Eleven

Good For Me

1999-2000

'I'm so close to heaven, it was such a surprise'
KIRSTY MACCOLL, 'GOOD FOR ME', 2000

K irsty had become very interested in learning Portuguese
after meeting so many Brazilian musicians through her
work in London. After recording 'England 2 Colombia 0', she
went to visit a musician friend of hers who had returned to his
home town in Brazil – Kirsty's trip was just one of many to Latin
America she made at this time. On arrival she first stayed for a
couple of nights with a student friend of mine, Denise Telles.

Denise was living on an island off the coast of Rio and after
studying the Laban technique for actors with me now worked
at the University there. She showed Kirsty the sights – including
an expedition to Copacabana beach to hear the music. I later
heard that she had then gone on to join her Brazilian musician
friend and that the two of them had spent time in a recording
studio listening to other musicians and trying out ideas.

Dave Ruffy later described Kirsty's vocal on 'England 2
Colombia 0' as 'a great performance... and you could never get
it better because it's so real. It was recorded when she felt it, and

it really came over. She was very honest, but not unkind. She didn't suffer fools because she knew that life is hard and she didn't dress it up in sentimentality. She's just got the power to say it like it is. She wasn't a girly girl. When Michele Drees came into the band on percussion - a very, very accomplished musician - there was someone who could do girly backing vocals and I think Kirsty really took some persuading. '

Pete says, 'She was a man's woman. She liked the company of men more than women, I think. Kirsty's whole way was much more geared towards men. I mean, she had quite a male sense of humour somehow, very witty.'

'I was aware that Kirsty didn't work with women very often,' remembers Michele herself, 'and I think Dave Ruffy told me Kirsty had said something along the lines of "I hope she's not a girly girl," so I knew she may be a bit tough - but that's cool. You have to be tough in this business. I was extremely excited to be asked to play in Kirsty's band':

… and I loved the way I got the gig with her. I run a little group called 'Sonhos do Brasil' where I sing in Brazilian Portuguese and play guitar - some very rare and unusual Brazilian and original songs. Kirsty was keen to have someone who could handle the background vocals as well as occupy the percussion seat. Apparently, she heard just ten seconds of one of my Brazilian songs and said, 'She's great, let's get her!' Kirsty never heard my percussion playing - just booked me on the strength of my love of Brazilian music. We had this in common: a great love of Latin music.

Just before I got that gig with Kirsty, myself and another woman-musician had been sacked from a TV house band because we were thought to be overweight! Obviously, I was furious about this and should probably have told the Musicians' Union. I am a dedicated and hard-working musician so when Kirsty asked me to play in her band shortly after this insult, without her either seeing me or it having anything at all to do with the way I looked, made it feel like justice had been done!

Kirsty had long battled with the sexism inherent in the music business. 'For women in the industry,' as Billy Bragg later reflected, 'it's much more based on looks and sexuality and the pressure to conform to that is overwhelming.'

And her first manager, Frank Murray, remembers that when she scored her first hit with 'Chip Shop' in 1981, some people in the record company:

came down like a pack of wolves and immediately tried to change her image – 'Let's make her into some kind of teen queen'. Kirsty wasn't into that. She would fight tooth and nail... A lot of record companies had this problem with Kirsty. They had a gorgeous-looking woman who could write great lyrics, who could sing, who could actually produce her own things – and they *still* weren't happy.

'When she was in the studio,' agreed Billy, 'she was clearly in charge':

Even when it was my record! She would come in and, you know, 'Do that,' 'Do this,' and 'C'mon, we're all going down the pub now.' She had a very formidable personality.

But despite Pete's wondering about 'how another female voice' might now work in the studio, Michele Drees became a treasured member of the *Tropical Brainstorm* sessions. 'With Kirsty,' she says, 'it was all about the music':

> This is always the shit part of the music business for women, which Kirsty was well aware of. There was a huge amount of respect between us. Kirsty was so generous and I am quite a naturally shy person; I express myself through music and Kirsty was always very kind about me. I remember one night after a concert, when we were all getting quite pissed in a bar of the hotel, we both connected about being alone for a long time. I had almost given up, but Kirsty advised me to keep all options open, as you never know where love will come from.
>
> One of the most nerve-racking parts of the gig itself was having to play 'How Insensitive' with just Kirsty and myself on guitar. God, she sang that song so beautifully; her pitching was perfect. I felt really exposed, but it was so exhilarating. It's always easy to hide behind the drums. I loved the fact that Kirsty didn't take any crap. She was a really strong woman, but also vulnerable, I think. I think Kirsty felt a bit awkward about performing live, and I always felt we had a connection about this.

'Mambo de la Luna' and 'In These Shoes?' were the first singles to be released from the new album in November 1999 and February 2000 respectively, *Tropical Brainstorm* itself coming out that March. It heralded a new, exciting and critically successful direction in Kirsty's musical career. She had overcome her early stage fright through a series of gruelling tours, she had found a way to blend her political commitment with her constant musical experimentation, she had discovered a brilliant 'new world' and she had fallen in love again. 'All her influences came together,' as Billy Bragg put it, 'on an album of which she was justly proud. Released to rave reviews, *Tropical Brainstorm* was the record on which Kirsty finally seemed to have found a way to mix her Latin influences with her natural wit, which as she got older was becoming nicely sardonic. She even toured with her band of mostly British musicians, including her partner James on saxophone. In him she had found the love of her life and her love for life again.'

She had even finally got to grips with the dubious art of the promotional video. 'She hated doing videos – she was not one for videos,' Dave Ruffy told me, and as her friend, photographer Charlie Dickins. put it, she sometimes needed a bit of 'Dutch courage' to perform in them:

In the video for 'Free World', where she is channel-hopping and you see her dancing around under an oil lamp – she came round to my house in Fulham and we got very drunk and then she got me to film her dancing to the Happy Mondays. This was then put in the video – but only we know she wasn't dancing to her own music! And she looked *fabulous*!

By the time she made the video for 'In These Shoes?', commented Pete Glenister, 'she only appeared at the end – she finally had full executive control!' Her old manager Frank Murray remembers the day the finished video arrived:

I am really proud of the fact that we were friends and also proud that I managed her career in those early years. We had some great adventures together, mostly laced with laughter... to this day I can still hear the sound of Kirsty's laughter. The last time I met with her, she had just received a copy of her

191

'In These Shoes?' video. We both watched it together and she thought it was so funny – she loved the fact that she barely appears in it. She came outside the house with me, and gave me a hug and a kiss. She told me she was off to Baghdad soon and would see me when she got back. I wished her well and drove off. I never saw her again.

As Pete Glenister and Dave Ruffy agreed – indeed, as all her many friends in the business have commented – Kirsty was never seduced by the glamour and idolatry of the music industry, and despite her dazzling talent always remained down to earth:

Pete Glenister: She just hated that whole part of being a 'celebrity', doing interviews and so on. At least in the beginning, she hated playing live, she was in blind terror at being on stage.

Dave Ruffy: It was only really on the last couple of tours that she really started to enjoy being on stage, after she met James. They had a really good relationship, they were very straight-talking with each other, they were very well matched like that. He was very good for her. Pete, you were around a lot longer than me – you used to have to deal with Kirsty's anxieties…

Pete Glenister: Yes, emotional support as much as anything…

Dave Ruffy: I remember, after James arrived she enjoyed the gig and she started to realise that people really liked her and she had a fanbase who really liked what she was. She was a really talented person, but she wasn't really a showbiz person.

Kirsty would support any fight against injustice, but was always unwilling to attend a social function just because of her celebrity. 'I loved Kirsty's capacity for loving the underdogs as well as the top dogs,' wrote her friend Marcia Farquhar (the artist wife of another Pogue, Jem Finer) to me recently, 'and for knowing that there is often quite an overlap in the most intriguing and lovable cases.'

I know that Kirsty would make herself available to the fans who would occasionally ring her or to the singers who would seek advice from her, but I also remember her feeling very annoyed with journalists who interviewed her about her latest release without having done their homework and asked questions which, with a little research on their part, need not have been asked in the first place. Often she also received letters to help various charities. I happened to be with her one morning when the post arrived, including one letter asking her if she would help endorse a charity event. She showed me the letter without comment but her expression said it all. The writer explained that she and her husband were fans of the folk scene, and had for many years been great friends with her parents: Ewan MacColl – and Peggy Seeger! Oh dear...This was definitely *not* the ideal tactic to use in a charity letter to Kirsty. The media could be just as easily confused. Kirsty heard a radio interview with Peggy which implied the same thing. Apparently Kirsty rang her up and put the record straight in no uncertain terms...

'Kirsty was very honest,' comments the broadcaster Janice Long, 'what you saw with her, that was it. No way was she ever hypocritical or two-faced. She would tell you to your face what she thought, but in the nicest way. Kirsty could take the proverbial out of herself, which she did loads of times. She had a sense of fun about everything. There was no way Kirsty was a rock star.'

And it was the same lack of pretension – and the same professional expertise – that made her a natural choice for the French and Saunders show in the 1980s, as the duo later remembered:

> In those days, because it was 'light entertainment', you had to
> have a song – a number – and also it meant we didn't have
> to write so much... We were fed up with all the pop stars
> wanting to just come in and do their latest hit and they were
> kind of humourless and all the rest of it. So we said, 'Let's just
> get Kirsty to do it and she could come and do a song every
> week, and we could have a good laugh.' Also, you could mess
> around with her and around her, because she was so game.

And there's that sound of laughter again, from which Kirsty was never very far. The same sound shines through every word of the memories her friend Marcia generously shared with me – 'the witticisms, quips and mostly just the atmosphere of the darling girl.' She remembered Kirsty as 'such a sassy, saucy creature, as well as one of the most sensitive and generous people I have ever known,' as well as a dear friend to her daughter Ella, 'who was a very shy and round child. Kirsty said she had a fellow feeling with her – their birthdays are a day apart':

> Obviously, it wasn't just the sparkly earrings and fluffy
> purses that she gifted upon me, but – far more deeply – she
> gave me enormous encouragement, and always supported
> my odd works with great enthusiasm. When I look around
> my room, there are so many of her gifts...
> One is the flimsiest, fluffiest black feather handbag you
> ever did see, which she gave me with the words,
> 'Something for your pills and your miniatures.' I always try

to keep at least one little bottle of brandy in that bag. And I have quite a few very sparkly earrings, which I shall horde forever because they were gifts from a firm believer in putting on the glitz, come what may. I once asked her what she wanted for a birthday present. 'Something very small and expensive,' she replied in a droll tone.

Kirsty was one of the most generous champions of other people – me included. She always came to as many of my exhibitions or shows as she could, and would always introduce me to others as an artist – never as 'Jem's wife', which of course at the time of The Pogues' heyday was a huge gift in itself... And on the subject of gifts, she once played a mischievous trick on a handsome young man at one of my birthday parties. He was (and is) a quiet American, for whom both she and I had a soft spot, but he had arrived at the party without any card or gift – and Kirsty must have noticed my obvious dismay. Anyway, he told her he thought he might have offended me and she told him he most certainly had – but that it could be put right if he were to make something for me there and then. She told him how much I appreciated homemade gifts and suggested he make me a glove puppet out of a paper bag. Under her instruction, a rudimentary origami puppet was made and presented to me. I accepted the gift most ungraciously (of course) and it was only when I saw the brains behind the project giggling mischievously in the background that I understood how had I come by such a gift!

Kirsty and I would phone each other up for no particular reason, and ask each other how things were going – you know, the 'How's it going?' question that can be answered in brief or at length. She rang me one night and asked the question.

'Well,' I said, 'I'm finding myself hanging out alone at night a lot, drinking wine, smoking fags, and listening to your records.'

'Me too!' came the reply, as quick as a diva's dart, and for the next few minutes we just laughed and laughed together at the joke.

So much laughter; so much respect; so much love. And always singing. The voices of Kirsty's many friends form a dense harmony almost as beautiful as one of her own arrangements:

Lyn Boorer:Another lovely memory I have of my great mate Kirsty was when I had my second child Pearl May. She was around four days old, and I hadn't been anywhere since she was born. It was near Christmas time and Kirsty called me on the phone to see how we were. She then said, 'Why don't you bring over the baby so I can see her?' She said it had been a long time since she had held a new baby, and for us to drive over. That we did, and to this day Pearl is very proud that Kirsty was one of her first friends – and remained great friends.

James Knight: Kirsty wasn't a fan of public transport, although I did manage to get her on the tube a few times. She preferred to drive and was into cars, although to Kirsty driving was really just singing with a steering wheel in front of you. I remember, having not been with Kirsty for very long, taking Jamie and Louis somewhere and being in stitches at two young boys sitting in the back singing along with Kirsty to most of the Beck album *Odelay*. There's nothing like a 12- and 13-year-old choir singing the whole of 'Devil's Haircut' perfectly, while a proud mother joins in on the chorus. Kirsty was a huge fan of lyrics but one of her favourites really sticks in my mind. It's a Steely Dan lyric that's in 'Kid Charlemagne'. For some reason, Kirsty found joining in on 'Is there gas in the car? Yes, there's gas in the car' *utterly* hilarious and would rewind and sing it again as we trundled along, louder each time with increased mirth.

Jools Holland: Looking back, there are two things which had an important effect on what I've learned about music – I'm not talking about her as a friend, I'm talking about her as a professional, another great artist who I've learned from. I learned about how singing a song could transform it into something that was great and the other thing she did which was interesting is she said, 'I want to put some horns on this thing and I could get Rico.'

I'd heard of Rico, but I hadn't met him, the trombonist who came over to England in 1962 from Jamaica and played with Bob Marley and on all the original ska records. He played on 'Ghost Town' by The Specials. He's the greatest trombone player that Jamaica has ever produced... Anyway, he came in – he'd got a bit plastered so he was a bit late – and it started off maybe on the wrong foot. It was like so many things.

He said, 'This [chord] chart isn't written out properly,' so we had to look at that. Then we got him to play the solo on the end and he said, 'I like this solo, but I really like the piano part. I don't want to get in the way of the piano part – who did this?'

And Kirsty said, 'Oh, that was Jools.'

Rico said, 'Oh!' and suddenly became my friend, once he'd realised it was *me* playing and not just bossing him about – which I hadn't realised I should have pointed out.

Kirsty rolled her eyes and said, 'Why didn't you tell him that in the first place?'

The other important thing was after that I bumped into Rico from time to time and he'd always ask after Kirsty. Whenever we met, Kirsty would be our reference point. Then, about 12 years ago, I said, 'We're about to go on tour,' and he said, 'I'm around at the moment if you want me to come' – and he's been with my Big Band ever since. He's played longer with us than he has with anybody. A lot of the music that we perform is the stuff that is part of his ska repertoire. Without Kirsty that would never have happened.

Often when we play – and we *do* enjoy ourselves – we play the song 'Enjoy Yourself', which has a version in Jamaica and also happened to be my grandmother's favourite song but that was by Geraldo or somebody different. When we play that song, people love it and I often think of Kirsty, because without her those people wouldn't be singing that song with us.

She was a great catalyst for things; she had this gift for being around and bringing people together because of the energy that she had. Musicians loved her because she could not only write great songs, but she also had this great voice. She understood how to get the best out of people as well, I think. So once there was someone she knew she wanted to work with, she would be very amusing. 'I want to work with X – I'm just going to make him my new best friend.' And within minutes you could see them roaring with laughter and her new best friend thinking he was becoming very amusing because of that thing that she had where she could make someone become more amusing themselves. That expression, 'getting blood out of a stone' – she could get somebody to be amusing who had never told a joke in their life, which is a great talent in itself.

Charlie Dickins: Kirsty and I were in LA once, doing promotional work following the American record deal and we went to some smart do. The drive back to our hotel on Sunset Boulevard (me driving, Kirsty drinking) involved going through Beverly Hills at 1.30am. We shared a passion for The Smiths and Morrissey and I happened to have my 'Best of' cassettes with me. So on it went and we cranked it up – very loud.

We were singing away at full tilt when the dreaded siren sounded and we were pulled over by a stereotypical Beverly Hills cop. The music was switched off abruptly. A very stern, smart and officious young man knocked on the window, which Kirsty wound down – both of us now rather anxious. Before the cop could say anything we apologised for the previous volume of the music, assuming we were about to get into trouble for disturbing the peace.

'Good evening, officer,' said Kirsty, undoubtedly fluttering her eyelashes. 'I am so sorry – was the music too loud?' Her accent betrayed her.

'You guys from England?'

'Yes,' she replied. Neither of us knew whether this was going to be a good or a bad thing. We were certainly unprepared for his next question.

'Do you like Morrissey?'

'I've sung with him!'

It turned out the cop was a massive Smiths fan and that he hadn't heard the music from the car, but had pulled us over for some registration misdemeanour – of which we were totally absolved once he knew Kirsty had sung with his hero.

I knew Kirsty so well and we spent so much time together over several years... She was always very loyal and pleased to see me, and always I felt very close to her, though we had very different upbringings. We had a real affinity with each other. I miss her not being there, and I resent her friendship being snatched away from me.

Morrissey once sang, 'It's so easy to love, it's so easy to hate. It takes strength to be gentle and kind.' We both loved those lyrics, and how the sentiment sits with Kirsty. She had qualities and strengths that were not the norm. And let's not forget, she's the only pop star to ever get Edward Tudor Pole and Lionel Bart in the same promo! Only Kirsty!

Marcia Farquar: I loved her shyness and her boldness, her laughter and her humanity. Obviously I loved her voice and her songs, but the person I miss is the girl who could lighten life with the greatest wit and compassion. She was no fool, Kirsty, and it was an honour to have known her.

•　　•　　•

In early 2000, at a time when Kirsty was busy finishing off work on *Tropical Brainstorm*, I was invited to teach a course for actors and dancers on Laban technique in San Francisco by a man called Ed Hooks. Ed gave classes on TV, film and stage work and I had previously advised him on Laban for a book on actor training. We agreed that my friend John Dalby should come along with me to provide singing lessons and to accompany some of the musical exercises.

Since my eyesight had by now deteriorated further and since I also found currency conversion into dollars complicated, John was put in charge of our financial arrangements – as it turned out, rather disastrously, since we went to every concert and every event that was going, and barely broke even.

'You wouldn't have done this on your own' was John's view, and I certainly wouldn't – though I must admit it was much more fun in such good company. We were away for three weeks, and when we returned, the boys were back at Bedales and Kirsty was now at work promoting the new album in a series of gigs with James in the band. He was also living with her at Mount Park Road.

Kirsty's band was the support at what turned out to be Ian Dury's final concert that summer. It was a great evening, which had MP and former outspoken Secretary of State for Northern Ireland Mo Mowlam for one rocking and rolling from her seat. Backstage after the concert, Mo and Ian were talking and I recalled that both were then suffering from cancer. I got a lift home with Kirsty and James and I remember feeling so very grateful that Kirsty was in such good health.

By the end of the year both Ian and Kirsty would be dead and Mo Mowlam lost her battle with the disease in 2005.

On what turned out to be Kirsty's last birthday, in October 2000, we all went to a Café Rouge to celebrate the occasion with James and the two Johns, Dalby and Thompson. A week later, I went off on holiday to Spain and missed Kirsty's last concert in London on the 28th, but we spoke a few times on the phone and she told me it had gone very well.

The weather in Spain was atrocious. I was happy to get back home and start working on my new book about Laban and was looking forward to the run-up to a Christmas with Kirsty after what had been an extraordinary and exciting year for her.

She flew off with James and the boys on Monday, 11 December 2000 for a well-earned holiday in Mexico, diving off the beautiful island of Cozumel.

A week later she was dead.

James Knight: Being with Kirsty seems like a dream sometimes and, although it's five years ago, I can still remember everything. The way she looked at me, her kindness and her love. It does get easier but she's never far away from me, in my head and in my heart; strange things remind me – tunes that I'd think she'd like that she'll never hear, problems I have that I'd want her advice on. The last thing Kirsty ever said to me was 'I love you', just before she left to get on the boat to go diving. I am forever grateful for the fact that we often told each other how we felt, and meant it totally. I hope that she'd be proud of me.

Sitting on my garden bench by the pond, on that April morning in 2006, the words of one of Kirsty's very last songs – a demo only released in the previous year – came back to me:

Sun on the water
Lapping around my feet.
Sun on the water
Making it hard to see.
It was the place where she felt free
And heaven lies under the sea
Hell is just dry land to me
When I'm dreaming.

As the tears on my face dried in the sunshine, I reflected that I was now more than twice Kirsty's age and that I could only begin to make sense of her terrible loss if I used what time was left me to fight, with all my remaining strength, for justice. Justice for her many adoring friends; justice for her two brave sons, whom she had died protecting; and above all, justice for Kirsty.

Chapter Twelve

Quietly Alone

2001-2002

'The pigeons shiver in the naked trees.'
KIRSTY MACCOLL, 'SOHO SQUARE', 1994

John Dalby returned from his holiday on 14 January 2001, having missed Kirsty's funeral on the 5th and every day of the next week he joined the musicians who were preparing for Kirsty's memorial service, coming over to me in the evenings. One night I played the music from the funeral service and I ended up in tears.

Kirsty's memorial service took place at 11 o'clock on the Saturday morning of 20 January 2001 at the church of St Martin's-in-the-Fields in London. Kirsty's very close musician friends were in charge of the programme, but the first music I heard that morning, when the taxi driving me from Ealing reached Trafalgar Square, was the sound of the church bells of Saint Martin's ringing out across London. For a moment or two, I was overcome by a powerful mixture of emotions. Overwhelming sadness, of course, because the bells were announcing a death – my darling's death. But at the same time, I also felt proud that their glorious sound was in honour of Kirsty's life.

Crowds had gathered on the church steps waiting for the doors to open. I didn't see a single face I recognised. Then I saw a familiar figure: Murray Melvin, an old friend and colleague of mine from our Theatre Workshop days. He gave me a hug and told me he had been asked to escort me through the doors. Dave Ruffy was waiting for me inside. He gave me his arm and with a proud smile on his face walked me down the aisle to my seat next to John.

The music before the service was by Bach. The vicar welcomed us and then Billy Bragg came forward to play 'New England', the song Kirsty had had such a success with in 1985. I think his voice sounded much softer than I had remembered – it must have been very hard to start the tributes off, especially since they had been such good friends.

Phill Jupitus and John spoke next. I followed them and as I looked out across the grieving throng of friends, my heart went out to them too. I shared their shock and pain and wanted to embrace them for being there for Kirsty. I spoke about Kirsty's childhood, her delight at feeding foxes and watching badgers. But I did say how much she had loved her many friends, and what an important part of her life they had been. There was so much love in the gathering that I felt Kirsty must be there touching all our hearts and I told them so. I was determined to be calm and not let everyone down, especially my darling.

When I finished, the musicians played Kirsty's song 'Us Amazonians'. Her dear friends Pete Glenister and Dave Ruffy and her partner James Knight read and spoke briefly and Holly Johnson sang another of Kirsty's songs, 'Don't Come the Cowboy with Me, Sonny Jim'. The hymn was 'Jerusalem' ('And did those feet in ancient times...'), but I don't remember the sequence clearly. The musicians had arranged this memorial to their friend and colleague themselves and with so many of them attending, there was a powerful feeling of love throughout the church.

After the ceremony, I remember shaking the hand of the Cuban ambassador Federico Dominguez. I recognised Jools Holland and Bono in the distance; other faces were familiar, but I couldn't put a name to them. I was given a message that some of my actor friends had booked a table at Joe Allen's restaurant. Hamish went off to have coffee with friends of Kirsty, while most of the musicians went to the pub. Jamie and Louis went off with their school friends and the rest of us went to Joe Allen's. We were a mixed bunch: actors, singers, Philip Hedley, the director of the Theatre Royal, Murray Melvin, friends from the Laban Guild and even three fans from America. As more people arrived, extra tables were added to one end and soon our table extended the length of the room.

Despite the sad occasion, there was a feeling of warmth and camaraderie that was quite extraordinary – complete strangers were chatting to each other like long-lost friends. It made the enormity of the day easier for me to deal with. I came home full of clear images of the day and once again marvelled at the great love so many people had shown for Kirsty.

•　　•　　•

My memory of the next few days and weeks is fragmented. Corinne from the BBC asked for photos, videos and home movies for her scheduled programme, *The Life and Songs of Kirsty MacColl*. Meanwhile Steve had to fly back to New York, where he was working and his partner Patti was pregnant with their second child.

The pattern of my life had now changed. James and the boys were living in the house – but suddenly there was no Kirsty to take charge and I dreadfully missed her frequent calls. The boys were coming home most weekends as usual and returning to Bedales, where they were still weekly boarders. On Sundays, after lunch, I would drive up to the house and run them to the station just to have a little time with them and to see how they were.

On one occasion they seemed to be short of money and wanted to get something from the station buffet at Waterloo. When I asked them if they had had lunch they replied that they hadn't – I thought this was odd because Kirsty had always cooked a proper Sunday lunch before they returned to school. The boys had never complained about missing this meal and it was only when I spoke to James about it that he had any idea that they didn't get a meal at school until the following morning. As a working musician, of course, James would have been busy working at a gig on the Saturday night and sleeping late on the Sunday morning.

A little later, James did actually invite me to Sunday lunch, and I found that while the roast lamb was very nice, there was a great shortage of vegetables – I think I had one carrot – and, since I prefer vegetables to meat, I pulled his leg. I am pleased to report that over the years he has become something of a champion of 'real' food.

James also said he had bought new clothes for the boys. Although I felt that was my job, knowing how Kirsty would have gone about it, I didn't say anything. After all, what did it matter who bought the clothes? And James was only carrying out the responsibilities he thought were expected of him. There were enough of us to look after the boys and the most important thing was that we all worked well together. Kirsty's friends Kieran and Annie were her executors and they were also the boys' godmothers. So although they had only met James for the first time at the funeral, and then only briefly, it seemed quite natural for all three of them to represent Kirsty and Steve on parents' day at Bedales.

Later Hamish and I took on that role and I remember a marvellous Saturday in June that year, when Hamish, Annie, Kieran and I attended and supplied a lavish picnic. The boys were delighted that we had come and invited their friends to meet us and share the masses of food we had brought. I felt particularly pleased as Louis bought me a raffle ticket and I won a bottle of wine – but of course my real pleasure was that my efforts to stand in for Kirsty had been so much appreciated by the boys and their friends.

As it was necessary for me now to contact the boys regularly, Hamish bought me a voice-operated mobile phone as my sight was continuing to deteriorate. He very kindly set it up for me so that I only had to say a name for the call to go through. At this time I was still able to drive my car.

After the memorial service there were endless requests from journalists for stories and photographs. As I looked them out, the memories flooded back. They weren't in any beautiful order but jumbled in boxes and spread across the years. There was Kirsty in a push-chair in Regent's Park, Hamish on his new bicycle, Jamie and Louis playing and sleeping in a tent, Kirsty as a schoolgirl… And as I looked through these piles of photographs, I began to reflect over her life, remembering the highs and the lows, and the joy I had felt when the asthma was finally conquered.

On 7 February 2001, the first of a series of radio programmes for the BBC, *Kirsty MacColl's Cuba*, was broadcast. Despite the success of her TV programme *Don't Go Near the Water* a few years before, I knew this project had been a new and exciting departure for her. Presenting the story of Cuban music, assisted by a group of local musicians called the Smooth Operators and with contributions by the musicologist Jan Fairley, then on a visit to Cuba, I was struck by how confident, relaxed and happy Kirsty sounded. It was almost unbearable to hear her voice.

Less than a week after the first programme went out, I heard from my publisher, Nick Hern, on 12 February, telling me that he was sending me a new contract. He had published my first textbook, *Laban for Actors and Dancers*, in 1993. It had sold very well and was still going strong eight years after its original launch in Australia. Before Kirsty's accident I had suggested to Nick that it was time for another book aimed at a wider readership. It was intended equally for those who had heard of the name Laban but who knew nothing about his work and for those who wished to extend their technique and knowledge further.

We had verbally agreed to do something but he had thought I would not be up to it after the accident. John encouraged me. He had remained a tower of strength and we met or phoned each other on a daily basis. Without his constant support throughout this crucial period, I don't know how I could have carried on with any sort of daily routine, balancing family demands with the fight for justice and working on the new book with him.

'I think this kept Jean sane,' John says. 'We even had some amusing times with illustrating the movements we were writing about. She got into awkward positions. At one point I thought the mantelpiece would come away from the wall as she grabbed at it for support.' But during these first two years – and in the years since – it wasn't my mantelpiece I clung to for support: it was John.

With his musical knowledge, we teamed up to make it a joint effort. We decided to call the book *Laban for All* – which caused a good few battles along the way. As far as John was concerned, the 'All' included a fictitious reader whom he called 'Mary of Milwaukee', who knew absolutely nothing of Laban's work and to whom we had to explain every detail in the book.

I saw the situation slightly differently, since I was primarily concerned that most dancers' training in Laban's method had stopped at a relatively basic level and I wanted to demonstrate to them that there was a great deal more to his theories than are usually explored. What I do know for sure is that working on this book with John helped keep me focused during the terrible aftershock of Kirsty's death.

The day I got the letter from Nick Hern about the contract

was a Wednesday, I remember, which was a half-day at Bedales and so that day I went with Jamie, Louis, Kieran and Annie to have lunch in nearby Petersfield. I seemed to be getting a lot of back pain at this time and when I couldn't sleep I used to play backgammon on the internet. I remember Kirsty telling me she had once entered an online backgammon contest, expecting to drop out in the first round, but she had kept winning each game and was duly pronounced champion at around five in the morning. She was rather surprised that she had won each round – and more than a little embarrassed that she had wasted half the night doing so. I remember thinking, everything I do now is a reminder, and then I thought, what must it be like for the boys? Suddenly I felt very aware of being the only female in the MacColls' little family; I still do.

On 27 February I received photos and a letter from Anita Quinta, whose house Kirsty had rented in Cozumel. Jean Berg, an American minister, had held a small memorial service for Ivan the dive-master and the other scuba boat people to attend. Anita Quinta, also an American, was then the wife of Gonzalez Nova's nephew (though the couple later separated). Kirsty's friend Ronnie, her co-executor with Annie and Kieran, was told that the travel insurance company would not honour the policy until they had received a statement confirming that Kirsty had been staying on the island of Cozumel. Kirsty had rented a house from Anita Quinta, but she was unwilling to provide any documentation to say that Kirsty and her family had stayed with her, even suggesting that her accountant had advised against it, saying that in Mexico bills couldn't be presented such a long time afterwards – though of course we were merely seeking confirmation of a bill that had already been paid. Nevertheless, Anita Quinta refused to speak to Ronnie, apparently on the grounds that, since Ronnie was an accountant, in her view he qualified as a 'legal representative': the house had only been rented out 'unofficially', and she was nervous of the implications.

Fortunately Jean Berg told me that her husband had returned the hire car Kirsty had used during her time on Cozumel and had kept the paperwork, so we were finally able to show proof that Kirsty had stayed on the island. This frustrating and upsetting delay held up payment from the travel insurance firm for some time and it was then that I began to have some doubts about other aspects of the accident. There was nothing that I could pinpoint exactly, but I heard that a local Mexican newspaper had printed an article saying that the MacColl family were not going to take up the case. This presumption made me very angry and I remember telling Ronnie that I wanted to be kept informed of everything.

Ronnie enlisted my help but it took several phone calls and weeks of correspondence before the travel insurance was settled. Almost immediately on settling the travel insurance claim, however, the firm employed a lawyer to seek to recover that money by prosecuting those responsible for the accident. To my horror, though, the lawyer then told me that he thought this process would take at least five years and if the case remained unsettled after that time I was given to understand that we would be expected to continue financing their case from our own pocket. This caused real problems for us because until the case was settled, the travel insurance could not be paid. I also heard from Ronnie that a witness statement appeared to have gone missing. It appears that it was a matter of uncertainty to the Mexican *medico* whether it was the front of the boat or its propeller that had hit Kirsty; the boat's speed was reported by Gonzalez Nova and his family to have been only one knot. Later, it became evident that the boat had been travelling at greater speed. Witnesses stated that the bow was up out of the water – and the extent of Kirsty's injuries showed that she could only have been hit by a propeller of a boat travelling at speed.

As these problems and obstacles began to mount up, the BBC's *Tribute to Kirsty* programme was shown on 3 March. Louis, James and I watched it. Jamie and Hamish chose not to watch it. We all grieve in our different ways. It was well done, but so terribly sad, of course. The programme at least stimulated a great increase in public awareness of the circumstances surrounding Kirsty's death and once again the press came for more interviews and photographs and I received many kind emails of sympathy and support. The website was also inundated with enquiries.

Soon after *Tribute*, Lyn and Jen, wives of musicians Boz Boorer and Dave Ruffy, came over to see me and we had a nice time chatting about and remembering Kirsty. They were great company, and managed to joke and laugh about the times they'd spent with her. We raised our glasses to her. Although I had met them before at parties, I felt now that we were also becoming friends.

On the evening of 13 March, Philip Hedley, Director of the Theatre Royal at Stratford East, came to see me with his team to discuss the possibility of a musical show based on Kirsty's songs. I returned to find five messages from Hamish on my answerphone: he was in hospital after suffering a minor heart attack the previous night. We had actually spoken earlier that evening and he had gone on to the gym to use the exercise cycle. Later, he had a lot of pain and rang for an ambulance. Hamish couldn't go home immediately so Neil, the husband of Kirsty's friend Fuzz, offered to come up from Brighton and drive me to Gloucester to see him in hospital. Louis also turned up with some magazines for him. Hamish was eventually discharged, and after some more tests, went home to Stroud. Apparently he had been so angry about Kirsty's death, and so unhappy, that he had overdone the cycling. He said he felt as if his heart was being nailed to a piece of wood.

Louis and I discussed Mother's Day. As I would not get a card from Kirsty and he and Jamie could not send her one, we decided to have a grandmother's day. I received a lovely card with 'Grand' written in before the 'Mother'. I think it helped us all at the time.

•   •   •

I always thought I could meet challenges, and often I welcomed the opportunity to test myself. Back in September 1991, I went on an Outward Bound course in the Lake District. I don't think anyone understood my choice of holiday. Acquaintances seemed politely mystified, but if Kirsty and Hamish thought it an unusual choice, they didn't mention it to me. It was something that had always attracted me and it was a chance to meet another challenge by overcoming my vertigo. I also wanted to make sure that I could rough it if necessary. I joined a group of recruits who were 50 and over. We covered the same course but took a little longer. It was only after I had been there a few days and we had bonded that I realised that I was, at 68, by far the oldest. But I climbed and abseiled with my colleagues and zipped through the air on a rope to the top of a tree from a wooden platform. I swam in a very cold lake and slept while wrapped in a plastic sheet under heavy rain.

But it was a different kind of strength – or endurance – that I needed after the accident and I was trying to stay busy and focused while at the same time always being ready to be there for the boys whenever they needed me. The new Laban book took up a lot of my time, though it didn't seem like particularly hard work for me. John's insistence on the 'For All' part of the title kept me on my toes, however, as literally did some of the drawings he made of me for the illustrations. I had to stand in one position for what seemed like hours. I am still very pleased with how the book turned out.

I was also still keeping up my singing lessons, which followed an uncertain course. Even if I'd been Joan Sutherland – and I wasn't! – the late 70s wasn't the ideal age at which to start, but I practised at every possible opportunity. I was at least learning what it takes to make a good singer and how much energy it requires. I came to appreciate, from a technical point of view, Kirsty's amazing ability to harmonise her own voice – what Johnny Marr called 'layering it'.

As I once said to Kirsty, 'I like learning,' to which she had replied, 'So do I.' She never asked me why I wanted to keep learning any more than she asked me why I was going on my Outward Bound course and I never questioned her judgement or the decisions she made in her own life. So I persevered with my singing, while Kirsty's photograph sat on John's piano smiling at me.

For Easter that year I decided to cook a Christmas turkey for Steve, James, the boys, Hamish and Kieran. It was a way of trying to maintain a normal family life. I was also the only capable cook at the time, so I knew it was something the boys would enjoy – and we all knew that Christmas dinner was Kirsty's favourite meal.

When Hamish came down from Stroud to visit and to see if he could help, he asked as usual to stay at Kirsty's house, telling James he'd be arriving quite late in the evening. Just to make sure everything was all right – he had recently had a heart attack, after all – I drove over to find Jamie alone in the house, but no provision having been made for Hamish. James's brother Bob had taken over the two free bedrooms with his furniture and musical equipment. He had been staying there for some time as he was in the process of moving house. In the early days of bereavement, when emotions are raw, it is all too easy to imagine all sorts of slights which do not in fact exist. I believe James was working hard, as was his brother, and he was simply not experienced in running a large household. Suddenly he had responsibilities which were entirely new to him. Certainly over the years our friendship has mellowed, despite the difference in age. One thing I had always to keep in mind was that Kirsty loved James and had been very happy in their short relationship. With that in mind other domestic problems faded away. Steve would often come over, and he, Hamish, the boys, James and I would go out for lunch. Somehow we were bonding afresh now Kirsty had gone, now we had lost such a central figure in all our lives.

•   •   •

On 8 May I took it upon myself to ring Bob at the crematorium and asked if I could collect the urn. He kindly came over himself with Kirsty's ashes in an urn in a velvet bag. A dreadful sadness overwhelmed me when I thought of the times I had been there for her, especially during her childhood. She in her turn had been there for her sons, but the price she paid was much greater than mine: in saving her sons, she paid with her own life. Momentarily, anger took over when I remembered the pathologist's report: 'This was an accident that should never have happened.' To this day, neither Guillermo Gonzalez Nova – the owner of the speedboat that killed Kirsty and the man who left her children swimming in the unspeakable horror of its aftermath – nor any member of his family on board has ever expressed a word of remorse or offered condolence on her death.

I showed Bob round Kirsty's beloved garden (which Peter the gardener is still maintaining) and then I took the urn home with me and sat in my own garden with it. I had not asked Hamish or the boys what they wanted me to do with the ashes, feeling it was all too soon. James did not want them at Mount Park Road, and I could understand that. But I am a mother, and I was not going to leave my daughter any longer alone in an anonymous crematorium. She belonged with me.

Chapter Thirteen

Soho Square

2002

'Do what we can and ought to, let's start today.'

'Don't Go Near The Water', The Beach Boys, recorded by Kirsty, 1991

I dreaded the day of my actual birthday in May. There were just too many memories of past parties, like my 70th in 1993, or even just the quiet restaurant meals, like the time Hamish and Kirsty had taken me out to their favourite tapas bar. On another birthday they took me to watch a polo match in Windsor, with Prince Charles playing in one of the teams.

Because my birthday was on a Tuesday, I decided to throw a party on the preceding Saturday at Mount Park Road. It was a thank-you to all the friends who had supported me over the previous months and an opportunity for people to get to know each other.

Joan came with Victor Spinetti and they arrived with Miriam Karlin and Philip Hedley. Ann Beach and her husband, Philip Rambow and his wife, Charlie Dickins, Pete Glenister and Dave Ruffy also came, along with many others who were joining the campaign. James was there and Jamie and Louis had invited some of their school friends who had been so supportive to them when they had had to return to school after the accident. The party went well, and I felt somewhere in the middle of this crowd, Kirsty was also there, laughing and enjoying everyone's company. But I missed seeing her, listening to her. When I laughed at some remark, there was a sudden moment of silence nearby and someone said, 'That laugh sounded just like Kirsty.'

Two days later my old friend the actress Ann Beach rang me to say that she had just heard *Desert Island Discs* on the radio and that the eminent geneticist Sir John Sulston had picked Kirsty's 'Don't Come the Cowboy with Me, Sonny Jim' as one of his eight records. Ann said she had sat on her bed and cried, but she felt I would like to know the song carried on.

Sarah from Major Minor Records had also telephoned to tell me that the fans wanted to do something in memory of Kirsty. She thought that as Kirsty had loved Cuba and visited many times, it might be nice to raise money for musical instruments to offset the rather stupid American embargo in force there. That embargo meant that many of Cuba's musicians were unable to play their instruments because they lacked simple parts like strings and reeds. We had all heard the story of the American who, when he discovered that the Cubans lacked pianos, collected a container load which went to Cuba via Canada. It seemed – and still seems – ridiculous to me that such a large country as the USA can refuse a tiny island such things as musical instruments just because they disagree with its politics.

I woke up on my actual birthday with a heavy heart and played Kirsty's music on my new CD player as I opened my cards from Joan, John, Hamish and Tom Willingson (a friend and Laban student of mine). In the evening I met John at Acton Town tube station and we went to see a dreadful opera, glad that we had not paid too much for the tickets. Returning home to his house, his partner John Thompson had prepared a special meal for us with champagne. I was grateful for the kindness and support of friends. The dreadful gap in my life was, and always will be there, but it would be churlish not to make the effort to respond to all those helping hands. And with these thoughts I finally fell asleep.

In a very short time Alan Officer, who had been running Kirsty's website for a number of years (and is still doing so today), announced the foundation of the Kirsty MacColl Music Fund for Cuba and invited all those who wished to make a contribution in Kirsty's memory to send their donations.

It became a larger organisation and I am now the chairwoman of what is called the Music Fund for Cuba, run by Cuban Solidarity. Its origins in the Kirsty MacColl Music Fund and the generosity of her fans is still acknowledged. We are presently renovating a theatre in Havana where young musicians will be able to perform. I believe Kirsty would be very proud of this wonderful enterprise by her fans and friends.

The Cuban Embassy in London was notified of our intentions and we asked them what musical instruments and parts were most urgently needed. The Deputy Ambassador, Oscar de los Reyes, came over with Sarah to meet me. He was delighted at the offer and told me that Tania Domingues-Rosas, the Ambassador's wife, would be in touch. In fact, I invited her to tea. I was happy to tell her that the fans had already raised £12,000. We got on very well and I learned that she too was a grandmother.

I was invited to lunch at the Ambassador's residence with Oscar and his wife. It was Tania who subsequently planned the trip John and I were to make to Cuba in March 2002, taking with us the much-needed musical instruments, guitar strings and a framed portrait of Kirsty to the Havana School of Music.

•   •   •

The travel insurance company's lawyer had enlisted the help of another lawyer in San Francisco. Ronnie engaged a lawyer for our family to file a civil claim against the owner of the boat. We expected to hear that a court case against the driver of the boat was imminent but in fact it was to be another two years before it came to court. I began to realise that the powers that be in Mexico were using extremely slow and inefficient tactics – perhaps in an effort to delay proceedings – and I wondered whether it had anything to do with the owner of the boat being one of Mexico's wealthiest men. One would have imagined that where a death had occurred, a formal investigation would have immediately followed; amazingly, this was not the case, and it was left to us to find out the truth. Tosh Rapoport told me that she had a friend who might be able to help us, and so it was that I got in touch with an investigator who, together with his aide, was experienced in dealing with such matters.

He began with a visit to Steve, who was living and working in New York and had the boys staying with him at the time. He made a good impression on them, and the boys told him as much as they could. Inquiries were set in motion. Although I was greatly relieved to finally get some help, it came at a price: his fees were considerable. I offered to take on the responsibility for the investigator myself as I was pursuing a criminal case against the owner of the boat, Guillermo Gonzales Nova. Ronnie felt that the estate could not help much because they were pursuing a separate civil claim. I on the other hand was determined to bring those responsible for Kirsty's untimely death to justice. Steve kindly paid the first bill, but afterwards I began to think seriously that I might have to sell my home.

As spring turned to summer, Alan Officer emailed to tell me that Kirsty's fans wanted to know if I would be happy for them to erect a bench in Soho Square in her memory, inspired by her beautiful song of that name. I thought it was a lovely idea, and was touched that they wanted to include me in their plan. The fans took the initiative and contacted Westminster Council for the requisite permission and in due course the new bench appeared with a plaque in her name, quoting the song: 'One Day I'll be Waiting There. No Empty Bench in Soho Square'. John Dalby later wrote about accompanying me to the unveiling:

We arrived in Soho Square in good time and we were surprised to see a large number of people had already gathered for the occasion. It was raining as we approached the throng and it was all Jean could do not to burst into tears as she tried to return the sympathetic smiles that greeted her. Chris Winwood, who had organised the event, welcomed her and took her to the bench which was decorated with flowers. A microphone and sound system had been set in place for what was to be a highly important occasion: not only were we dedicating the bench in Soho Square to Kirsty's memory, but this was also the occasion when £12,000 was to be presented to the Kirsty MacColl Music Fund for Cuba. For this we were honoured with the presence of the Cuban Ambassador and his wife Tania. After various speeches and dedications, Jean presented Tania with a ceremonial cheque. It was a most moving and impressive event and we were touched by the number of people who had come from abroad. One young man, John Miranda, proudly told us he had come especially from California. He had brought his guitar and readily joined in the singing that followed. Afterwards, many of us repaired to The Pillars of Hercules, a small but welcoming pub, where the singing continued.

It was the first time that Jean had spoken directly to

Kirsty's fans and she confided to me she did not want to become too emotional. After all, we had to remember this was a joyful occasion – that because of their love for Kirsty and her music, the fans had supported Cuba.

Soho Square certainly seemed an appropriate place to remember Kirsty, since the area lies at the centre of the London music business. Since that day in August 2001, fans from around the world have come to sit on and photograph the bench and its plaque. Every October, on the Sunday closest to her birthday on the 10th, the fans gather round about midday and meet the family. The ever-faithful John Miranda from San Francisco usually plays his guitar to accompany the singing. Afterwards we all go to a larger pub just off the square and renew old friendships and everyone continues with more singing. Some regular visitors come from as far away as Holland, America and even Australia. There are signs of a second generation of fans arriving to enjoy Kirsty's music. I think this particular meeting is very heartwarming for the boys, who proudly bring their friends to see the love and respect that so many people continue to have for their beautiful and gifted mother.

Meanwhile, I had made a small private memorial of my own, clearing a little patch of waste ground in my own garden near a pond and calling it Kirsty's Garden. I planted spring bulbs and vinca for ground cover and a buddleia by the wall to attract butterflies and bees. Dragonflies enjoy the warm spot in the summer. Near the pond's waterfall feature there are now masses of wild strawberries nestling between the mint and the chives. The birds seem to enjoy the strawberries; they also leave cherry stones on the slabs around the pond. Since I don't have a cherry tree, I like to think that they fly over to my spot to eat and drink and otherwise refresh themselves. Sometimes there are as many as eight or nine stones.

At the same time, though, I was beginning to be concerned about Kirsty's own garden and conservatory. Peter the gardener was doing a good job, but the maintenance of her pond, with its ecologically friendly water-treatment system, wasn't really his responsibility. The pond was leaking and needed regular topping up for the few fish still there. James, for completely understandable reasons, didn't show much interest. The plants in the conservatory were also slowly dying off and only the cacti still survived. I did what I could on my visits but it wasn't enough.

The days I spent gardening in Kirsty's new plot or on the patio gave me a sense of peace in an otherwise busy and constantly demanding period. I recently asked Peter about his memories of Kirsty. 'If she hadn't done what she did,' he told me, 'she'd have made a great gardener' – which is praise indeed.

Earlier in the year, I'd been invited to run another summer school, but my heart really wasn't in it and John and I were still busy with the Laban book. The staff told me that they wanted to work on excerpts from Mozart's *Magic Flute* and I felt it was too much to do in a week. Eventually I bit the bullet and accepted the engagement – though in retrospect I wish I hadn't. This was a dreadfully low period for me, and I wish I had followed my instincts and turned them down – though I thought any dampening effect I might have had on the students' spirits was offset by John's magnificent coaching.

At the same time, after much discussion with Philip Hedley at the Theatre Royal, we decided not to go ahead with the proposed musical based on Kirsty's songs. I just thought it was too soon and none of the ideas we discussed seemed worthy of her – though I know Pete Glenister was disappointed with our decision.

One of Kirsty's old schoolteachers rang me to say that he had been contacted by a journalist interested in following up a brief interview he had given to the local press about Kirsty. He told her he couldn't agree to being interviewed without my agreement. This journalist also wrote to me about her plans to write a book about Kirsty's life. It was obvious to me that she knew nothing of Kirsty's work (though she did mention that her father liked Ewan's folksongs). She was one of several would-be writers that I felt I had to put off. Why should they write about Kirsty when they had never even met her – or ever seen her perform? Another writer contacted me later that year, via her agents, with a similar proposal and I agreed to meet up with them. The writer seemed pleasant enough, but knew almost nothing of Kirsty or her music and I again turned it down. The agents were interested in me doing the book alone, but I couldn't see that happening for a long while.

In the summer Steve came over from America and took the boys out for weekends. Hamish also took a break and caught a ferry to France, driving down to Limoges with a friend. I think it was around this time that he first started thinking about moving to France, where he now lives. I was keeping myself busy with the Laban book, but I also found time to see many friends and acquaintances, old and new.

I particularly remember a lunch with Olga Betko and her husband, John and his partner and two friends of Kirsty's. I had originally met Olga at the ballet in London a couple of years before, when the Bolshoi company were performing Prokofiev's *Love of Three Oranges*. We had started chatting about the production and the Bolshoi in general during the interval. I mentioned that I had seen the ballerina Galina Ulanova perform in Moscow when I was attending an International Youth Festival in 1957. I had taken some dancers over there to compete and won a medal for choreography.

Olga was a news announcer and journalist in the Russian branch of the BBC World Service and expressed interest in doing a live interview about the Youth Festival. When I arrived, she was excited because she had managed to get hold of some sound effects she was going to use to illustrate our interview, in particular what she called 'old trains'. These turned out to be the puffs and whistle of steam locomotives: I hadn't realised I was *quite* so ancient!

It wasn't just Olga's sound effects that reminded me of my age. My doctor wanted me to have my blood pressure tested and sent me to hospital to be fitted with a contraption that would monitor it over 24 hours. In the taxi on the way back the device went off with a 'beep' every time it drove over a speed bump. The driver eyed me suspiciously, but I decided to be a woman of mystery and offered no explanation. An eye condition flared up again and I took myself off to the hospital for painful treatment - and returned after two or three days as an emergency case, since it was discovered I was allergic to my medication; this was a worrying time. I was already concerned about my central vision and although my sight is now very restricted, I can still more or less manage to write these words.

At around this time I also met Jean Berg, the American minister, and her family in London. She couldn't tell me much about the progress of the inquiry, but gave me news of Ivan, the dive-master on the day Kirsty died, who had been, she said, terribly affected by the accident and was no longer able to follow the career that had previously been his guiding passion. Before Jean returned home to Cozumel, she and her family went to Soho Square and took photos of the bench.

Kirsty's birthday on 10 October - the first since her death, what would have been her 42nd - was never going to be an easy day. Everyone was very kind, though, and the fans even sent me flowers, which was utterly unexpected and very touching. I asked Alan Officer to thank them for me on the website. Later in the day, the Johns took me to see a performance by Trockadero, an all-male ballet company ('The Trocks'), with the well-intentioned hope that it would cheer me up. Then we met Kieran and Denise, and we consoled each other with reminiscences. It seemed incredible that, only a year before, I had met up with Kirsty and James and the two Johns at the local Café Rouge for a celebration. It was always a convenient choice for our family get-togethers; now we never go there.

A little later that month, Hamish came down from Stroud, and took me for a day out with the boys. First stop was the London Eye, which I thought was a great way of seeing the city. I didn't find the great height to be much of a problem – perhaps thanks to my Outward Bound course ten years before. That autumn I was also invited to Goldsmiths College, to celebrate the inauguration of a university scholarship in Kirsty's memory to cover the fees for an MA course in Culture, Globalisation and the City. According to Dr Les Back, who runs the MA course, many aspects of Kirsty's life and career resonate with its key themes – music, culture, politics – and the award is reserved for those students whose combination of 'local insight and global resonance' matches the commitment of Kirsty's own work.

In early December I was asked by the psychotherapist Dr Tom O'Connolly to go to Nuremberg and take a Laban course for his patients. I took one of my old diploma students, Jenny Frankel. It was a great success – despite the long journey, which involved a flight to Frankfurt and then a three-and-a-half-hour train journey. But when Tom met us at the station wearing a costume with a tricorne hat and presented us with flowers while playing music from a small tape recorder, our tiredness momentarily evaporated. Tom had been a student on a number of my courses and had recognised the value of Laban's movement analysis in his own therapeutic practice. Despite living in Germany for some 25 years, he was still very Irish. His daughter Fiona speaks

English perfectly, of course – but with the most beautifully soft Southern Irish accent. Tom made us very welcome.

The run-up to Christmas seemed to be a constant series of sad anniversaries. On 10 December, it was a year since I had had supper with Kirsty and her family. She had run me home, we had said goodnight and as I got out of the car I remembered I had forgotten to take with me the large saucepan I had asked to borrow. She said she'd go back for it and returned a few minutes later. I thanked her, and as she left I called out 'I love you!', and she called back 'I love you!' before getting into her car. That was the last time we spoke to each other; the next time I spoke to her was in a funeral parlour.

Suddenly it was 18 December, a year ago to the day when I first heard the dreadful news of Kirsty's death. What a painful year that had been – but the fight to find out the truth had to carry on. That night, I invited Steve and the boys, Joan, Denise and the two Johns to dinner: it was time to remember Kirsty and celebrate her life.

I spent Christmas that year with Hamish up in Stroud, where Joan and her friend Peter Rankin joined us. Hamish was the perfect host and made us all feel very welcome. He had decorated the main room with little lights and filled a small sock for each of us to wake up to on Christmas morning. Joan offered to help cook the turkey dinner, but we politely declined, knowing that to accept would have involved all manner of delays, as dear Joan did have a tendency to get sidetracked! We all did our best to keep cheerful, but the strain was obvious. I developed a terrible cold and on 27 December I returned home to London, and went to bed.

• • •

It had been a bleak winter, but the spring of 2002 offered the promise of some proper sunshine. John and I had been invited by Tania, the wife of the Cuban Ambassador in London, to visit the music school of Havana, where a library had been named after Kirsty. Following the marvellous fundraising campaign, the Kirsty MacColl Music Fund's total of £12,000 was spent on a huge collection of musical instruments, together with strings, reeds and other much-needed equipment.

We were invited over in the week before Easter to say a formal thank-you to Kirsty. We took with us a CD of *Tropical Brainstorm*, her BBC Cuba documentary and a framed photograph of Kirsty herself. John and I were welcomed with flowers at the airport on Saturday, 23 March and driven to the Plaza Hotel in Havana. Walking down the Avenida on a gloriously sunny morning, there seemed to be music everywhere we went. No wonder Kirsty had loved the place. We were introduced to our two friendly guides who spoke excellent English.

Our main priority was to see some dance! On the Sunday we attended a Ballet Gala at the Great Theatre of Havana. The standard of dancing was very high, even among the children in the cast, and we were also impressed by how many men there were in the audience. Our guides introduced us to some of their friends, who were very interested to learn about the reasons for our trip. A group of us went back to our hotel after the second half, where we tried a drink which Kirsty had recommended in her radio programme and given full instructions on how to mix, specifying it should be served with crushed ice.

During our week in Havana, we were invited to visit several dance schools, ranging from classical ballet to extremely energetic modern dance. We were inspired by the high artistic standards and dedicated commitment both among the students and the teachers. The Ballet School, the Higher Institute of Art (where we attended a lecture on Laban) and the National Dance School... it was a frenetic schedule, though John and I also found time visit the beach and explore some local restaurants on our own. One of these was a very grand house, I remember, where we were shown up a magnificent staircase to a table next to a balcony, open to the warm evening, where we sat like an elderly Romeo and Juliet. We were the only customers. The food wasn't bad, and was also extremely cheap - unlike the tourist restaurant we visited another evening, where we drank wine in a courtyard patrolled by strutting peacocks. We wondered if they ever ended up on the menu!

On 27 March, we visited the music school as its guests of honour. This was the centrepiece of our trip and an enormously touching occasion. The staff and students welcomed us warmly and took us to the front of the music library where, before Kirsty's portrait was unveiled, the school's choir - each holding a single flower - sang beautifully for us. In a moving ceremony, the students placed their flowers in front of the picture, below which was a bronze plaque. The inscription, in Spanish, read that Kirsty MacColl was a famous singer-songwriter and a great friend to the people of Cuba. We were then shown into the brand new library named in her memory, which still had to be equipped. There, we heard a short orchestral concert, followed by two or three solo performances. Kirsty's fans had wanted to remember her in a very positive way and it was marvellous to reflect that their enormous generosity was now being translated into the universal language she adored: music.

John and I were very sorry to leave Cuba and the warm artistic vigour of its people behind us as we flew home after our week's stay to carry on working on our book. It had been the perfect inspiration. Nick Hern had published my first book, *Laban for Dancers and Actors*, in 1993; *Laban for All* appeared in early 2003, when John and I both attended the party to celebrate ten years of Nick Hern Books. It was hard to contemplate how much had changed in my life over those years. The book sold very well, but there was a definite sense of anticlimax, a dip in the spirits, after finishing it. Our energies were in any case needed elsewhere, as the struggle to find justice for Kirsty gathered momentum.

I made up my mind to share the pleasure John and I had enjoyed in our visit to Cuba with other friends, planning a return trip to Havana for April 2003. This time it was much more of a working holiday, since the plan was for us to actually direct some classes. We were a large and happy party. Along with my old friend Denise Keir, there was Mitch Mitchelson, a practitioner of Physical Theatre and an authority on the Commedia dell'Arte, who was particularly interested in Havana's circus school. Sarah Aucott had studied as an actress at the East 15 Acting School and was now its Head of Movement. Lindsay Royan, alongside Sarah, had taken my Laban diploma course and was now working as a qualified psychologist and Lindsay's husband Richard also came.

Denise already knew Lindsay, Sarah and Mitch's work from the summer schools we had organised in Europe and across the UK, and was 'very keen', she said, to see my 'teaching techniques put into action in such an interesting place'.

There was also another member of our group, the journalist Karen O'Brien, who was then working on a biography of Kirsty. Several people had approached me with plans for such a book, though it was obvious that while most of them had no experience of writing, the others knew nothing about either Kirsty or her work. I was asked to write a book about her myself but everything was still much too raw. The fans wanted to know more about Kirsty's life, though, and when Karen O'Brien recommended herself to me, I decided to trust her. She had been anxious to accompany us on the trip, but when we got there she kept to her own schedule – though she did come with us to see the plaque at the music school. Karen's book, *The One and Only*, was eventually published in 2004. I saw very little of her after our return from Cuba, but she had promised that she would let me read a draft of the book before it went to print to check on its accuracy. For some reason this never happened.

Our trip to the music school, which we did on our first day in Havana, was a really special occasion. We were all warmly welcomed by the staff and I introduced my friends to the senior staff, who took us to see Kirsy's plaque on the wall outside the music library. I had brought some photographs from Kirsty's childhood which they had asked for, to introduce her to the young students at the school, as well as a few small gifts such as pens and pads of paper, which were difficult to get hold of in Cuba. These were all much appreciated and, while enjoying some refreshments we were told that there was a surprise in store for us: we were led into a concert room where the school's orchestra had assembled to entertain us. The standard was very high and these young students gave an impressive performance of a number of pieces, including Ravel's *Bolero*, played on the instruments donated by the Kirsty MacColl Music Fund.

That evening we all went to the ballet to see a performance by children of all ages and once again the standard was remarkably high. The auditorium was absolutely packed with many enthusiastic supporters and it was encouraging to see that there were as many young male dancers as girls. What was so thrilling for me was that the Cubans accepted so readily that dance was a natural form of expression for everybody, with none of the silly stigma attached to boys wishing to train as dancers back at home. I was told there were many dance schools training professional performers throughout Cuba.

The next day we went to see Havana's Circus School, where

the whole ring and outer space were filled with such an amazing range of individual activities and skills that it was difficult to decide what to watch. Denise was fascinated by the way the expertise gained by the more advanced students was then shared with the less experienced ones, leaving the tutors to work on finer points of technique on a one-to-one basis. I remember watching a young boy and girl, each about 14, practising a complicated routine with backward somersaults. Sometimes they did it beautifully; at others she didn't land properly; but their focus was so intense that they continued throughout our visit to work it towards perfection. After about an hour, they got it exactly right. Mitch was enormously impressed, telling me that in his opinion the standard of these students was higher than anything comparable at home.

During our visit we also took in some of the sights around Havana – *La Floridita*, the famous haunt of Ernest Hemingway, the various museums and Castro's boat, by now regarded as a historical icon, as well as the bronze statue of John Lennon sitting on a park bench, where like many tourists we had our photographs taken, returning each evening to have a meal or just a last drink in the hotel bar. Denise Keir remembers it fondly:

Sometimes as we sat in a colourful little restaurant serenaded by musicians or sipped our final *mojitos* in a rooftop bar (they were always the 'final' ones), we admitted to each other that we felt slightly guilty about enjoying the holiday so much. But then, almost in unison, everyone would say, 'Well, it's what Kirsty would have wanted – let's drink to her.'

When the trip had first been suggested I asked my doctor if I needed a jab. He laughed and said, 'Try to find something you need treating while you are there! The medical services are wonderful.' I certainly envied everyone their teeth, and realised it might be something to do with the entire absence of sweet shops.

The school was eager to learn more about Laban's methods, and in particular they wanted to see a practical workshop. I suggested that the class should be equally comprised of dancers and actors. This was a very unusual experiment for the Cubans – and would probably also have been considered strange in the UK – but I wanted to demonstrate that Laban's work crossed the divide between movement training for both disciplines. I was introduced to a class of 50 students with an equal split between the sexes and disciplines. Privately, I thought these young actors were very brave coming into the dancers' territory without knowing what to expect.

I began the class by working on the 'efforts' (Laban's system of loosening-up exercises), before Mitch, Sarah and Lindsay joined the class. We had a good interpreter and I asked the dancers to sit and watch the actors, who used the techniques beautifully to flesh out a series of devised characters. Mitch was in his element. The actors were especially delighted too by the enthusiastic reaction and clapping of the dance audience. Then it was the dancers' turn.

With Mitch and the actors watching the movements from the back, I choreographed a short movement study based on a musical scale, again assisted by Lindsay and Sarah. Richard had brought a portable cassette player, which he plugged into a very dangerous-looking socket at one end of the classroom. As a finale, my helpers withdrew with me to join the spectators and the young class went through a short choreography of their own devising. It had been a marvellous afternoon – and I shall never forget something Denise let slip afterwards:

Jean was brought a huge bouquet of flowers and given a standing ovation. The staff stayed to talk and were very keen to persuade her to return to run a two-week course the following year. They could find us accommodation, they said, but unfortunately there were no funds for travel. 'If you want her to come again you'd better not wait too long,' I found myself saying, 'she'll be 80 next month!' There were, literally, gasps of disbelief among our hosts, after watching this human dynamo expending so much energy to make the session a success.

We all contributed to the simple pleasure of enjoying a shared experience, but it also gave me a practical opportunity to give something back to a country that had given Kirsty so much pleasure and inspiration, recognising kindred souls among its people whose love of the arts is recognised as a necessary part of everyday life.

We had one final lovely afternoon on a pristine sandy beach, swimming in the clear water – and then suddenly, inevitably, there was music: one musician after another appearing out of the blue. In no time a typical Cuban beach party had begun, with about a dozen musicians at least – people of every size, age and shape dancing and laughing together in the sun. Wherever one went there was music and singing, laughter and dance.

'I know an island where the people are kind,' Kirsty had sung on the first track of *Tropical Brainstorm*, 'and the rest of the world seems far away.' I now felt I knew exactly what she meant.

But it was soon time to return to 'the rest of the world' – and to the campaign seeking justice for Kirsty which, by the time we arrived home in April 2003, was about to make some important strides.

Chapter Fourteen

Hard to Believe

2003-2004

'It's all lost in the blink of an eye.'
KIRSTY MacCOLL, 'TOMORROW NEVER COMES', 1994

It had become clear to John and myself that the authorities, both in Mexico and the UK, had from the outset been extremely reluctant to get involved with either the investigation into Kirsty's death or the prosecution of those responsible for it. Put simply, they just didn't want to know and we were at a loss to know how to proceed until Fred Shortland joined our newly-formed committee in 2003.

In the years since then, the story of our campaign has grown, though it is still a story without a proper ending. Telling it has not been easy, but it remains necessary – if only to provide a warning to others of the lax attitude towards holidaymakers displayed by the Mexican authorities and of the power of wealthy individuals. Our fight for justice goes on.

In December 2003, I received a long, hand-written letter from the USA. Postmarked 5 December, it was from Ivan Diaz, Kirsty's dive-master on the day of her death. Enclosing a copy in his original Spanish, Ivan's undated letter was a slightly imperfect

English translation. I read the letter in its terrible simplicity with a mixture of emotions: renewed grief at Kirsty's senseless loss, but also with the hope that we might at last help achieve justice for her. These are Ivan's own words:

Dear Jean,

Hello, how are you? I hope when you get this letter that it finds you doing well, I am okay. Well, first of all I want to apologise if I didn't write to you before but I have been thinking about what I was going to tell you. We did receive your message on which you were asking me some questions, well, now that I am writing to you I will try to answer the best I can to your questions, okay?

That day of the fatal accident, before the accident, that morning I went to work as usual. I was hoping to get a dive trip that morning but I didn't, so I was a little disappointed. After all the boats went out Michael told me that there was a dive trip at 1.00pm and he asked me to take it. I told him that, 'Yes, I would take out that trip but I needed to go downtown to do something and I would be coming back later on to get everything that we were going to need, like the equipment we were going to need for my divers.'

At first I didn't know who were the people that I was going to take out to dive. Michael had told me that they were a family: a mother and her two sons. When I got back to the dive shop I got everything ready and put it on the boat. I waiting for my divers, then I saw a woman and two kids getting off a car, I think it was a taxi, but I am not sure of that, anyway, I saw them walking towards the pier. When I saw Kirsty I thought she was a beautiful woman and I have had a nice impression of her from the first moment. Once she and the kids got on board we left the pier and we were going to the reef where we were supposed to make our first dive. When we got there I was talking to Kirsty about the place and she suggested that we should go out to the further reef to make our first dive and on the way back we could do the closer one, so we decided to go to Chankanaab Reef. We got there and made our dive plan. We all agreed that when the first diver gets at 1,000 psi [pounds per square inch pressure] we must all go up and we will be making a safety stop at 15 feet for three minutes, then we go up to the surface and get back on board the boat.

We did have a real nice dive, as matter of fact. While we were diving I noticed that there was a larger group of divers were coming behind us, so we stopped and I signalled to the other dive master to go ahead and he did, so we stayed behind that group. By doing that it kind of confused a little bit the crew members of our boats because they didn't notice that it was us who got behind.

However, when we finished our three-minute safety stop at 15 feet, I signalled to Kirsty and the kids that it was okay to go up and so we did get to the surface. When we all came up I was looking around to find our boat and I noticed that the other boat – it was much closer to us and ours it was watching the other divers. I was starting to make signals to our boat to come to pick up us when suddenly I noticed that there was a fast private boat that was coming at high speed directly over us. I do remember telling to Kirsty and the kids to watch out because there was a speedboat coming. There was nobody on the front of that boat watching where they were going, and the front, it was way high so they could not see us.

Everything happened so fast. I was screaming and waving my hands trying to get their attention but with the noise from the engines and the speed that they were going they couldn't hear me and they just ran over us. I felt the bottom of the boat hit me on my chest and pushed me away. I was lucky to pull with me one of the kids and I heard the propeller hitting a [oxygen] tank and I saw blood all over us. The boat that hit us tried to keep going but it couldn't because it got damaged, one of the propellers. They turned around and started to tell me that I was a stupid and I didn't have a buoy marker. I told them that they were wrong because we were in a protected area and they were not supposed to navigate at high speed around there, and also they were supposed to be on the deeper waters out of the protected diving areas.

When the authorities came I asked them if it would be okay to send the kids home because I didn't [think] it was okay to see the way their mother it was. They let me send them home, so we picked up the body and brought it to shore. While we were at the pier I heard Gonzalez Nova said that he was driving the boat he told that to the police chief and the Harbour Master's officers.

Later on at 7.00pm, I went to give my testimony to the Public Ministry of Justice Department. Anyway I was alone because I didn't have a lawyer or any legal representative with me. While I was giving my testimony, next to me it was the crew member of the *Percalito* [the speedboat which hit Kirsty]. He said that he was driving the boat at the moment of the accident. When I heard him saying that I turned around and I told him he was a liar because earlier Mr Gonzalez Nova admitted that he was driving the boat and now he was changing the story. I was so angry and I wanted to strangle him right there. The Public Ministry told me to stay calm or he would send me to jail. He got that guy in the back office to keep him away from me.

I saw Mr Gonzalez Nova with his two sons accompanied by two or three lawyers. I didn't see them coming in to give their testimony before I got out of there.

On next day I had to go at 9.00am at the Harbour Master's office to give my testimony. At first it was the captain of my boat who went in to give his testimony. We were there from 9.00am until 8.30pm and I was still waiting for my turn. While I was sitting on the waiting room I saw a person who came in and sat down next to me. He started talking to me and told me that he was a newspaper reporter and asked me for an interview. At that moment I was feeling so stressful and I feel that I needed to talk to somebody, so I gave him an interview. That was when I found out who was Kirsty MacColl! I didn't have the least idea of who she was – too bad, I really liked her from the very first moment that we met and we started talking.

Later on that night when the Harbour Master Chief finished taking our captain's testimony, he was a little angry at me because I gave the reporter an interview before I even talk to him. Anyway, he told me to come on next day to give him my testimony.

On next day I went at 9.00am and I started giving my testimony. I spent the whole [day] too and didn't finish it yet, so I had to come back again, by the way, during the first day.

While I was giving my testimony one of the guys who [I assumed might be] helping the Harbour Master Chief told me to signed up a piece of paper blank and later on they will take care of that to fill it up. I refused to sign it, I told him that I will not sign up anything that I wasn't able to read it and know what I am signing for. He got mad at me because I didn't want to sign what he want. From that moment on I noticed their attitude change at me. They were telling me all kinds of things that I was supposed to have with me while we are diving around. I told them that when we took the course to get our seaman's credential or card, nobody of the Institution told us that we needed those things.

As a matter of fact I heard one of the guys told the Harbour Master Chief that Mr Gonzalez Nova could not come to the office because he was resting and he didn't want to be disturbed.

Honestly, I do not know if he and his family ever come to give their testimony, what I doubted they did because their lawyers were taking care of that. Some time later a friend of mine told me that he saw the mate of the boat *Percalito* getting drunk in one of the local bars around town and he said that he just got a good amount of money from his boss to take the responsibilities of the accident and he was going to get a nice house. Then I didn't hear anything about the case until April second when I was required to show up at the Court House to give my testimony to the Judge and one of Gonzalez Nova's lawyers, this guy tried to confuse me and made me to admit that I abandoned the divers for about two minutes, but I told him that I never left them until the kids and I got on board our boat.

That guy Cen Yam got convicted in jail because he was [charged with] driving the boat.

Some people told me that when the Gonzalez left the beach where they were, they were drinking some beers and when they pulled out they did it at a high speed and [a] few boat captains noticed they were navigating right over some of the reefs where there are some divers and snorkellers. Unfortunately they got us!

Jean, this is the very true about what happened that fatal

day. I hope this answered some of your questions. Hope to
hear from you again.

Take care.

Love from Diaz

PS I am enclosing a copy of my testimony from the very 1st
day of the accident. It is written in Spanish but I did
translate it in this letter. I hope it helps you in what so ever
you might need it. Okay? Contact me on our e-mail for
anything else please.

Love Ivan

I am 48 Y[ears] O[ld] of age not 28.

Ivan's letter is a central piece of evidence in the case it has taken us
so long to piece together in the sad years since Kirsty's death. As far
as we are concerned, that is the truth of what happened, a truth
that has never been acknowledged in the official investigation.

My personal quest for justice had grown into an international
campaign, and we were preparing ourselves for our first trip to
Mexico in the new year of 2004.

The following chapters tell the story of the Justice For Kirsty
campaign, which has benefited from the invaluable contribution
made to it by Fred Shortland, who has worked tirelessly on our
behalf ever since joining us in the spring of 2003. Widely
respected as an outspoken and deeply knowledgeable human
rights advocate, with extensive experience in Latin America, Fred
has kindly agreed to tell part of our story – so far a story without
a proper ending – in his own words.

That story really began, as John Dalby remembers, one day in
the bleak January of 2001, the month of Kirsty's funeral and
memorial service:

Jean and I sat down on the sofa and I said to her, 'We ought to fight this,' as it looked as though we were just accepting the situation. What was it that triggered this remark? In my naivety, I thought that the British Foreign Office would be up in arms and would do something about it – this was in January 2001, when every day was going by and nothing was happening. Then the lawyers began to take over – there was an awfully long wait, but I think that what really triggered things was an account in the Cozumel paper along the lines that the MacColl family were not going to contest the case. This surprised and outraged us. We always thought it was a case we had to pursue. We still hadn't heard from the British Foreign Office, or from the Mexicans; for the lawyers, it was just another case, and we thought it could take several years.

The legal team employed by the travel insurance people needed the assistance of a lawyer living in the States who had a knowledge of Latin American legal matters; this American joined the team briefly. At the same time a civil case was being pursued by Ronnie which involved the boat's insurance. There was a problem here as well because the boat appeared to be registered in Guernsey... but apparently things weren't as straightforward as they might have been.

That is putting it mildly. We had been told almost nothing in the months following Kirsty's death and I had begun to suspect that we were being deliberately kept in the dark. Towards Easter 2001, I confided in my old friend Tosh Barron (née Rapoport), who strongly advised me to seek the services of a lawyer. She recommended a top American investigator. This was an expensive move, but Steve Lillywhite generously paid the first instalment. What this investigator found out in the first few months of his work, however, was chilling: a catalogue of conflicting statements and unsubstantiated claims that called into question the workings of the formal investigation and the judicial process itself.

John and I took part in a four-way phone call later that year between the American travel insurance lawyer, Kirsty's accountant and executor Ronnie and the American investigator we had taken on. During the course of the conversation, I said I thought that the travel insurance side of things was taking a very long time to be resolved. Unfortunately, we were told this was rather typical.

Ronnie told me that his central concern was to tackle the civil case on behalf of Kirsty's boys, but he was not prepared to endanger the estate by taking on a criminal case at the same time and that if I wanted to go down that route, I would have do so alone. To be fair, he did give me some initial support, along with our investigator. It was then that I began to realise that I might have to sell my home.

John and I were left in despair, and our first impulse was to travel to Mexico and try and do something about it ourselves, since the methods being pursued by the travel insurance lawyer and the American investigator seemed to me to be at loggerheads, and much time was lost. I decided to carry on with our US investigator.

As mentioned above, the delay by the civil lawyers in part arose because proof was needed of Kirsty's residence on the island in the time leading up to her death. But since she had taken out travel insurance for the ten days she was spending on Cozumel Island, this was quite ridiculous. The problem came with the refusal by Anita Quinta, the American woman who had rented her house to Kirsty for the trip, to offer any formal acknowledgement or written receipt for the time they had all stayed there. Her excuse was that her accountant had told her it was illegal to give a receipt after so many weeks – which I thought somewhat odd. She also refused to speak to Ronnie on the grounds that she considered him part of a 'legal' team.

It later transpired that Anita Quinta had only unofficially rented out her house, and we only managed to establish proof of Kirsty's stay through Jean Berg, an American minister of religion whose husband had finally taken Kirsty's hired car back to the garage and been given an official receipt. It also turned out that Anita Quinta was actually related by marriage to Gonzales Nova himself (she was the wife of one of his nephews).

It was being claimed that the *Percalito* was travelling at just one knot (less than one mile an hour) when it struck and killed Kirsty. We were later to hear that various witnesses had placed the speed at something more like 18 knots, 'with the bow up'. Meanwhile, John and I tried to find out more about Gonzalez Nova. The internet provided some information about his commercial interests and great wealth.

From the very first, John remained a tower of strength, and as described above, we remained in close contact, travelling to Cuba together in March 2002. Over the course of those first two dreadful years, we both came to the obvious conclusion that there had been a sort of whitewash and we were determined to find out the truth. The evidence we gathered made two things clear to us: first, that Gonzalez Nova was a person of great power and that the local people on Cozumel were wary of that power. And second, that the findings of the official court case represented a grievous miscarriage of justice. John and I had spent two years enlisting support and getting as much publicity as possible for our growing campaign. We were essentially on our own, with limited resources at our disposal and still less experience. As far as the wider world was concerned, Kirsty had been killed in a tragic accident. It was very sad, but we should put it behind us and move on. However, as the private investigator's report had begun to reveal, 'simply a tragic accident' was far from the truth.

The case was heard in a Mexican court in March 2003. The Mexican legal system is based on the Napoleonic Code, whereby judges alone decide on cases. José Cen Yam, the deckhand on board the *Percalito*, the speedboat that killed her, was conveniently convicted of Kirsty's culpable homicide, sentenced to two years in prison, and ordered to pay £1,450 compensation to her sons. With no appeal forthcoming, the case was closed and under local State law could not be reopened. José Cen Yam walked free after paying a fine of £61 in lieu of going to jail, calculated at the rate of one Mexican peso for each day of the sentence, based on the current minimum wage in the State of Quintana Roo. Meanwhile, Guillermo Gonzalez Nova, the captain of the *Percalito* and one of the wealthiest individuals in Mexico, was neither charged nor even implicated in the events surrounding Kirsty's death, despite the fact that the boat was owned by one of his many global companies, and that he was on board, and responsible as captain, when it ploughed into her. Indeed, the court proceedings had been dominated by Gonzalez Nova's lawyers, who strenuously cross-examined a key witness, Kirsty's dive-master Ivan Diaz, even telling him to 'shut up' as he tried to give evidence.

José Cen Yam's testimony included the crucial detail that the accident took place within an area of water prohibited to speedboats, and this was supported by a number of other witnesses – but not by Guillermo Gonzalez Nova and his son Gustavo, who claimed it took place outside that restricted zone. Cen Yam also testified that this was the first time he had ever driven the *Percalito* – but according to Gonzalez Nova, the deckhand had been driving the boat for five years.

Meanwhile, however, a separate maritime investigation by the Port Authority had been convened, and this had found Gonzalez Nova guilty of allowing an untrained person to drive the boat. He was also found guilty of (1) the boat being driven at excessive speed, and (2) an environmental breach for being in a restricted area, for which he was charged nominal fines. It appeared that none of this information was significantly taken into account during the criminal proceedings.

It is our firm belief that the case somehow went through the system quickly, with minimal reporting, in order to minimise the damage to Gonzalez Nova and Cozumel's lucrative tourist industry. Without my family's knowledge, or our representation at the trial, a gross miscarriage of justice was committed that should have been obvious to any legitimate legal system.

Of course, Gonzalez Nova isn't the only one responsible for Kirsty's needless death – merely one of the most powerful among them, and the single most obstructive force in our quest for the truth. As Fred Shortland explains, there is a chain of negligent responsibility for that tragedy:

An experienced diver herself, Kirsty selected a package offered by Papa Hog's, a 'Scuba Emporium' on Cozumel, owned by Caribbean Heat SA de CV, and run by the experienced dive-shop operator Mike Gerus. The boat in which Kirsty and her sons went diving on 18 December 2000, was the *Scuba Shack II*, owned by Rosa Molina and operated via Papa Hog's, with Jesus Fernandez Che at the wheel and Ivan Diaz as its dive-master. (Rosa Molina's Port Authority licence to provide 'nautical tourism services' was non-transferable, and was therefore cancelled in the wake of the accident, when she was also fined.)

The *Percalito* ploughed into Kirsty's dive group at

approximately 2 o'clock that afternoon. On board the speedboat were its captain, Guillermo Gonzalez Nova; his sons Luis Guillermo Gonzalez Fernandez and Gustavo Gonzalez Fernandez; Gustavo's wife Norma, and their ten-month-old daughter; and its deckhand, and alleged driver, José Cen Yam.

Three months after Kirsty's death, in March 2001, Cozumel's Acting Port Captain, Vicente Moralez, issued his investigative report to the Prosecutor. Among his findings was the view that the owners and operators of Papa Hog's were themselves partly responsible for a lack of supervision, having failed to observe normal safety procedures. No marker buoys had been set; the *Scuba Shack II* had not flown the necessary 'Alpha Dive Flag' (the internationally recognised signal to indicate the presence of divers); its two crew members were below the specified minimum for such a trip.

The Port Captain's report also found Guillermo Gonzalez Nova responsible, as captain of the *Percalito*, for a number of breaches in navigational laws, including the consent given to an untrained person to drive the boat, and the more general failure to ensure the safe operation of the vessel.

José Cen Yam was found culpable of having navigated the boat with neither proper accreditation nor practical capacity to drive or control the boat; and of having allowed one of the party onboard to be seated leaning against the windscreen, so impairing the boat's forward visibility.

Two expert witnesses – one of them Elvira Hinojosa, Director of Cozumel National Park – supported the Port Captain's report, finding further fault with the *Percalito* for its violation of the rules of the National Marine Park: boats such as the *Percalito* were strictly prohibited in waters specifically reserved for swimming and diving over coral formations.

In May 2003 the Port Authority Head Office issued their official findings, ruling that the *Percalito* was at fault in the accident on the following grounds:

(1) Violating Condition 22, Section XVI of the Management Programme of the National Marine Park: 'Navigating in these areas or over coral formations is only allowed when the boat is guarding divers or is going to pick them up. Speed may not be over 4 knots.'

(2) Violating Regulation 30: 'Navigation in the National Marine Park must take place strictly outside the diving and swimming areas.'

Guillermo Gonzalez Nova was found guilty of these maritime offences and given two nominal fines, based on 1,000 days of the general daily wage of the Federal District of Mexico City.

Kirsty and her sons had been diving at the Chankanaab Reef in the maritime park area of special protection, where speedboats are banned. What's more, the *Percalito* has a top speed of over 30 knots, driven by two 315 horsepower engines; although Gonzalez Nova was certified as a yacht captain in 1976, his licence permits him, in coastal waters, to operate a vessel with engines up to only 100 horsepower. So how on earth had the *Percalito* been allowed into its waters? And why had this not been properly taken into account during the trial? After all, the Prosecutor and the Judge had the Port Captain's report supported by two expert witnesses. It was beyond comprehension.

At the very heart of the case lies a very simple question: Who was driving the *Percalito* when Kirsty was killed? Was it really José Cen Yam? Or was he simply the fall guy? Despite six long years of legal and political scrutiny, this key question still remains unanswered. Will wealth and greed always triumph over truth and integrity?

On 23 September 2002, a concert of Kirsty's songs had been given in tribute at the Royal Festival Hall in London. Many well-known singers who had worked with her performed together, including Tracey Ullman. The concert was a sell-out, packed with Kirsty's fans, and it seemed an ideal opportunity to inform them in the programme that her family were still fighting for justice and urgently needed support. The response was overwhelming, and resulted in the birth of the Justice For Kirsty campaign.

Our first committee meeting took place in November 2002. We were a small but committed team: myself and John Dalby, Kirsty's musical collaborator and lifelong friend Philip Rambow and her close friend and favourite photographer Charlie Dickins. Alan Officer, who had created Kirsty's official website in 1995, was also elected to the committee and set up www.justiceforkirsty.org.

I had recently found a drawing of a bird Kirsty had made when she must have been about 15. I suppose it was really just a doodle in felt-tip and on the back she had written a note to her boyfriend at the time, 'I have just gone to a guitar class – will be back soon'. I thought this was very touching and we used it for the campaign logo.

Joan Littlewood, who had come to my summer school in Ealing that August, had told me she would not be able to attend the tribute concert in September. In the end, she actually died the night before, as she sat going through my old letters to her. Her funeral was on 6 October 2002, at Golders Green Crematorium and I went with Hamish, Jamie and Louis. Joan had a cheerful send-off, as she would have wished. She had stipulated 'No priests!', so her friend, the actor Brian Murphy read a eulogy. Joan's little cap sat on top of the coffin. During the tribute, something rattled near the coffin. 'She's there,' said Brian, 'taking notes!'

Two of Ewan's songs, 'I Met Her in Venezuela' and 'Dirty Old Town' were sung and there was a party afterwards with a buffet, a band and much more singing. There were many performers and musicians from the Theatre Workshop days and they led the singing of songs from the old shows. Some we hadn't seen for years – Ann Beach, Harry Green, so many old friends.

At Joan's request, her friend Peter Rankin arranged to take her ashes to France, to join those of her lifelong partner Gerry Raffles. Ewan's 'Venezuela' song had always been a favourite of Gerry's and Peggy Seeger had sung it down the phone to Peter in advance of the funeral. Peter thought he might run into difficulties in customs, but he and his small rucksack were waved through onto the train. Arriving at Viennes, an occasional place of pilgrimage for Joan in the years since Gerry had died on the river towpath in 1975, he was met by a couple of Joan's friends. They arranged to meet him later that night to scatter Joan and Gerry's ashes into the river. Peter arrived at the middle of the bridge in the pitch darkness, the two figures materialised out of the shadows to join him and the little ceremony was done. Later, Peter told me he left Viennes rather quickly since he wasn't exactly sure of the legality of his actions!

A week after Joan's funeral, I received a gracious visit from Japan by the father of my dear friend and student Kami. A professor of Japanese literature and a choreographer at his wife's dance studio in Tokyo, he had come to England to pay homage to our great master Laban. He described the new Laban institute in London as 'a building for Laban, but he doesn't inhabit it' – a view with which I must say I agreed. The institute neither embodies the spirit and philosophy of his work, nor adequately promotes or teaches it, and is therefore badly misnamed, disappointing many students hoping to study Laban techniques there.

I remember fondly his visit to my flat, where he carried out a traditional Japanese tea ceremony. He had brought all the utensils and equipment with him, lighting the small primer-stove for the water and making the tea. We talked about Laban and he came to one of my local classes, moving very well for an elderly man. I tried to spare this gentleman all the time I could.

He sent me two beautifully painted marionettes and in due course I sent him a copy of *Laban for All*. I later learned from Kami himself that his father had died shortly after his return.

I had a meal in early December with Steve, Patti, Hamish and the boys – Steve was now working in England until the boys finished school. I said my goodbyes to Louis, now 16, who was flying to New Zealand to stay with a school friend. It was a quiet Christmas that year, with the two Johns and our neighbours, Peter and Jill. The more people there are, the easier it is to cope with such occasions, but we did well enough together. I was even without my old cat Solomon – the third of that name I had owned – who died quietly at the great age of 19 in October.

Also in December, a powerful article about the case appeared in the *Mail on Sunday* written by Pete and Leni Gillman. Leni was an old friend of mine and an early member of the campaign committee. The article triggered off a great deal of media interest and I was asked to give interviews on both radio and television programmes. The response was extremely heartening, and many offers of support, along with the first donations to the fund, came in.

There were also offers from two separate documentary film-makers: the independent Robin Bextor, and Trevor McDonald's team at ITN. However, the latter offer came with a warning that if war broke out in Iraq they would immediately have to go to Kuwait to cover it. In the event their departure was almost immediate, following the invasion of Iraq in March 2003, and we agreed to go with Bextor (whose documentary about a boy from Peru I had seen and admired). These were all important steps forward, but we still struggled to make a broader impact. I was getting emails from many people unknown to me who asked how they could help the campaign. One of those who contacted us was Fred Shortland.

Fred had lived in several countries in Latin America, including Mexico, worked with Amnesty International and was the Chief Executive of Casa Alianza UK, a charity providing care, rehabilitation and legal-aid services for street children in Guatemala, Nicaragua, Honduras and Mexico. Casa Alianza also has a formidably successful track record not only of campaigning on human rights abuses against street children but also of prosecuting perpetrators, including police, high court judges and even countries at the Inter-American Court of Human Rights.

By the time Fred Shortland joined us, our campaign was slowly gaining momentum, but it was an uphill battle. Fred brought a much-needed professional expertise to our faltering efforts and I shall always be grateful to him for his tireless work on our behalf. Casa Alianza's logo is a bird held protectively in the palm of an open hand: a good omen for Kirsty's felt-tip bird! Painstakingly reviewing the findings of the private investigator, Fred developed and implemented the campaign strategy, taking on the British Foreign and Commonwealth Office and moving the campaign's focus to the President and the Attorney General of Mexico, calling for a judicial review. This was a bold and courageous strategy, but one that depended on getting the British Government on side. This seemed unlikely, since the

British Embassy in Mexico had been noticeably silent in the time following Kirsty's death. They had offered no practical support or assistance, and had not even paid the family the courtesy of a phone call, in spite of the fact that Kirsty's death had made headline news around the world. This can only be described as a serious failing of the British Government to assist its citizens abroad. With an Honorary Consul stationed in nearby Cancun, my feeling was there was absolutely no excuse.

'I was aware of Kirsty's death from the BBC News,' remembers Fred himself:

I was numbed and greatly saddened. I recalled meeting her with my old friend Glynn Wood, Kirsty's live sound engineer, at the after show party following her performance at the London Forum on 18 May 2000. We chatted for a short time and when I left to say, 'Thank you for the invite', she gave me a huge hug and thanked me for coming to the show. Little did I know that this would be the last time I would see her – or that in the years to come she would become an important part of my life.

In January 2003 I noticed a posting about the Justice For Kirsty Campaign on Suzanne Vega's website 'Undertow' and its call for all volunteers with experience in campaigning. I responded to the request via the campaign website but never had a reply. Several weeks passed and still no answer, so I contacted Glynn Wood whom I had known for several years, as he was also Suzanne Vega's sound engineer and tour manager. Suzanne Vega was involved with Children's Rights and I had worked with her both at Amnesty International and Casa Alianza. We had become good friends over the years, keeping in regular contact, so I now asked Glynn to make an introduction on my behalf to Jean, offering help on campaigning as I was reluctant to make a direct approach. I was, after all, a complete stranger and did not want to intrude on the family's grief. Glynn knew me personally and could vouch for my track record on human rights and campaigning. It took some time to make the connection with Jean, but we did eventually by phone.

When Fred rang one evening, we talked for a long time. I was so pleased to find someone who had the expertise to help and we arranged to meet up with John Dalby at the local Italian restaurant in Ealing, on 12 March 2003, along with Robin Bextor, who gave Fred a lift from Roehampton University, where he'd given a lecture on human rights. We all got on very well and I allowed myself to believe that we were making progress. Fred could see we needed help, so we invited him to our next meeting, when he was introduced to Charlie Dickins, Philip Rambow and Leni Gillman, who had now also joined the committee. Along with Alan Officer – now we were seven!

Fred's expertise on human rights and his knowledge of campaigning was invaluable. We learned that he had lived in Mexico for many years and could speak Spanish. He told me that our case would take time, but that we would be following the letter of the law. One of his first suggestions was a leafleting campaign. A flyer was designed explaining our cause, with a tear-off slip to be posted to the President of Mexico. Charlie Dickins helped with the layout and photography and Alan Officer promoted the leaflet on the website. Thousands of fans responded by asking for leaflets for themselves and their friends. And of course the newly designed Justice For Kirsty logo was used. Fred Shortland:

Attending my very first Justice For Kirsty campaign meeting, it became clear that the campaign had no clear goals, objectives, or strategy, and very limited funds. If I became involved, then, it would mean starting from scratch: a formidable undertaking. I was very surprised that it was really a 'campaign' in name only - but what did I expect? Here was a dedicated group of people who were very close to Kirsty: her mother Jean, consumed with anger, desperately searching for the truth, Philip Rambow, Kirsty's co-writer and musical collaborator. the photographer Charles Dickins, the journalist Leni Gillman, Alan Officer, creator of Kirsty's website, and the composer and performer John Dalby, a long-standing family friend. It shouldn't have surprised me, of course, that none of these members of the campaign committee had any actual experience of campaigning - though they had certainly worked hard to raise awareness.

They had valiantly tried to obtain support, for example, from various diving associations, including the PADI [Professional Association of Diving Instructors], of which Kirsty was a member, but although such groups generally expressed sympathy, they nevertheless failed to lend active support to our campaign. Jean was totally focused on having Guillermo Gonzalez Nova account for his actions, both to her personally and in a court of law, but this could never be the sole basis for a meaningful campaign.

My first task was therefore to examine the facts and the findings of the private investigator previously hired by the family. Initially the investigator was somewhat reluctant to have myself - a total stranger, after all - fire so many detailed questions at him, and as we delved deeper into the case the answers he gave were gradually slower to arrive, until we eventually reached a point where we were getting no responses at all. It soon became clear that while the initial reports were excellent, the investigator had little new to report and, being on a monthly retainer, the family were now getting little value by retaining him.

As Fred discovered, the New York-based investigator I had hired was reliant on sources with experience of undercover narcotics investigations in Mexico, as well as on a Mexican lawyer who provided him with advice on legal matters. Over a period of several months, Fred worked with both the American investigator and the Mexican lawyer, in particular, seeking to establish whether there were any business connections, in the background, between the lawyer and the Gonzalez Nova family, as I simply wanted to be reassured. Fred Shortland:

This was an essential enquiry because of the myriad of companies owned by the Gonzalez Nova family, the principal being the holding company, Controladora Comercial Mexicana (CCM), which consists of a group of supermarkets and restaurants throughout Mexico and a joint venture with Costco Wholesale Co of the United States. Quoted on the US Stock Exchange, CCM's 2006 turnover was 45,628,000,000 MX$, the equivalent of £2.1 billion, and employed 38,437 people. Guillermo Gonzalez Nova, now 74, is the chairman of the holding company, and while his personal fortune is unknown, he is ranked amongst the richest individuals in Mexico.

Among CCM's numerous companies is Percal Ltd, the official owner of the *Percalito* – the speedboat that killed Kirsty. This high-powered, twin-engine speedboat, purchased in Miami in 1994, entered Mexican waters illegally, without paying duties, and while it was supposedly registered in Guernsey, in fact that was not done until November 2004, almost four years after Kirsty was killed. The word 'Guernsey', however, had been prominently displayed beneath 'PERCALITO' on the boat's stern before this date, implying registration. But has anything been done about this? Has anyone been called to account for these criminal activities of tax evasion and the falsification of documents? Not as far as we are aware.

The Comercial Mexicana Group is no stranger to controversy. Since 2001 its joint venture with Costco USA has been at the centre of a bitter controversy over a million-square-foot Costco warehouse store and shopping mall. The Costco-Comercial Mexicana complex in Cuernavaca stands on what used to be 24 acres of beautiful woodland, surrounding the Casino de la Selva, a hotel and arts centre, an architectural gem from the 1930s. After the land was purchased in 2001 from the Mexican government at the grossly undervalued price of $10 million, Costco very quickly moved in and devastated the area, destroying 46 rare plant species, cutting down hundreds of ancient trees and concreting over the unexcavated archaeological remains of a 3,000-year-old Olmec site.

Peaceful protests followed by campaigning groups and thousands of local residents, many of whom were violently attacked, arrested and imprisoned by the state police. Environmental and human rights organisations, including Amnesty International and a United Nations Commission, condemned Costco-Comercial Mexicana for gross violations of a wide range of basic rights. In a damning indictment, the UN High Commissioner's Report on Human Rights in Mexico accused the company of civil rights abuses and of violating the Mexican people's right to a healthy environment and depriving them of their artistic, historical and cultural heritage. By contrast, CCM's website promotes its corporate ethical policy. Adopting a policy is one thing, implementing and upholding it quite another.

A high-profile case will always attract all sorts of people with an axe to grind, and we certainly had our share, chief among them those people and campaign groups who had issues with Gonzalez Nova's business empire and wanted to add their grievances to our campaign. While it was tempting to join forces with them in order to increase awareness in Mexico of our campaign, I was reluctant since I thought such a coalition might dilute the campaign's message, weakening both our position and our case. After all, we had enough problems establishing the simple truth of Kirsty's death without taking on wider issues, no matter how worthy. After long discussion and careful thought, we opted to 'go it alone' and focus solely on our own campaign.

It was around this time that I was contacted directly from Mexico by a mysterious woman who offered all manner of general advice and specific suggestions. She claimed to have personal contact with President Fox and guaranteed us a private meeting with him. Free accommodation, transport and office space were also offered to the whole team. The direction she kept pushing us towards was to follow the case via Mexican human rights legislation, but her credibility became increasingly suspect.

She claimed that Bono had personally called her, for example, and that she was a personal friend of Prince Charles and the Irish Ambassador to Mexico. Although we were very sceptical and remained extremely guarded in our dealings with her, we kept the dialogue open in case she was indeed able to secure a private meeting with President Fox. As the date of our proposed departure drew close, however, our contact with her became less frequent and when we finally asked her to liaise with our lawyer, all communication ceased. When we pushed her for the presidential contact details she had promised, the phone number she reluctantly gave us turned out to be for the switchboard of the president's official residence, Los Pinos, a matter of public record. And then, all of a sudden, she was unavailable for our visit to Mexico City and her offers of assistance were withdrawn.

The last we heard from her was a message, some time later, not to contact her. She could not get involved, she explained nervously; she had been warned off. No further information was forthcoming and she simply disappeared. Was she a genuine well-wisher? Or a time-wasting crank? Or was she in fact a plant, part of a botched attempt from Mexico to infiltrate the campaign to gain privileged information and to steer us away from pursuing a legal criminal approach? Whatever the truth, the episode brought one thing home to us. We had to be absolutely sure that we were dealing with principled people who could not be bought off and who would not be intimidated by wealth or power.

'What was very difficult to understand,' comments Fred Shortland, 'was that the MacColl family had no knowledge or representation at the trial of José Cen Yam [in March 2003] and were only made aware of the outcome after the event, thus making it impossible to appeal. The case was deemed closed. This was a major problem which should have been monitored and picked up earlier by the private investigator and legal council.'

After a great deal of discussion, we decided to stand the New York investigator down and work directly in Mexico. While the investigator's work had been invaluable, we needed to move forward – and this could only be accomplished in Mexico. With some of the facts established, Fred was in a position to develop the campaign strategy by pulling together all the various strands, the first objective being to raise awareness at the highest level in the United Kingdom and Mexico by systematically lobbying the Foreign and Commonwealth Office (FCO) and the Mexican Embassy in London. For our campaign to succeed, it had to force the Mexican authorities to re-open a closed case, open a new investigation and review new evidence, while monitoring judicial proceedings to ensure a proper hearing with no undue influence. Fred remembers:

Given President Fox's publicly-declared commitment to human rights, these aims did not seem to me to be overly ambitious. Under his presidency, after all, Mexico had for the first time signed and ratified International Human Rights treaties and allowed the UN and Non Governmental Organisations (NGOs) like Amnesty International and Human Rights Watch into the country to conduct research, access which had previously been denied under his predecessors. This was certainly a positive step, and greatly encouraged us in developing the campaign strategy.

We simply felt that, if we could create awareness at the highest levels of the Mexican government and judiciary, their new-found commitment to human-rights protocols would lead them to agree to conduct a thorough review of our case, determine who was driving the boat that killed Kirsty, and prosecute accordingly. In the event, however, those hopes turned out to be ill-founded.

Vicente Fox was now in the second half of his term as President, by which time promises of new reforms on a whole range of issues, including human rights, were starting to slide down the political agenda to an increasingly disheartened electorate. Vicente Fox had managed to break seventy years of PRI one-party government with a populist agenda that he was now failing to deliver.

The legal approach alone would not succeed: it seemed to me critical to get the British government on board to bring pressure to bear on the Mexican authorities, from President Fox's office down to the relevant Ministries, including the Ministry of Tourism, and persuade the Mexican Attorney General's Office to intervene and conduct a judicial review.

This was a very tall order for someone with limited resources, no budget, their own business to run, as well as a charity for Latin American street children. So why did I take it on? I have been asked that question many times by those close to me, who know my heavy workload. 'It's an impossible case', 'You will never win', 'It can't be done', 'You can't afford to do this pro-bono work' – these and many other, even more valid, reasons were thrown at me. There have been many times, I must admit, when it would have been easier to throw in the towel, admit defeat and simply walk away. But somehow I just dug my heels in deep, and kept on going. It has been very difficult, as in my human rights work to date I had worked with Amnesty International and Casa Alianza – but this time I was having to work alone, with no organisational support.

The Mexican tourist industry represents approximately 10 per cent of the country's GNP. In 2006, for example, it attracted over 22 million visitors (over two-thirds from the USA, and 400,000 from Britain), generating $12 billion and employing 1.95 million people. As such, the industry would be highly sensitive to the negative effects of any adverse publicity. We nevertheless chose not to deliberately target tourism, since we did not want to engage in negative campaigning that would reflect badly on our case in Mexico. In the event our restraint was indeed appreciated by the Mexican Minister of Tourism, Rodolfo Elizondo, whom we later met on two separate occasions.

In the UK, we discussed our case with a Foreign Office official. Our first meeting with Rachel Cooper, Head of the Protection Section at the Consular Division, was on 10 April 2003. It was a bitter disappointment. We wanted to enlist the support of the FCO in securing appointments and pressuring the Mexican government, but essentially they offered little more than tea and sympathy.

As the minutes dragged by, I could see that Fred, who had a great deal of experience working with the Foreign Office, was getting increasingly agitated. Eventually he complained that their response was totally unacceptable and requested a meeting with Baroness Amos, the Minister responsible for the Consular Section. This was refused. I again felt extremely let down by those who were supposed to be helping us. As we were getting ready to leave, the official asked me directly, 'Mrs MacColl, what did you exactly expect to get from this meeting?'

'Frankly, nothing,' I replied, 'and that's exactly what I got.'

Then, in almost a throwaway remark, she said something I shall never forget: 'Don't quote me on this,' she said, 'but it's those who shout loudest who get heard.'

I didn't reply, but I remember thinking to myself that those few words were the most helpful I had yet heard. I haven't stopped shouting since.

Fred was furious and said he would take the matter to a higher authority where we might find greater support. Two weeks later he was as good as his word. Previously scheduled to attend a meeting for Casa Alianza with Bill Rammell MP,

ove: On stage with Mark Nevin, writing partner and session musician on 1983's
rry', and Kirsty's 1991 release *Electric Landlady*.

ow: Appearing with Shane MacGowan, Eddie Reader and Blur on her friend Jools
lland's 1994 Hootenanny.

Kirsty MacColl

©1994 I.R.S. Recor

Above: Hamish and Kirsty with their godmother, Joan Littlewood, the groundbreaking theatrical director of the Theatre Workshop.

Below: My great friend John Dalby, musician and composer, sharing a drink with us all in the back garden in happier times.

Above: Holly Johnson designed and created this stained-glass window in Kirsty's house – Kirsty loved it. It represented the 'angel flying round this house' in one of her songs, 'Angel'.

Below: She was very fond of her cloud-painted wall at home! Many fun times were captured in front of that background.

ove: Hamish on holiday with Jamie and Louis in the chilly south coast sunshine.

ow: Now the boys are fine young men, pictured here with their father Steve, and me.

Above: Kirsty found renewed happiness and energy in her life with talented saxophon
James Knight.

Below: On holiday in Cuba. She fell in love with Latin rhythm and lifestyle and it grea
infused her own music.

ove: John Dalby, our Mexican lawyer Demetrio Guerra, me, dive-master Ivan Diaz
1 campaign linchpin Fred Shortland in Mexico, with hope – and steely determination
1 our hearts.

ow: The Justice For Kirsty Campaign committee, London, 2007. I will never give up
fight for justice for my daughter.

The beautiful, talented, unique and irreplaceable Kirsty MacColl, 1959-2000.

Parliamentary Under Secretary of State for Latin America, regarding the killings of street children in Guatemala and Honduras, he took the opportunity to voice a strong complaint about the unhelpful and obstructive attitude of the consular staff at our meeting and pushed very hard for more substantial support from the Foreign Office. Soon afterwards, the FCO appointed a specific case officer, Colin Leeman, and regular meetings followed. Our relationship improved dramatically and has now become an excellent working relationship. Meanwhile, in Mexico the British Embassy would in time become part of our team, along with our new lawyer, Demetrio Guerra, and start to work in earnest on our behalf within the diplomatic and political system.

Conscious that the campaign was developing media interest, the FCO were no doubt concerned that they had done nothing to assist us at the time of Kirsty's death and were presumably anxious to appear more helpful now, especially since they were also aware of our plans for a documentary film. In fact, the Consular department of the FCO is no stranger to adverse publicity in this regard, having earned something of a reputation for lack of support in several other cases. Nevertheless they had to be pushed very hard indeed in the first instance.

Due to Fred's efforts we slowly turned a very negative situation with the Foreign Office around, raised awareness at the highest level in the United Kingdom and had the British Government on board adding considerable weight to the campaign. Fred reviewed the findings of the private investigator, developed and implemented the campaign strategy, and took on the British Foreign and Commonwealth Office. He moved the campaign focus to the President and Attorney General of Mexico, calling for a judicial review. This call was included in leafleting strategy which brought a new lease of life to the campaign.

As a result of the heightened awareness, that summer of 2003 I became well used to speaking on radio (including Radio 4's *Woman's Hour*) and television (whether the local London networks or Sky News). A favourite spot for the TV interviews was inevitably Kirsty's memorial bench in Soho Square. I remember having to ask two elderly gentlemen sitting on the bench if they would mind moving for a few minutes for one of those filming sessions. When I explained who I was, one of them said, 'We were fans of Theatre Workshop, Jean, in the old days, and we knew your work and Ewan's. We wish you all the best for Kirsty – she was a great songwriter.' I remember feeling extremely moved by those words; it was as if they had summarised my whole life in a single sentence.

• • •

But progress still seemed terribly slow, especially after August 2003, when *Laban For All*, the book John and I had been working on since before Kirsty's death, was finally published, leaving us with more time to focus on the campaign. We had some more campaign meetings and I did a few more radio interviews. Meanwhile Robin Bextor's plans for a documentary film were also running into trouble. Robin continued to attend our campaign meetings, but after several months it became clear that he was having difficulties in securing firm commitments from commissioning editors. This was a major concern to us since a high 'media profile' was essential, not only to publicise the Justice For Kirsty campaign but also to put pressure on both the British and Mexican Governments. 'Governments behave quite differently when under the gaze of the media,' comments Fred, 'none more so than the Blair administration.'

When Robin's six-month contract came up for renewal in September 2003, we parted company and decided to start again.

Our plans to travel to Mexico in the new year were still in place, but we were left with the prospect of having no documentary – or doing it ourselves. For the next few weeks we thought that Charlie Dickins would have to shoot the Cozumel trip on his own and John drafted a working script. But this would have been an enormous task and since we would have had to hire most of the equipment, we were also worried about the strain it would place on the campaign funds. We were all too aware that we needed all available funds to pay for the criminal case itself. In the event, however, and to our enormous relief, none of this was necessary and Robin Bextor's prevarication proved a blessing in disguise.

Among the main aims of the Justice For Kirsty campaign was to raise awareness of the corruption and lies that surrounded the case – though we remained unable, for legal reasons, to quote much of the evidence for this we had unearthed. The journalist Alix Kirsta wrote an excellent article for the *Daily Telegraph* on Gonzalez Nova's business empire – including the decision to demolish a museum to make way for a supermarket, against the wishes of the local people – and his behaviour over the accident. It was Alix who suggested the names of a few other documentary film directors, and it was on her recommendation that I first contacted Olivia Lichtenstein, a freelance television director who agreed to take on the role if she could get the BBC to finance it.

As soon as I met Olivia I knew she was the right person for the job. After a series of meetings she came on board and I introduced her to the rest of the committee. Although then working as a freelance, she had experience of working for the BBC, as well as being full of enthusiasm and challenging ideas. She quickly secured a commission from BBC 4 to make the documentary that was eventually titled *Who Killed Kirsty*

Sun on the Water

MacColl?. With her would be her assistant, Louise McLean, who was equally enthusiastic and had the further advantage of being a fluent Spanish speaker. Fred was nevertheless slightly wary of this involvement, since 'you could never be sure of how they would portray those involved or the campaign':

> It was important to have the campaign as an integral part of the documentary but not at any price. The last thing we wanted was an emotive piece of light entertainment. We had to maintain our focus in going to Mexico and the priority had to be the campaign not the documentary.

I understood – and was grateful for – Fred's concerns. One evening in October 2003 he invited John and me to attend a charity dinner for Casa Alianza at the House of Lords where we met a number of human rights workers as well as some of the consular officials then liaising with human rights activists in Latin America. It was 9 October, the day before Kirsty's birthday, and we felt that our case was at last being given a sympathetic hearing. Three years before, to the month, Kirsty herself had, with Steve Wilkinson of the Cuba Solidarity Campaign, handed in a petition of 25,000 signatures to Baroness Scotland at the Foreign and Commonwealth Office, and Steve told me how Kirsty had forcefully stated the case against the American embargo of Cuba.

In the run-up to yet another Christmas without Kirsty, we were bracing ourselves for our trip to Mexico in the new year, though our travel preparations were subject to constant uncertainty. 'Getting to Mexico for the first time was extremely difficult,' remembers Fred:

> Time and time again dates were missed due to repeated setbacks and numerous obstacles... at one point it looked as

though it would just never happen. In the end we decided to take a leap of faith, fix the date, buy the tickets, go it alone and just make it happen.

The Mexican Embassy and Consulate in London were proving extremely difficult, if not downright obstructive, by not processing our formal requests for meetings with the various Mexican authorities. After a great deal of planning and organisation, we applied for our visas, explaining that the reason for our visit was to inquire into Kirsty's accident. Fred had advised us to be quite frank about our visit. I was told that, since I was not going on business or as a tourist, I would have to wait several weeks for a special visa. But our flights had already been booked and dates could not be changed and everyone in our party was working to a deadline. They also insisted that we required special visas that could only be issued in Mexico, which could take up to six months to obtain, and we further learned that they were not granting visas to journalists.

The BBC film crew did not receive their visas until the very last day before departure. After last-minute consultations with our Mexican lawyer, Demetrio Guerra, it was decided to take the risk and travel on tourist visas and then, once safely arrived in Mexico, change my legal status so that I could appear in front of the Federal Prosecutor and conduct official business. It was a risk, but a risk worth taking – and one which thankfully we managed to pull off. It did however cause John and I a great deal of anxiety, as we were the advance party, travelling alone into unknown territory, with no knowledge of Spanish. Even when we finally passed through Mexican immigration controls on arrival in Mexico City, we were fully expecting to be denied entry – or even arrested.

It was during the chaotic uncertainty of these setbacks and

tribulations that I received the letter from Ivan Diaz, postmarked 5 December 2003, I have quoted above. It focused my energies and renewed my determination to see justice for Kirsty.

Meanwhile, an extraordinary coincidence had occurred: John discovered that Moya, the sister of a friend of his, was living in Cozumel and was married to a diving instructor. Armed with the couple's telephone number, it was arranged that he would call Moya on our arrival. Now, however, disaster struck: Olivia Lichtenstein's father died suddenly, which meant that she was unable to make the trip. However, she kindly found the time to recommend an excellent replacement director, Tom Anstiss, who agreed to stand in for her, much to our relief.

It had been arranged that John and I would arrive in Cozumel a couple of days before everyone else, and I think John found this a bit daunting, now that Jean Berg would no longer be there to greet us: just before leaving, we had heard that she had been called away. John felt this was rather strange. We had been told of the widespread corruption on the island, of a former governor being jailed for involvement with drug trafficking and other offences, and of Gonzalez Nova himself as a sort of local 'Don', one of the most influential men in Cozumel.

When John and I set off, ahead of the main party, on Saturday, 6 March 2004, the others were still experiencing great difficulties with their visa applications and we actually left not knowing whether they would be able to follow us. Their key party included Tom Anstiss, our new film director, our cameraman Stephen Foote, Charlie Dickins (stills photography), Leni Gillman, who would co-ordinate press coverage with Elizabeth Mistry, herself also fluent in Spanish, Pete Gillman (for the *Mail on Sunday*) and last – but definitely not least – Fred Shortland himself. It was also arranged that the production coordinator Louise McLean would later join us, along with a local soundman for the documentary, Gabriel Barberis.

As John and I embarked on our trip, we left Heathrow on a wing and prayer, with no real idea of what to expect, or what we might achieve. We didn't even know if Fred, let alone the BBC crew, would be able to join us. But we had generated a great deal of media interest in our visit and I was determined that nothing would prevent me achieving justice for my daughter.

The flight to Mexico is extremely long. To pass the time, John brought out his phrasebooks and a Spanish dictionary and laboriously took me through all the words and phrases we might need in the various encounters we envisaged. When booking our flight, I had asked for a wheelchair to be available on arrival in Mexico City as I was suffering from a back injury and had been told that the walk on arrival was an extremely long one. I had injured my knee during an aerobics class when I was in my mid-70s and this had subsequently required treatment on my back. I should have stayed faithful to my Laban work: in nearly 60 years of practice, I had never had an injury.

Sure enough, when we arrived at Mexico City Airport, we were greeted by not one, but two smiling attendants, each with a wheelchair. I was only too thankful to sink into one of them but John was too proud to accept the offer and insisted on walking beside it. My guide walked so quickly, though, that John was soon grateful to take advantage of the other chair. A race ensued as our attendants skilfully dodged passengers and rushed us through customs and immigration to the exit, where they kindly deposited us. It was a relief: we had fully expected to be denied entry – or even arrested. We hailed a taxi, asking to be taken to the Plaza Hotel – now apparently renamed the Fiesta Inn. After a few hours' sleep, we were back at the airport, boarding a flight to Cozumel.

The heat hit us on arrival and we were glad to reach the hotel that Jean Berg had recommended to us. The Flamingo Hotel was simple but comfortable, and the American manager made us welcome. It was built around three sides of a courtyard that served as the dining room and the bar, and where we would hold many meetings over the next few days.

We were naturally very anxious to get in touch with Moya but when John telephoned, her husband said she was 'out', but would contact us on her return. We didn't hear from her that day (which seemed a bit odd) but the next morning at 8.30, Moya telephoned and invited us out to breakfast. Shortly afterwards, she arrived in a Land Rover and, after we'd introduced each other, she drove us to a spacious garden centre where tables were set for breakfast on a large lawn. There would have been no chance of getting a table had it not been for Moya's husband, Sergio, who had arrived early and was sitting there waiting for us. Sergio was friendly and charming, and insisted on treating us to a 'full monty' breakfast. After breakfast, and with children laughing and playing in the background, we told them about the Justice For Kirsty campaign and about the documentary film that we had come to make. They were both very sympathetic and Moya said she would do everything she could to help.

Returning us to our hotel, she asked us what we wanted to do. We had no plans until the following day, when the rest of our party were due to turn up, so she offered to drive us quite a long way to a delightful beach, with fine sand and palm trees, where we stayed for some time before she took us on to Corona beach, a lovely spot with smooth sands shaded by trees. It was now late afternoon, and a few people were sitting on chairs and loungers, catching the last of the sun. Moya led us towards the water where there was a small wooden pier. She said very little to indicate that it was from this pier that poor Kirsty's fatal trip had begun and ended. By now, the sun was low in the sky and people were departing for home, leaving a solitary beach attendant quietly raking the sand. Without a word, Moya fetched a chair for me to sit on – it was a sensitive gesture – and she and John left me to my thoughts for a few moments.

She then drove us to the marina where Gonzalez Nova's speedboat was moored. By now it was pitch dark and the marina was lit by overhead lamps. And there it was, gleaming in the soft light, the wretched boat that had killed my darling Kirsty. I cannot describe my feelings as I stared at it. As we looked helplessly at this chilling sight, we were aware of a solitary car slowly passing nearby. The thought occurred to me that we were being followed.

The next day, Ivan, Kirsty's dive-master, came to my room at the hotel, and John and I recorded his account of the accident. He was very emotional as he recounted the horror of that day, and burst into floods of tears. His genuine grief and anger affected both of us, and it was obvious from his emotional outpouring that he had never been given the opportunity to give such a full account of the accident. It was a most harrowing experience. He also made some very disturbing revelations which, even now, we are advised not to disclose. One thing is certain: he was a man of integrity who had longed for the day when he could tell the truth to people who would listen. Since the accident, Ivan had abandoned his diving career, which had been his passion, and earned his living in other ways, far from Cozumel Island.

Moya also managed to contact Anita Quinta, the woman who had unofficially rented her house to Kirsty, and after some prevarication she agreed to meet us the following morning over breakfast. Moya introduced John and I to her and then left. I remembered that Anita Quinta had described the British media as the 'Yellow Press' in her phone calls to me – she wanted nothing to do with them. She had twice rung me in the run-up to our trip – which I found rather odd – asking me if I was coming to Mexico, and whether I was bringing Kirsty's sons with me. I had said they would certainly not be coming with me and it was then that she had claimed that Gonzalez Nova's family had experienced difficulties with the 'Yellow Press' and asked me if I was intending to bring *them* with me. I had told her that the British press had behaved impeccably, but I hadn't told her when precisely we were due to arrive (and I didn't mention the BBC documentary team). She was obviously very concerned about adverse publicity – but it all still seemed very odd, especially when she complained bitterly about the cost of transatlantic phone calls. Since I had never asked her to ring me in the first place, I wondered why on earth she should say such a thing.

When John and I met with her that morning in Cozumel, Anita seemed a very nervous woman. She told us that she thought 'Mr Gonzalez Nova', her ex-husband's uncle, was a very nice, well-respected man – which was certainly news to us in the light of his behaviour since the accident. To justify her remarks she told us that on the evening of Kirsty's death he had called his whole family together to say that they must tell the truth about the accident. If there was nothing to hide then surely there was no need to remind people to tell the truth. I also bore in mind that Gonzalez Nova had immediately brought his lawyers down from Mexico City. We tried to arrange another meeting with Anita but she was very unwilling, and that was the only time we ever saw her. We have had no further communication since that day. She had been a very nervous woman, and it seemed clear that she had no wish to get involved in 'Island politics'.

After lunch a bus turned up outside our hotel and the rest of our party spilled out noisily with all their equipment. They told us that they had been met at Cozumel airport by a reception committee, claiming to be from the local tourist association – but how had they known which flight they were on? It was all very strange. I was greatly relieved to see them, and it was a joyful reunion after all the hassles with passports and visas. Eventually, when their rooms had been sorted out, we at last had our first meeting 'in the field'.

We also met with our lawyers, Demetrio and Carlo Guerra of the Mexico Legal Group, for the first time. The other lawyers we had encountered had treated us as just another case. When we met Demetrio, though, he immediately impressed us with his dedication and commitment. He understood the importance of the campaign and proved an invaluable ally and friend during the legal processes to come.

The first thing we had to do was change my immigration status to enable legal work to proceed. Demetrio, Fred and I simply went to the local office in Cozumel, without even an appointment, and the whole process was completed in no time. So why had the Mexican Consulate in London given us such a hard time, since they deal with such routine matters on a regular basis?

Preparing the new evidence, and developing the legal strategy, had been partially accomplished prior to departure by Demetrio in Mexico, and Fred in the UK, but there was still a great deal to finalise in Cozumel, including interviewing Ivan Diaz.'As the case was formally closed,' explains Fred,

> our strategy was to present new evidence to the Federal Prosecutor requesting that a new and proper investigation take place and the case be reopened under Federal Jurisdiction, as opposed to the State jurisdiction under which the case had been heard. We had no confidence in the legal process under the jurisdiction of the State of

Quintana Roo due to the obvious mishandling of the case. It was well known to be ineffective, with a former State Governor in prison for complicity in drug running.

We certainly felt uncomfortable and on edge in Cozumel (where some of the FBI's 'most wanted' apparently reside). Everything had its price and some of our party were quite concerned for our personal safety – but not me: I was prepared for anything, and more than anything I wanted to confront Gonzalez Nova himself.

•   •   •

The BBC film crew were pursuing the story in parallel to our legal efforts. To an extent, they had come to Cozumel with their own agenda. Filming started with me interviewing Ivan on Cozumel beach from where Kirsty's boat set off before the accident and they also filmed Gonzalez Nova's boat, the *Percalito*, in harbour and local people, some of whom had witnessed the accident. One boat captain said he had tried to divert the course of the *Percalito* but found that it was travelling at such high speed he couldn't keep up with it. At no time, he added, did the people aboard the *Percalito* attempt to help the two children left in the water calling for their mother.

They failed to track down José Cen Yam, the boat-hand who took responsibility for driving the boat, though director Tom Anstiss felt sure that if they could have stayed another week they would have unearthed him.

They called at the house of Gonzalez Nova himself, only to be told that one of his sons could not be disturbed as he had had a night out on the town and was still asleep. Apparently no one else from the family was there to talk to the film crew. All this was valuable work, but as Fred remembers, it also brought disadvantages:

We started experiencing problems with the journalists and film crew endangering our mission by chasing leads and witnesses, and competing amongst themselves for a good story. I had been extremely cautious of the media and my worst fears were being realised. I gathered them all together, explained the potentially difficult position they were putting us in and read the riot act, threatening to withdraw media access if they did not respect our position. Thankfully they understood our point of view, thus avoiding a potential disaster. We had a job to do and, while media coverage was important, it was not the first priority.

On the Friday morning of 12 March 2004, after a final meeting at the hotel, we set off en masse for the office of the Federal Prosecutor in Cozumel to present our new evidence and formally request a fresh investigation. We had not made an appointment in advance (since we thought it was likely to have been refused), so we simply turned up, doorstepping them with our BBC film crew in tow. The effect was one of total confusion and disbelief, and the film crew was immediately barred – before they even knew what it was doing there. After we explained who we were, Demetrio, Fred and I were reluctantly allowed into the outer office.

Demetrio was then called into the Federal Prosecutor's office and a rather heated one-to-one discussion ensued while Fred and I were asked to wait in an adjoining room, wondering what was happening inside. This outer office was piled high with box after box of case-files, chaotically stacked in no apparently discernible order.

'No wonder evidence gets lost,' muttered Fred, who then took the time to chat with the bemused staff. He was told that the backlog of cases amounted to between 18 months and two years. One box-file, gathering dust on a high shelf, was labelled 'Incompetence'.

We were at length shown outside and told to wait while they reviewed the file and considered what to do. Things certainly didn't look very promising, and we feared that the evidence would be rejected since the case was formally considered closed. After an agonising wait of three hours, Demetrio and I were called inside – but at first Fred was barred. Demetrio had to think on his feet and got Fred in as the formal translator. It's a good job we weren't all searched as we re-entered the building since each of us was wired for sound for the BBC crew. I'm not sure I quite took in what was happening as document after document was given me to sign, but Demetrio cautiously advised me that the file had indeed been formally accepted for review. My spirits immediately lifted, and I whispered to the film crew outside, via our mikes, 'Get the drinks in!'

We eventually emerged from the office triumphantly waving the formal receipt for our documents. After over three years of painful frustration, here was the breakthrough for which we had waited so long. It was a fantastic feeling and that night we allowed ourselves a celebration at a nearby restaurant, where we were superbly entertained by John Dalby. I felt that Kirsty was most definitely with us, urging us on and in a strange way celebrating with us at each and every step of the way.

Towards the end of our stay on Cozumel, we organised a ceremony at sea, at the spot where Kirsty had died. Lizzie Mistry had obtained a beautiful wreath and I asked for the words 'Goodbye to an Angel' to be written across it – a reference to Kirsty's song 'Angel' ('There's an angel flying round this house...'). We all threw flowers, and then John helped me to drop the wreath. It was very moving. The camera crew were in another boat and filmed it. Fred remembers:

As we approached the reef, Ivan Diaz froze, stared intensely into the crystal-clear sea and, fighting back the tears, placed his arms around Jean. He was trying desperately to be strong but he was reliving that terrible day. Paralysed by grief, he simply broke. We stood in silence as Jean, supported by Ivan and John, placed the wreath in the sea. Speaking as best she could, her words laced with the tears of anguish and grief, she cried out, 'Goodbye, my angel, I love you. Why did you have to die like this?'

Each one of us kissed a rose, the most beautiful red roses I have ever seen, and dropped it in the sea. As they floated gently away into the sunset, John Dalby, eloquent and steadfast, read the second verse from Kirsty and Hamish's 'The Hardest Word', written on the death of their father Ewan:

'On the horizon the eagles are flying
And I mean no more than a cloud in the sky
I never know if I'm laughing or crying
The hardest word is the word goodbye.
Teach me the old ways, I'm ready to learn
Be kind to the sister, be kind to the brother
The writer, the singer, the poet, the clown,
Be good to the man and be kind to them all
And we are ancient, built from bones.
Make time for the young and make time for the old
Be kind to each other, O that's what I know,
Be kind to the mothers, daughters and sons.'

The boat returned to shore in the fading light, each one of us silent in deep reflection. Later, when I remarked how very moving and beautiful the ceremony had been, Jean told me, 'I just didn't want to let go of the wreath. I wanted to pull it out of the sea.'

It was now time to press on with the second leg of our journey to Mexico City. The day after our wreath-laying, which had secured some local media coverage, my visit was made 'official' when I received a surprise late-night telephone call from Cozumel's state governor, telling me he was fully sympathetic and would do everything he could to help. We had made our presence felt on a very small island of a thousand eyes and ears. What a pity I had had to wait over three years for this offer of assistance.

We accepted the State Governor's offer, requesting that he both broker a meeting with Gonzalez Nova and push the authorities to secure meetings in Mexico City. A few days later we were told that Gonzalez Nova was not then on Cozumel Island, but we were given a contact number for a Minister of Government in Mexico City, who would supposedly co-ordinate our meetings there. Despite a series of formal requests (via the Foreign Office and the Mexican Embassy) for official visits with the authorities, not a single meeting had yet been confirmed and with only days away from our scheduled arrival there, Fred worked tirelessly, phoning and emailing, and phoning again.

Communication from Cozumel was difficult and I felt that our calls were being monitored, if not bugged. In one typical exchange, Fred received a terribly polite phone call from the British Consul in Mexico City, who courteously advised us that no meetings had been confirmed and that it was highly unlikely that we would be able to arrange any at such a high level. Fred was furious and demanded that the Embassy insist – but whether they would was another matter. In addition to the protocol of these formal requests – which anyway seemed to result in our constantly being fobbed off – Fred had also established direct contact with a presidential aide, whom he was pushing every day, but still getting nowhere.

He left Cozumel for Mexico City a few days ahead of the rest of our team to take a well-earned break with some old friends. He looked exhausted – physically, emotionally and mentally drained – as he took me aside before leaving to warn me that, despite his best efforts, no meetings had yet been confirmed. Before he left, he fired off a final email to President Fox's aide: 'We have a BBC film crew and the international media wanting to know the status of our visits next week. What do you want me to tell them? It's your call!'

As he flew out of Cozumel, everything was up in the air.

• • •

We arrived at the Hotel Majestic in the historic quarter of Mexico City on Sunday, 14 March 2004, travel-weary and now also suffering from altitude sickness. It would be a long week and we were anxious about what it might bring. Would we be able to secure the meetings with the key players that we so desperately needed in order to make things happen back in Cozumel? Or would it all be a waste of time, as we were so often told it would be? If we couldn't secure those meetings, all the progress we had made in Cozumel could be lost since, left to their own devices and without pressure from the Federal Government in Mexico City, perhaps the Cozumel Prosecutor's Office would lose the file...

On the morning of 15 March 2004, Fred again established contact with Lic. (a courtesy title, the abbreviation of *Licenciado*, to indicate the holder of a higher academic qualification) Gonzalo Altamirano Dimas from the Ministry of Government and to our great surprise and relief was advised that our first meeting would be at the Ministry of Foreign Affairs later that same day at

6pm. The Minister herself, Deputy Foreign Secretary Lourdes Aranda Bezaury, would meet us there in person. From that point on, all the meetings we had requested, with the Ministries of Tourism and Human Rights, with President Fox's Office and that of the Attorney General, all fell into place. I could hardly believe the turnaround. Fred's persistence, his dogged determination (as well as his direct line to the Presidential aide), had finally paid off – and it was now that the British Embassy sheepishly got back in touch with us, confirming all the meetings that only the previous week they had advised us were impossible.

'Planning the meetings was critical,' remembers Fred, 'and it was important that we controlled all the meetings with clear and concise requests in a logical and orderly manner':

I was accustomed to such high-level meetings, none of our team had any experience and I was concerned that if we did not present our case well enough all could be lost. After all, this may well have been the only opportunity we would get to engage at the highest level in Mexico. We could not afford to fail.

I set out a meeting plan, assigned roles and rehearsed and rehearsed until we were polished. At each meeting the approach was consistent. Jean provided an update of what we were doing in Cozumel; Demetrio Guerra provided a summary of our legal position and I provided an overview of the campaign, including our intention to take the case to the Inter-American Commission for Human Rights if the authorities did not process and resolve the case properly. And finally we made two requests: first, that regulations to protect divers and tourists would be enforced and second, that the various authorities would monitor proceedings on the case to ensure that no further irregularities took place.

At every meeting, and without fail, formal apologies were made to Jean, and agreement was secured to monitor those legal proceedings.

After the usually rather awkward introductions at each of these meetings, Fred would initiate proceedings by laying out our proposed agenda, which all the officials agreed to, putting us in the driving seat. I think they were somewhat taken aback by this approach, but at the same time relieved to have a structure to the meeting. All of the meetings were conducted in Spanish, which I found very hard going as I wanted to fully understand what was being said. An official translator was supplied for each meeting, some of whom seemed to struggle, but whenever they did Fred would intervene to ensure that I understood what was being said. I'm not sure I remember Fred's repeated 'rehearsals'; I just tried to tell the truth, each time.

'Our meetings would start off with us all sitting around a table, everyone being very polite,' says John Dalby, 'and Jean would have her say':

On the first day she was very eloquent as she described the accident. She was reduced to sobs of grief – people were absolutely stunned, their jaws dropped in horror. It was not an act. On the next day it got to her turn and, equally spontaneously, she gave an account – just as moving as the day before's, but certainly not any sort of 'repeat performance'. Each time – and there were many meetings – everyone was impressed and visibly moved. Jean can't speak about this, but when she described a particular detail of Kirsty's death, there was an audible gasp of horror around the table.

Everyone was quite nervous at these meetings, including the various officials we met, who had obviously had these duties thrust upon them at short notice from a higher authority. They must have had some sort of brief, but it soon became clear that they hadn't mastered the details. No doubt they were also wondering exactly what our campaign had to do with their own ministerial portfolio, since they exercised no jurisdiction on legal matters, and I think they were rather on the back foot – though we had no idea how any of these very formal meetings would go. In fact, since they progressed so smoothly, our mood lifted a little, and for the first time we allowed ourselves to enjoy the trip. Since the film crew were not allowed into the meetings in Mexico City, they went home early, leaving us to our breakfast briefing meetings and group dinners on the wonderful balcony of the Majestic Hotel, overlooking the Zócalo (the city's central square) and its beautiful Cathedral. Spirits were good – especially after Fred, a few days into our stay, received a message that seemed to promise a meeting with President Fox himself.

There were daily – sometimes hourly – phone calls to Fred, with hurried arrangements for our many meetings, though we were never really sure who we would meet until the very last moment. We had of course formally requested a meeting with President Fox, though I realised this was always going to be something of a long shot, since (as Fred explained) he could not be seen to be personally involved in a matter of judicial process. We were therefore all surprised and delighted when on returning to the hotel one evening, the receptionist – with a rather curious and puzzled expression in her face – handed Fred a message:

It was a note telling me to call the President's Office – which I did immediately. After going through a detailed security check of every member of our group, we were instructed to be at door Number One of *Los Pinos*, the President's offical residence in Mexico City, at 10 o'clock in the morning of Thursday, 18 March – our last day in the country. When I relayed this to Jean and the rest of our party they were absolutely delighted: it seemed after all that we *would* be meeting President Fox!

On approaching Door One that morning, a rather sinister-looking group of heavily-armed guards gave us the once-over check of our ID, then waved us through to the immaculately manicured gardens, where we were met and escorted to the meeting room and greeted by the President's representative Doctora Laura Carrera Lugo. Doctora Lugo informed us that President Fox had been called away on urgent matters, apologised to us on his behalf, and advised us that the President had delegated her to take the meeting on his behalf.

We were naturally very disappointed but it was important to remember that we had nevertheless made it to the office of the President of Mexico – which only a few days before had seemed an impossible dream. More than any other of these meetings, this one remains ingrained in my memory for the frank and helpful attitude shown us by Doctora Lugo and in particular a very unexpected comment she made in response to my statement that if the judiciary failed us in any way, we would not hesitate to take the case to the Inter-American Commission of Human Rights (IACHR). It was not only our 'right', she told us, but our 'duty', if needs be, to take the case to the IACHR: we would be 'assisting Mexico fight corruption'. I took this to be an open acknowledgement of problems within the Mexican legal system, and an indication that judicial reform was high on President Fox's agenda. We were further advised that the President's Office would liaise with Mexico's Attorney General, its Ministry of Tourism and the Federal Government to see if the case could be reopened.

I must admit that, for once in my life, I was rendered absolutely speechless by this – and of course extremely encouraged. I truly felt that we had at least received a proper hearing, and that progress on legal matters would follow in due course.

Meanwhile, as we approached the end of our visit, we had also again been contacted by the British Embassy who were now anxious to meet with us. This, our last official appointment, took place late on 18 March. Although the Ambassador herself, Denise Holt, was then in the UK, we were made welcome by a somewhat confused (and maybe even embarrassed) consular staff, who were amazed by how much we had accomplished, both in Cozumel and Mexico City.

However, our requests for the authorities to broker a meeting with Gonzalez Nova failed, despite a direct approach from a Government Minister. At an off-the-record meeting at the Ministry of Government, which our lawyer was requested not to attend, I was advised that they had been in contact with Gonzalez Nova's people, but that he himself was not then in the country! I was also directly asked at this meeting what it was that I wanted. I think they thought I was after a financial settlement from Gonzalez Nova but, as I replied, all I have ever wanted was for him to tell the truth about the death of my daughter, to explain to me exactly what happened, and to offer an apology – that's all. I then asked the Minister to personally deliver a letter I had written to Gonzalez Nova and this he promised to do. To this day I have not received a reply – not even an acknowledgement, not even an expression of sympathy, which is the very least I expected.

We arrived back at Heathrow on 19 March 2004, exhausted but truly elated in the belief that we were finally making progress. There we were met by Hamish, Jamie and Steve, as well as a BBC TV news crew – and Olivia Lichtenstein, who would soon begin work on editing together the film crew's footage. It was a wonderful welcome home.

Chapter Fifteen

Treachery

2004-2006

'How could he treat me like this?'

KIRSTY MACCOLL, 'TREACHERY', 2000

W e felt our Mexican trip had gone as well as we had any right to expect - certainly better than we had been warned it might - so the months and months of waiting that followed, with no news of the Federal Prosecutor's findings, were frustrating. John and I remained busy, however, making a return trip to Cuba in April 2004, where we took some Laban classes, and revisited the Havana Music School.

A few months after our return, Olivia told me she was having difficulties on the documentary with the BBC's legal department, who wanted to edit out the testimony of some key witnesses. They were apparently worried that Gonzalez Nova might sue - and his pockets were certainly deep enough to do so. Given that the Gonzalez Nova camp had never gone public, however, and that he himself was something of a recluse, we felt this was highly unlikely. And after all, it was the truth that was being told.

Olivia invited us into the editing suite that summer to see a rough cut of the programme, where we were joined by Demetrio Guerra to review any possible legal implications. Although Demetrio was happy with the programme, the BBC lawyers still made some cuts which we felt weakened it, though we nevertheless thought the finished documentary a very powerful piece of work.

In early September that year I went up to Scotland with Olivia to attend a film festival as part of the publicity launch for the film. I was still having trouble with my back and my orthopaedic consultant had advised me to order a wheelchair.

'Have you come for the festival?' asked the nice man in Edinburgh on my arrival, as he introduced me to my wheelchair. 'What are you going to see? How long are you staying?'

'I'm going back home tomorrow,' I replied, and then of course I had to explain about Kirsty. It turned out that my helper was a fan of hers and a regular visitor to Alan's website. On my return journey, I had a different helper, who asked the same questions and showed me the same kindness. He was an older man, ex-RAF, and when I explained who I was, he told me that he had often gone to hear Ewan's concerts of folk songs. 'I remember Ewan,' he said, and left me with the words 'Don't give up the fight.'

I never have.

Olivia's film, *Who Killed Kirsty MacColl?*, was finally broadcast for the first time on BBC 4 on 24 September 2004. The BBC later wrote to tell me that they had been inundated with calls and emails, receiving more responses to it than any other documentary. They kindly sent me two folders containing over 400 letters and emails offering sympathy and support. I got more through the website and many people joined the campaign. Alan Officer said the hits on the site had increased by something like 500 per cent.

The documentary heralded another round of media

appearances. One of the more enjoyable of these involved my trip to Belfast for *The Kelly Show* in early October 2004. Gerry Kelly, the show's host, interviewed me before a live studio audience and when I said I had brought some campaign leaflets with me, he got up to distribute them among the audience, there and then. It was a warm and spontaneous gesture which I greatly appreciated. He also told me that Kirsty herself had once appeared on the show to promote her latest release. Even before I left the studio, the switchboard lit up with calls, carrying messages of sympathy and support from all over Ireland and requesting further information about our leaflets. I had to promise to send more when I got back home.

When I boarded the plane from Belfast Airport the next morning, I was immediately recognised and welcomed by the cabin crew – it seemed that everybody watched *The Kelly Show*. I was asked if I might 'like a drink'. When I suggested a cup of tea – bearing in mind that it was only eight in the morning – I was told that I 'must put something in it' and a few miniature bottles came my way. The plane's captain personally placed an order for some leaflets, gave me his address, then apologised for having to leave me, but it was time to depart. When another stewardess came round with a sandwich and I asked for a cup of coffee, she wouldn't hear of it and gave me another few miniatures 'just in case'. The Irish people have always loved Kirsty – they made her an honorary Irishwoman, recognising many of the qualities they shared. Perhaps it all had something to with the genes and my Irish grandmother! I certainly reciprocate that love.

Slightly less inspiring, perhaps, but no less necessary was an appointment I made with *Hello!* magazine a little later that year. A journalist had rung me up to propose exchanging publication of the story for photos of the family. Mindful of our constant need to raise money for the Justice For Kirsty campaign, I managed to coerce my two teenage grandsons into having their photographs taken: the price was my promise to cook them toad-in-the-hole for supper. The interview with me was done in advance, and the photoshoot took all day. The house looked great in the pictures. I did my best, but was only too well aware that Joan Collins had graced the pages in the previous issue as a proud new grandmother!

Six months had passed since our return from Mexico and there was still no news. We began to suspect that something untoward was going on. Fred arranged meetings with the new Mexican Ambassador, Juan José Bremer de Martino, and with Sir Michael Jay, Permanent Under Secretary and Head of the Diplomatic Service, to try to move things along. The attitude of the Mexican Embassy in London had dramatically improved since our visit to Mexico and the new ambassador, although guarded, was very helpful, and promised to relay our concerns to the Mexican Foreign Office. We had complained about the Consulate officials when asked in Mexico if their London Embassy had been helpful.

The Mexican Embassy were now no doubt also feeling the heat from the Foreign Office, following a statement from Sir Michael Jay, who had raised the case directly with its Government during a high-level visit to Mexico. When asked to define the FCO position, he stated that 'The Justice For Kirsty campaign is at the very centre of Anglo-Mexican relations'. In our meeting with Sir Michael on 18 November 2004, we also requested assistance from the FCO Pro-Bono Lawyers Panel, which led to the appointment of Parosah Chandran QC, a prominent human rights barrister with extensive experience in international issues. And meanwhile in Mexico City itself, the Consul Richard Morris and his staff became part of our team and started to work on our behalf within the diplomatic and political system alongside our lawyer Demetrio Guerra.

The campaign had now reached a point – nearly four years after Kirsty's death – where one of the key objectives had been accomplished: awareness had been raised at the highest levels in both the British and Mexican Governments. But justice continued to elude us. After exerting a considerable amount of pressure we were advised by our lawyer that the Federal Prosecutor in Cozumel had dismissed the new evidence and closed the case. Our lawyer had been refused a certified copy of the resolutions, without which we could not challenge the findings. It was a catch-22 situation that caused considerable distress and yet more delays. I was absolutely furious, and felt totally let down by all the ministers who had undertaken to monitor the case. Had they all merely been paying lip service, just to placate me and send me away happy? 'The Federal Prosecutor was clearly at grievous fault for his failure to register our appeal as a formal criminal investigation,' says Fred Shortland:

And for refusing to provide certified copies of the resolutions to our lawyer, Jean's legal representative with power of attorney registered in Mexico. What had happened to the Attorney General's commitment to monitor these proceedings? After months of protest a copy of the resolutions were finally made available to our legal team which revealed a litany of errors and incompetence:

- They had failed to register the proceedings as a formal criminal investigation.
- The case had been closed without interviewing key witnesses: subpoenas had been issued, but never served, as they claimed Gonzalez Nova could not be found.

- Allegations of perjury had been dismissed.
- Our lawyer had been obstructed and impeded.

To me, it seemed absolutely inconceivable that further irregularities were yet again taking place. It quickly became clear that we had to revisit Mexico and confront the Attorney General once again.

Meanwhile, however, there was a crisis closer to home. Hamish had been house hunting in France and in November 2004 he rang me to say that he had found a place and would be coming over to England to sort out the finances. I had always encouraged him to move to France – he spoke the language quite well and I could see myself having some happy holidays there! I looked forward to his arrival, though I knew it would be just a fleeting visit.

He arrived at midnight straight from the ferry, suffering from what seemed to be a very bad cold which lasted several days and prevented him from completing his business plans. At last he decided to go to bed for a few hours, but within a short time came down to ask me to ring for a taxi to take him to Hammersmith hospital. His car was outside and he was obviously feeling too ill to drive himself.

I called a taxi, which was promised within five minutes. It didn't show up. I phoned again. When a car finally appeared, the driver explained that someone else had been assigned the fare but had decided that the £8 wasn't worth turning up for, despite the fact that he was to take someone to hospital. Hamish said he would call me.

The call came through more quickly than I had anticipated: he was having another heart attack. I packed up some nightwear and toiletries for him and went to join him at the hospital. He seemed relaxed enough but I don't know whether or not this was a brave face put on for my benefit. The next few days were taken up with waiting for tests and diagnoses. I was glad to see his appetite slowly return and I, like the relatives of other patients in the ward, brought food in for him since much of the hospital food seemed inedible.

At first it was suggested that tubes called stents might be inserted, but at length a quadruple bypass was advised. The waiting time for this could be weeks. Hamish's immediate concern was that all his furniture was on its way to the new house, which had not yet been finally signed over to him. Then one of the patients in the next-door ward fell ill and was found to have contracted the so-called superbug MRSA. The patient was isolated immediately, though by that time he had been walking around all the beds chatting to everyone for some days.

I insisted that Hamish have the operation as soon as possible and enlisted Ronnie's help. Hamish was concerned about the financial implications, but the superbug had galvanised us into action. Transferred to another hospital, his operation was scheduled for 8.30am on 11 December. I tried to keep myself busy that day as best I could and the phone rang towards midday. The operation had gone well, the surgeon told me, but it was still early days.

When I went to see Hamish, he was just able to say, 'Well, I'm still here.' The surgeon asked me about our name and I told him who we all were and about Kirsty. He replied that he had suspected Hamish was her brother. I visited daily with the usual things one takes to patients, grateful that Hamish was still with us.

Hamish was due to come home on 17 December, in time for the anniversary of Kirsty's death. I just had to keep busy and my friend Denise came over to help me clean the kitchen thoroughly and prepare a bedroom for his return. We had a very quiet Christmas; I bought a tree and ordered a small turkey. I was told to feed the convalescent whatever he wanted. I had lost one child, but the other had been saved.

I was simultaneously publicising the campaign – on one occasion going directly from an interview on *Sky News* to visit Hamish in hospital.

Having heard the miserable news from Mexico, we held another committee meeting on its future policy. The reunited Pogues were on tour, and in the run-up to Christmas 2004 I went to one of their concerts in London, where I was delighted to hear Spider Stacy make an appeal for the Justice For Kirsty campaign from the stage. There was a collection at the end, organised and overseen by Philip Rambow, and Louise McLean – Olivia's assistant, who had come to Cozumel with us – was a brilliant and energetic bucket-holder. There had been collections throughout the tour and Philip's 14-year-old daughter Georgia had travelled when she could with her mother Jann to help out with them. A separate collection had been made in Dublin and the overall amount of cash raised was fantastic. When the time came for 'Fairytale of New York', everyone in the place joined in. Ewan's 'Dirty Old Town' was also part of the repertoire. Hearing those two songs in the same concert seemed to bring the two halves of my life together.

It never rains but it pours – almost immediately after Christmas, with Hamish making a steady recovery, I received a phone call from John Thompson, John Dalby's partner, to say that John had had a stroke and was in Charing Cross hospital. When I went to see him, I thought the conditions were better than at Hamish's, but the food was similarly poor. So when John Thompson went down with a heavy chest cold and couldn't visit, I was more than happy to resume my meals-on-wheels service. Since Charing Cross was so much further away, I couldn't take hot food, so I bought the patient a salad each evening before rushing home to cook Hamish's evening meal. Salmon salad, ham salad, chicken salad – soon I was running out of ideas for John's meals, though I tried to vary the menu and included a different dessert. One evening I asked John if he liked tinned sardines. Apparently he did – provided they were boned!

In time, John was discharged from hospital and home again, with a slight eye problem but otherwise in good shape. This didn't stop him complaining that he wasn't allowed to drink more than one glass of wine a day. Both Johns and my friend Denise came over for a celebratory dinner to toast his recovery.

After sorting out the delayed paperwork on his house, Hamish decided it was time to go back to France. I waved goodbye and he promised to ring me as soon as he got to his new home. When I visited him for his birthday the following July he was happy and well on the way to recovery.

•   •   •

It had been a testing few months, but the pressure upon me never let up, since I had to prepare myself for a second trip to Mexico in March 2005. John reluctantly bowed out of the trip, feeling he wasn't up to such a gruelling journey. He was slowly on the mend and attending our campaign meetings, though, and would continue to support the campaign from home. To my great pride, Louis now volunteered to take over John's place on the committee and it was therefore Louis, Fred and I who flew off to Mexico that summer. It was thanks to the fundraising efforts of The Pogues that the campaign had enough resources to organise this second trip, though I paid my own travel expenses out of personal savings.

Fred, Louis and I arrived in Mexico City on 30 May 2005 and this time our meetings – at the British Embassy, the Ministry of Foreign Affairs, the Ministry of the Interior and the Office of the Attorney General – were fully co-ordinated by the UK Foreign

Office and the Mexican Embassy in London. How different from our first visit to Mexico City when the British Consul had shrugged his shoulders and told us, 'Our hands are tied.'

This time we were invited us to the Ambassador's residence and officials made themselves available to us for our week's stay. We felt very supported and were even given an English breakfast with staff on our last full day. They were also very kind and courteous towards Louis, who impressed us all by the dignity and courage of his presence, even contributing a few points in Spanish during the meetings.

'We instructed our legal team to file an administrative appeal against the Federal Prosecutor and to file a constitutional appeal to underpin and strengthen our legal position,' says Fred.

We explained in detail what had happened during the course of the previous year and demanded to know why previous commitments to monitor proceedings had failed. The only ministry that had done anything to honour its pledges was the Ministry of Tourism:

- New Rules of Procedure had been passed for National Maritime Parks' Divers and Tourists areas, designed to strengthen and protect tourists.
- Limits on speed were tightened. Dive boats were required to lodge route plans prior to departure and communication and first-aid emergency procedures had been improved.
- On Cozumel Island, 32 illuminated buoys were installed, marking entrances to the National Maritime Park and an ombudsman for tourism had been appointed.
- The Ministry of Tourism had contributed £42,000 towards the cost of £184,000.

- A promotional campaign, explaining the new safety measures, was in place throughout Mexico, and the new laws were designated 'Kirsty's Laws' as a mark of respect to her memory.

If nothing else, then, at least our campaign had succeeded in protecting divers from a similar fate – as long as these new regulations were monitored and enforced.

Demetrio was meanwhile under a great deal of pressure, as the simultaneous deadline for the filing of our constitutional appeal in Cozumel and our appeal to the Attorney General's office in Mexico City fell at midnight on the evening of 2 June 2005. At 10 pm, Fred, Louis and I were in a taxi, apparently lost in the outskirts of Mexico City, with a very anxious Demetrio and a pile of legal documents. With the clock ticking, Demetrio asked to be dropped off on the side of the road and we made our way back to the hotel. When Fred later called him, Demetrio told us he had eventually found the right office, and deposited our appeals, just one hour before the deadline!

'The meeting on 1 June 2005, at the Ministry of Foreign Affairs with Lourdes Aranda Bezaury had been a very formal affair,' says Fred, 'with as many as twelve people assembled, including high-level representatives from the State of Quintana Roo.'

Demetrio opened the meeting with an update on the legal proceedings and the constitutional appeal and for the very first time the penny dropped with the Minister. While not a lawyer herself, she could plainly see that we had grounds for complaint against the Federal Prosecutor in Cozumel.

As legal matters were outside the jurisdiction of the Ministry of Foreign Affairs, she took the initiative to arrange a special meeting for our lawyer with the head of international legal affairs at the Attorney General's office in advance of a meeting the following day. At that meeting they accepted the basis of our legal position, advising us that they would re-open the criminal investigation and review the findings of the Federal Prosecutor in Cozumel.

Quite apart from the dubious rulings, the series of procedural errors and the refusal to provide certified copies of the resolutions to our lawyer, the statute of limitations now emerged as a key factor in our case – which may well have been exceeded by the unnecessary delays and obstruction.

We therefore immediately made it clear that we now had a case against the State of Mexico's judiciary at the Inter-American Commission for Human Rights for this latest series of irregularities. This time it was Jean's rights that had been breached. When Demetrio returned to the hotel with the news of this breakthrough we were all elated.

The Office of the Attorney General in Mexico City on Avenue Reforma is an imposing modern building with a very high level of security. When we first visited in March 2004, each member of our party had been body-searched, photographed and fingerprinted. Fred had been the last through, I remember, and politely declined the fingerprinting.

'You must,' the receptionist stated firmly.

'No, you have no authority to do so,' Fred had replied. 'It is a breach of my rights.'

'Okay, sir, just go through.'

I was flabbergasted at this. 'You mean to tell me,' I asked Fred, 'you had us go through all that palaver and you just walked through?' As a bit of a rebel myself, I was most impressed.

This time, though, it was very different. We were greeted on arrival and immediately issued with security passes. Someone asked about fingerprinting, only to be told that such a procedure would not be necessary since all our prints would already be on file from our last visit.

Fred smiled and whispered in my ear, 'It's a bloody clever system if they have mine.'

Once inside the building, we met the Deputy Attorney General, the Head of International Legal Affairs, Lic. Miguel Angel Gonzalez Felix and the Ministry of Foreign Affairs had each sent a representative to the meeting.

'We were advised that they were going to review the findings of the Federal Prosecutor in Cozumel,' says Fred:

> In addition, 'We are going to investigate all the issues and facts surrounding the case with imagination and creativity to resolve the case once and for all.' We were told that a working group would be established across the relevant ministries and this would include our lawyer, Demetrio, who would be able to review and report to us on a monthly basis.

We appeared to be making progress – though we were all aware that we had felt similar optimism before, only for it to be subsequently dashed. The minister certainly lost no opportunity to accompany us to the main reception area, where photos of our group were taken, much to the dismay of the hovering security staff. Once released into the streets, we made for the nearest bar in the Zona Rosa to toast our well-earned success before moving on to a farewell dinner at the hotel. We had made plans to go to famous Plaza Garibaldi after dinner to see the acclaimed mariachi bands, but by then I was feeling very tired and rather unwell and so I decided to get an early night.

I spent a very uncomfortable night indeed after that meal. The next morning we were all due to meet for a de-briefing breakfast – the special English spread the staff at the British Ambassador's residence had laid on for us – but by the time Fred looked in that morning, I knew I would never make it. He and Louis made me comfortable, left me with plenty of bottled water and then went to the meeting. My condition deteriorated while they were away and when they returned they discovered my blood pressure was rising: I had contracted salmonella poisoning.

I was admitted to the Santa Fe Hospital where they whisked me away into a private room while Fred and Louis took care of all the administration, paperwork and payment. As soon as I was settled they gave me a complete examination and undertook a whole series of tests. The doctor who attended me at the hotel spoke excellent English, but unfortunately none of the hospital staff did, so I was totally dependent on Fred. He very kindly stayed the night with me, sleeping on a sofa in my room and later sorting out the care and insurance details back in the UK – where he had to explain to his wife that he had spent the night with another woman! Fred adds:

They managed to control the infection overnight, but Jean's blood pressure remained worryingly high and was just not coming down. With possible complications setting in, it became clear this was no simple case of 'Montezuma's revenge'. We were booked on the Sunday evening flight to London and it was now Sunday morning – but would Jean be well enough to fly? The doctor who initially attended Jean was due to arrive around midday, and we had no idea if he would sign the release form that the airline would require.

While Jean wanted to make the flight, I was not prepared to take any risks – if we had to stay then so be it – but if she did not respond to treatment, there was no telling how

298

long that might be. Luckily, one of my friends in Mexico City was a surgeon and it was very reassuring to be able to call on an independent second opinion. To everyone's enormous relief, Jean's condition had improved slightly by midday and the doctor signed her off. Louis and I then had to rush back to the hotel to pack, and many of our friends accompanied us to the airport.

Fortunately, Jean had medical insurance – a nice little earner for the attending doctor who from the very beginning was impossible to tie down regarding charges, repeatedly brushing away our questions. In the event, for less than 24 hours' hospitalisation the cost was a staggering £1,600 – but Jean had received excellent care. It had really been touch and go, but we made it. By coincidence, we met one of the officials from the Mexican Ministry of Tourism on the plane. He had seen us only a few days earlier. When he learned of Jean's condition, he was acutely embarrassed.

Clearly, I wasn't the only one to feel a flood of relief when our plane touched down at Heathrow and we were met by Steve Lillywhite! My health problems aside, we all came away very hopeful that, at last, we were being listened to and that things would now change. We were even told that a satisfactory resolution might even be reached by October 2005. Some hope! At the time of writing, over two years later, we are still waiting.

On 13 September 2005 we were invited to meet Giles Paxman, the new British Ambassador to Mexico, at the FCO in London. We provided him with an update on the catalogue of failures, broken promises and continuous delays we had experienced. At this point our main concern was with the handling of the appeal, as Fred explains:

Having filed an administrative and constitutional appeal regarding the conduct of the Federal Prosecutor in Cozumel for failing to register the case as a criminal investigation and having had this appeal accepted, the Mexican Attorney General's office had sent the file back to the same person who had mishandled the initial appeal. We were also extremely concerned that the monthly review meetings we had been promised by the Attorney General's office were not happening and this was causing even more delays.

We expressed our gratitude for the excellent support we were receiving from the Consular staff at the Embassy, namely Richard Morris and Andrew Morris. Giles Paxman gave us his assurance that this support would continue and the Embassy would continue to press the Mexican authorities on the issues raised.

With none of the regular updates or reports that had been promised us from Mexico, despite our constant lobbying and complaints, proceedings were once again grinding to a halt. No news resulted in media interest in our campaign flagging. It was a waiting game.

The Pogues repeated their kindness in the run-up to Christmas, both publicly and privately. The band continued to publicise the campaign during their tour, once again organising collections among audiences, who were as fantastically generous as they had been before. Guitarist Jem Finer and his wife Marcia Farquhar wouldn't hear of me being alone over Christmas and very kindly invited me to join their family. Hamish had been asked to spend the season with friends in France and in some ways I was glad to be spared the memories of the anxieties of our previous Christmas together.

As 2006 began, it was to another group of musicians and

friends of Kirsty, the band U2, that we looked to bring further hope to our cause. Learning that U2's tour schedule included Mexico itself, Fred saw an opportunity for a big media push. This depended, of course, on being able to enlist Bono's help and he was extremely busy. Not only was there the tour but more immediately the launch of his Product Red initiative (to tackle AIDS, tuberculosis and malaria in the developing world) at the World Economic Forum in Davos.

We began to put out some feelers and Fred sent Bono an outline of the difficulties we were still experiencing with the Mexican authorities. Fred expressed the wish that Bono might raise awareness with the media while on tour in Mexico. We were taking nothing for granted, of course, but we remained hopeful.

U2's forthcoming tour of his country had also attracted the notice of the Mexican journalist Rodolfo Montes, of the national newspaper *El Universal*, who contacted us with a request for a campaign update as part of a feature on the band he was writing. We put him in touch with our lawyer Demetrio and the journalist then flew to Cozumel to seek out José Cen Yam – the deckhand convicted of driving the *Percalito*. We cannot, of course, be precisely sure what happened out there, but Fred has pieced together the following account.

Cen Yam seems to have become quite angry and refused to be interviewed, but the journalist did manage to question his wife, María Rosalba Ku, and father-in-law, who unloaded what was an obvious burden. They were both adamant that José Cen Yam was not driving the boat that killed Kirsty, María stating that her husband was bought off with promises of land and a new house if he testified that he was driving and took the responsibility. Gonzalez Nova subsequently reneged on his promises. He did purchase a plot of land – but not a house – and then fired José Cen Yam, leaving the family in debt for building materials that they could not now pay for.

Feeling bitterly betrayed, family members were now willing to tell all to a national newspaper. They stated that, burdened by his conscience, Cen Yam had returned to the authorities and the Port Captain a few days after giving his first witness statement in an effort to change his testimony, only to be told it was then too late to do so. Cen Yam was locally known on Cozumel as 'the assassin', which greatly depressed him – so much so that his family told the reporter he had on several occasions contemplated suicide.

Cracks were starting to appear in the official story of Kirsty's death and the truth was at last starting to emerge. When Cen Yam became aware of the interviews, the journalist was threatened with his life.

To our delight, Rodolfo Montes's article appeared in *La Revista* magazine on 6 February 2006, publicly stating, 'Several witnesses identified the driver... It is a prominent and rich man: Guillermo Gonzalez Nova, owner of the commercial chain Comercial Mexicana.'

A week later, at the U2 concert at Monterrey on 13 February 2006, Bono dedicated 'I Still Haven't Found What I'm Looking For' to Kirsty's memory and our campaign's long-overdue quest for justice. He repeated the dedication at all the venues on the tour and directly called upon President Fox to intervene in the case. It prompted a rather lukewarm response from Presidential spokesman Ruben Aguilar. 'The investigation has to offer results,' Aguilar announced at a news conference. 'The Federal Government is following this situation.'

Local and international media picked up the story within hours, at last providing the extensive coverage that we had always wanted. The Justice For Kirsty website took a record number of hits and the campaign was back in the news. Surely the explosive revelations of the alleged cover-up in the newspaper article, coupled with Bono's broadcast appeals and the worldwide coverage of the campaign they attracted, would finally get the authorities moving?

Unfortunately, nothing of the kind happened, and our only comfort was the considerable concern the coverage must have caused the Gonzalez Nova clan. But the alleged cover-up was now public knowledge, and the campaign's profile was at its highest. We were getting very close, and Fred seized the opportunity to keep up the pressure on the legal side of things:

Based on the newspaper article revelations, we applied to have Cen Yam's wife and father-in-law subpoenaed, along with Gonzalez Nova's daughter-in-law Norma Hajj – a key witness who was on the boat when Kirsty was killed, but who had never been interviewed or called to testify. Our initial applications were rejected, but our lawyer Demetrio Guerra persisted until the requests were granted. It remains to be seen whether the results can be submitted as evidence, since they may be considered hearsay, but at least the truth has been made public.

On 6 May, the Office of Public Affairs for the Federal Government of Mexico advised us that Emilio Cortez Ramirez, the Federal Prosecutor in Cozumel with whom we had filed our new evidence during our visit in March 2004, was found liable for breach of authority for his failure to register our appeal and proceedings as formal criminal investigations. The Office of the Attorney General was ordered to apply administrative penalties, fining the prosecutor and removing him from his post.

While this ruling may not have a direct impact on the outcome of the ongoing criminal investigation, it nevertheless confirmed that this Federal Prosecutor did not follow correct procedures, acted improperly and impeded our lawyer. This was a direct result of the complaints and appeals we had filed to the Office of the Attorney General on our second visit to Mexico in June 2005.

The ruling also strengthened our position with regard to other outstanding issues before the Office of the Attorney General that have still not been resolved and, should the case be filed with the Inter-American Commission of Human Rights, the negligence of the Federal Prosecutor has been clearly established.

All this recent progress, however, was now at risk of being jeopardised since Mexican Presidential elections were due to be held in July. With a change of president, we would have a tremendous problem of continuity at the end of the year, since the many different officials with whom we had established contact would be replaced with him. It was therefore essential to get a resolution as soon as possible.

On 12 May 2006, we had another meeting with the Mexican Ambassador in London, delivering to him a letter addressed to the Attorney General complaining of the lack of follow-up, and the failure of the authorities to properly control and monitor the case. As Fred explains, we were particularly disappointed at the Attorney General's silence, since he was personally known to us:

On our first visit to Mexico in March 2004, we had attended a meeting at the Ministry for Government, on Tuesday 16th, with Lic. Daniel F Cabeza de Vaca Hernandez, who was the Minister responsible for Human Rights. It was yet another very formal meeting conducted in Spanish via translators. He had listened intently as Jean gave her very moving account of that fateful day, and of the orchestrated cover-up that followed. The Minister had said little, merely commenting that Mexico needed better and stronger laws, but – since he had no knowledge of the case – he had also requested a copy of our appeal to the Federal Prosecutor in Cozumel, and stated that he would have someone check the facts and would intervene with the Attorney General on our behalf.

Cabeza de Vaca Hernandez was then highly regarded in Mexican political circles as a rising star, and we were of course encouraged by the personal interest he took in our case and the promise he had made. We were therefore subsequently delighted to learn that he had himself been appointed Attorney General and optimistic that with his personal knowledge of the case and stated commitment to assist us, matters would now move along in a more positive and speedy manner.

Unfortunately, however, our hopes were, once again, misplaced and in fact communication broke down completely. It was this inertia that led Jean to compose a letter to the Attorney General, Lic. Daniel F Cabeza de Vaca Hernandez and we both delivered it to the Mexican Embassy in London on 12 May 2006. 'How much longer do we have to wait?' it began, before detailing the numerous problems and intense frustration of the inactivity and constant delays we had encountered. Copies were also forwarded, among others, to the Mexican President Vicente Fox Quesada and the British Foreign Secretary Margaret Beckett.

The Mexican Embassy in London confirmed to us that the letter was delivered to the Attorney General, but to this day no acknowledgement or response has ever been received. To us this was yet another and very clear indication that even the Attorney General himself was either unwilling or unable to respond in a proper manner and complete his personal and professional commitments to Jean.

On 12 May 2006, we had another meeting with the Mexican Ambassador in London, delivering to him a letter addressed to the Attorney General complaining of the lack of follow-up and the failure of the authorities to properly control and monitor the case. We were particularly disappointed at the Attorney General's silence, since he was personally known to us and we had made concerted efforts to maintain contact with him.

Two months after delivering our letter, on 2nd July President Fox's term came to an end followed by extremely controversial elections where Felipe Calderon Hinojosa was eventually confirmed as the successor to take over in December. The change of administration would undoubtedly bring yet more delays unless the Attorney General concluded the case before leaving office. This was highly unlikely, however, since although we had at last achieved a high profile for our case, it was a political hot potato and the chances were that the outgoing officials – including Cabeza de Vaca Hernandez – would want to leave it to someone else to conclude.

During this frustrating interim period, progress ground to a halt, and even our lawyer Demetrio was left with relatively little to do. We invited him to London that October as an honoured guest at the Soho Square celebration of Kirsty's birthday, where he addressed the fans with a review of the campaign's progress. Later that month, on 25 October 2006, Gonzalez Nova's daughter-in-law Norma Hajj at last presented her official testimony, as Fred explains:

Norma Hajj confirmed that she had been on board the *Percalito* with her 11-month-old daughter on the day of the accident. When specifically asked who was driving the boat, she stated, 'I could not tell, as I was taking care of and looking after my daughter.' What is very interesting is that this statement fails to support or verify the witness statements of both Gonzalez Nova or Cen Yam. Does this imply that she wanted no part in the original story as told to the authorities?

The great-niece of Guillermo Gonzalez Nova, Andrea Gonzalez, was killed on 5 February 2005, by a speedboat ploughing into an unlit sailing boat at night in Valley Bravo. The incident itself went largely unreported in the Mexican press, though the many obituaries ran to many pages, emphasising the importance of the Gonzalez Nova family in Mexican society. Surprisingly, however, the family took no legal action: the perpetrator, who was known to the family, was neither charged nor prosecuted. Had the Nova dynasty deliberately suppressed matters so as not to draw the all-too obvious parallels to Kirsty's death?

Felipe Calderon Hinojosa took office as President of Mexico in December 2006 against a backdrop of civil unrest, mass demonstrations and even a protest sit-in in Congress that prevented departing President Fox from making his final address. After promising so much in the area of human rights, Fox left office with many pledges unfulfilled. Our worst fears were realised, since we now had to deal with an almost entirely new administration. The only minister to retain his office was responsible for tourism, Rodolfo Elizondo Torres. He was the one official to have honoured his stated commitment to our campaign and his personal promises to us.

As so often during the long and terrible years since Kirsty's death, it was a case of one step forward, and two back. Were we now back to square one? Fred says:

The Justice For Kirsty campaign has been an emotional rollercoaster for all of us, with as many twists and turns as a cheap detective thriller. Elation followed by moments of despair and intense frustration – time and time again, year after year.

For me personally it has been an incredible and testing journey. I have been challenged in the extreme, both personally and professionally. My initial intention was only to provide strategic guidance to the campaign, but I ended up running it, immersed in every detail, scrutinising investigators, instructing lawyers and lobbying the Foreign and Commonwealth Office, the Mexican Ministry of Foreign Affairs, and the Mexican Attorney General on behalf of Jean MacColl and the campaign.

Since I became part of the team, hardly a day has passed that I have not been in touch with Jean. She has amazed me with her tenacity, energy and single-minded determination – she is truly an inspiration to everyone involved with the campaign. Faced with these ongoing and constant obstacles, most would have given up a long time ago... but not Jean!

Rather to my surprise under the circumstances and given that we are both hard-headed individuals, we have developed a remarkable working relationship, which I confess has at times been difficult. Many times I suspect Jean has gone against a mother's emotional instincts to follow reason and logic. By the same token, I have occasionally overruled my own instincts, gone against reason and logic and thrown caution to the winds. Sometimes you have to take big risks to make things happen.

Numerous attempts to close the case have been made by both Gonzalez Nova and the Mexican authorities, yet we battle on, countering every legal argument and their very questionable interpretations. What is difficult to understand is why, in the face of such intense international pressure and scrutiny, the Mexican authorities have not simply charged Gonzalez Nova and let the courts decide. We meanwhile await the findings of the new Attorney General.

If we have to take the case to the Inter-American Commission of Human Rights, there is no doubt in my mind but that we will win – yet our victory will be a tragedy for the Mexican people, since the inevitable consequence will be a ruling against the State of Mexico for judicial incompetence.

The Justice For Kirsty campaign is not alone in criticising the Mexican judiciary. In 2007 Amnesty International issued a report entitled 'Injustice and Impunity: Mexico's flawed criminal justice system'.

I can only hope and pray that in the end we can secure justice not only for Kirsty, her family, her fans – but also for the people of Mexico.

As I come to the end of this book and write these words, I am no closer to my goal than I was when I began it. Despite many years of hard work, despite the many and various contributions of dozens of her friends and despite the constant and inspiring support of thousands of her fans, we are all of us still seeking justice for Kirsty's tragic and untimely death.

I have already described the beautiful ceremony that took place in April 2006, when Kirsty's ashes were scattered on the waters off Havana. There was sun on the water that day, but the brilliance of Kirsty's life has for too long been clouded and debased by the behaviour of the man directly responsible for her death on 18 December 2000.

Kirsty's voice and music will always sing to us and will continue to shine when we are all long gone. But it is now time to bring to justice all those who have denied for ever the music, love, life and fun that Kirsty MacColl would have brought into the world if she had come home safely with her boys to Cozumel beach that day.

It's as simple as that.

Epilogue

Still Life

*'I always look at the last page of the book:
how will it end?'*

'OTHER PEOPLE'S HEARTS', 1995, BILLY BRAGG, RECORDED BY KIRSTY, 1995

I have never been one to spend too much time reflecting on things. Even when the great writer Stan Barstow suggested to me in all seriousness that I should write my autobiography, somehow I never got round to it, extremely flattered though I was.

'You have something to say,' he told me, before mischievously adding, 'And put my name in the foreword as having encouraged you to write it!' (I hope Stan will forgive me for not mentioning his name until the epilogue!)

But in those days I was much too busy leading my life to think about writing about it. 'Maybe one day,' I thought to myself, 'but only when I'm *much* older.' Perhaps the millennium – if I ever made it that far – would be a good time to start. As Kirsty sang in 'They Don't Know', her first hit single, 'There's no need for living in the past' – and maybe the same went for me too.

Well, I made it to the year 2000 – but I could never have

311

imagined the terrible circumstances that have led me to write this book. Luckier than most, I had kept myself busy, fit and cheerful, happy in my career and deeply proud of my children, each of whom was by then busy getting on with their own lives.

So when the millennium arrived, I had much to be grateful for, celebrating the occasion with friends, with family and with Kirsty (who always fitted into the categories of both friend and family). She, Hamish and I have seen out some dark times together, but were now a strong, happy and healthy family unit.

Before the year was out, however, the lives of our tight and happy family circle had been destroyed: Kirsty had been killed in 'an accident that should never have happened', her children had been bereaved and traumatized, and Hamish's grief was soon to transform into severe illness. It is at times like these, when a mother feels her family to be threatened, that she will fight back with all her strength. Kirsty's last, instinctive action had been to save her children. I have been fighting for her, and them, ever since.

As Fred Shortland explained, on 12 May 2006 we submitted a letter, addressed to the then Mexican Attorney General, Daniel F Cabeza de Vaca Hernandez, to the Mexican Embassy in London. We were assured that the letter had been delivered – but to this day neither he, nor his successor under President Felipe Calderon Hinojosa, has had the decency to reply to it, or even acknowledge its receipt.

12 May 2006

Lic. Daniel F Cabeza de Vaca Hernandez
Attorney General
Mexico City

Dear Sir,

<u>Re: Justice for Kirsty</u>

How much longer do we have to wait?

My daughter Kirsty MacColl was a visitor to your shores enjoying scuba diving with her two young sons. They witnessed their mother's horrific death at close quarters. She saved their lives as she pushed them out of the path of a powerboat captained by [Guillermo] Gonzalez Nova, being driven at high speed in a restricted area. At no time did Gonzalez Nova offer assistance to the two young boys calling for their mother as they swam in her blood. These memories still haunt them to this day and will no doubt remain with them for the rest of their lives.

Nothing can be done about my daughter's unnecessary and violent death, but as Kirsty's mother I look upon your government and judicial system for nothing less than *justice* in this crime. It appears that the person responsible for my daughter's death is immune from prosecution, and there is considerable reluctance from the Mexican authorities to prosecute.

In 2004 I visited Cozumel with supporters of the Justice For Kirsty campaign and a BBC film crew. The authorities did not undertake a proper investigation and the first case was considered closed. Only Gonzalez Nova, one son,

313

Cen Yam, and Ivan Diaz the dive-master, gave evidence, despite the fact that we requested the taking of additional evidence to their testimonies.

On our visit to Cozumel we discovered additional witnesses who were surprised not to have been called to provide a witness statement or to give evidence: evidence which differed considerably from that of the Gonzalez Nova family. I assume you will have seen the BBC documentary, which was made available to both British and Mexican governments and judiciary. During the visit in 2004, I went to the Federal Prosecutor in Cozumel to present new evidence and a case of perjury against Gonzalez Nova. A very reluctant prosecutor finally accepted the appeal.

My group then visited Mexico City where the ministers all expressed deep sympathy but stated they had no knowledge of the accident. We also met with you personally at the Secretaria De Gobernacion in your position as Subsecretario De Assuntos Juridicos and Derechos Humanos. We were given assurances by all ministers, including yourself, that matters would change and they all undertook to monitor the new investigation and proceedings carefully. I returned home trusting that those commitments would be honoured. Sadly, they were not.

I heard nothing at all from the Mexican authorities until forced to return to Mexico City one year later in June 2005. During that time, the Federal Prosecutor in Cozumel had rejected the request for a new case in June of 2004, without advising us, and refused to give my lawyer copies of the resolutions. It was not until some eight months later in 2005, and after considerable pressure from ourselves and the British Government, that my lawyer received copies of the resolutions so that we could continue with the case.

The resolutions were nothing less than ludicrous and it was clear that the Federal Prosecutor in Cozumel had acted improperly and impeded proceedings. This matter has now been substantiated, as Emilio Cortez Ramirez has been found liable for a breach of authority for failing to register our appeal as a formal criminal investigation: a matter that will strengthen our case at the Inter-American Commission of Human Rights.

Having still heard nothing from your government, despite both my lawyer and the British Foreign Office being in constant touch with your office, I returned to Mexico City [in 2005] to receive yet more apologies. It was clear that little monitoring of the proceedings or case had been done. Only the Ministry of Tourism had taken action to protect your very lucrative tourism industry – but what of the safety of the tourists themselves? Once again, promises were made. My lawyer would meet with ministers once a month to discuss progress, and an undertaking was given that a resolution would be determined by October 2005.

Little progress has been made, no meetings have taken place and there has been no resolution despite continued requests.

Through malpractice, inefficiency or undue influence, the case is not progressing and has clearly not been monitored as promised. This has caused lengthy and unnecessary delays which may have an adverse effect on the statute of limitation and serious implications for the Mexican judiciary.

Why weren't *all* the Gonzalez family interviewed? Why has it taken so long for an innocent family to get justice from a country that depends so much on its tourist industry? Do we have to start a campaign warning tourists to stay away until I get justice for Kirsty?

Kirsty has a worldwide following and people around the world are following the case. Since the accident, Gonzalez Nova's behaviour with regard to the accident has been appalling, but it is far too late for messages of sympathy now. He, as captain of the powerboat, is responsible for my daughter's death and has clearly committed perjury with complete impunity.

We are not going to accept any more excuses or delays: my patience has been exhausted.

Yours sincerely,

Jean MacColl,
The Justice For Kirsty Campaign

Everything I wrote then remains true today – in fact it is even truer, since I increasingly suspect that the Mexican authorities are simply waiting for me to 'go away'. But as they should know by now, after nearly seven years of campaigning, I'm not one to go quietly.

Over those years, I have learned at first hand that corruption is endemic throughout certain sectors of Cozumel and that Gonzalez Nova appears to have the law on his side. The 'accident that should never have happened' for which he is responsible and his subsequent, apparently uncaring behaviour, will tarnish his reputation for the remainder of his life.

However, I have also come to learn more about the value of love, from the thousands of people all over the world who continue to support the campaign and from the many friends I have gained who have helped in so many different ways. Once more I would like to thank everyone who has expressed their love by supporting us.

These days, I go to a pilates class every week and my back has improved tremendously over the last two years, thanks to my instructor, Alan Herdman. 'There's life in the old girl yet!' he recently joked, and I certainly do still feel like the 'human dynamo' Denise calls me when working with my students. I'd prefer to do much more physically and not to have to rely on others to demonstrate. With my eyesight the way it is now, however, I'd probably end up falling flat on my face.

I have earned one name that I am very proud of, though. Louis and his friends have always supported the campaign and attended the parties I have regularly held for campaigners. Louis told me recently that I had a nickname among them: they all call me 'The Warrior', he said, adding that they thought I was 'cool' – which is high praise indeed. I like that and I can hear Kirsty laughing at my honorific title – and willing me on to continue the battle, wherever it takes me.

I am sometimes asked what I will do when the campaign is over. I only wish the end *was* in sight, but until justice is finally achieved for my daughter, I shall battle on. And then, I suppose, go back to my lifelong Laban work, passing on what expertise I have to new generations of dancers. There's even an unfinished novel I began 30 years ago: John pulls my leg about it, but who knows, maybe I will surprise him (and myself) one day, and actually finish it. My grandchildren are a constant source of love and inspiration and we enjoy a good relationship. I am in constant touch with Hamish and take my holidays with him. As I keep trying to tell myself, I am still very fortunate. And then suddenly, unbidden, my eyes fill with tears and I find it difficult to retain my composure. I remember something Ewan once said to me, what seems now hundreds of years ago: 'Education taught us everything except how to deal with our emotions.'

After writing that memory down, I come across another letter: a now-fragile yellowing parchment, which Ewan wrote to me in pencil over 60 years ago, in our early courting days, when he was in a prison cell for going absent without leave shortly after the war ('I managed to get some paper from a Lance Corporal'). On the back of the letter is a poem in Scots dialect he wrote for me ('For Jean, my love'). It's called 'The Forge':

THE FORGE

It'll no' be aye lik this, lass, dinna greet.
The luve that we ha'e lit will burn the mirk
Wi' sich an unreal flame that folk will greet
Each 'ither in the street wi' news o' a new, bricht bleezing
    comet i' the ligt.
Ach, let their ghaistlike legions trauchle roond
An' roond the glowing core o' life.
They canna hurt us wi' their stinking breith
For we will temper luve intil a dirk,
And point it at the very hairt o' grisly deith.*

Something about Ewan's poem reminds me of a moment during one of Kirsty's concerts with The Pogues in the late 1980s that I shall always treasure. I was quite new to this sort of thing, and sitting in the dress circle of the arena before the lights went

---

'Greet: weep; *mirk*: darkness; *trauchle roond*: wearily trundle; *temper luve intil a dirk*: shape love into a dagger.

down I became aware of the odd quizzical glance in my direction. I must have seemed as old as Methuselah to the other members of the audience – and the courtesy backstage pass I wore aroused greater curiosity in my nearest neighbours. As the concert got underway it was marvellous to look down over the huge gathering of youngsters standing below and dancing to the music – and *how* they danced! – and joining in on all the choruses. They loved Kirsty and Shane's 'Fairytale of New York' – and then the next song was 'Dirty Old Town', one of The Pogues' biggest hits, written, of course, by Ewan MacColl. In the band's introduction to the song, it was dedicated 'to Kirsty's mum, who's in the audience here tonight'. And I remember seeing the audience sway gently from side to side, singing along to Ewan's words – and then out came the cigarette lighters and hundreds of tiny flames lit up the dark around us.

It was a strange and very moving moment for me. Having heard the song so often in the theatre and in Ewan's own voice on the long rambles we used to take together, now here it was being sung by The Pogues and our daughter Kirsty. Light years seemed to have passed. I remember thinking to myself that for all the obstacles, tribulations and sadnesses I had experienced in my life, I would not have exchanged a single second of that unhappiness for the pride and fulfilment I felt while listening to that performance. I don't know how much of my feelings I showed on my face, but a little while later a girl sitting nearby whispered to me, 'You're Kirsty's mother, aren't you?'

Well, so I was – and so I will always be. 'I used to dance and I knew romance,' sang Kirsty in one of her last songs, 'Golden Heart' (co-written with her half-brother Neill), ''till a dagger of glass tore my world apart'. The same goes for me. Perhaps this book is my attempt to light another flame and forge another glowing blade against the darkness.

I don't expect to meet Kirsty when I die. I would, of course, love to give her a big hug and tell her so much, but I believe we all of us return to the earth in an everlasting cycle of life. Kirsty is with me every day, and I like to think that when I get to the pearly gates, St Peter will let our spirits join forces for another of her great parties – where all latecomers will be welcome!

Kirsty's own music in any case will always continue to bring light into the darkness. 'As long as there are Christmases, her incredible voice lives on,' as Carl Chase wrote, and it is strange to see now how much of Kirsty's story has to do with that season of winter light. But she is with me every day; I feel her presence; and I remain grateful for the endless treasure of her life, her music, and her love.

> One day you'll be waiting there,
> No empty bench in Soho Square.
> No, I don't know the reason why.
> I'll love you till the day I die.

UK Discography

Singles

Many of Kirsty's singles were issued in a variety of formats with different track listings on each – these are marked with an asterisk (*). All remixes refer to the main song on the single unless otherwise stated. Please visit www.kirstymaccoll.com for full details of all releases including international pressings and promotional releases, with full author and producer credits.

'They Don't Know', Jun 1979
Stiff Records, 7" single BUY47, 7" picture disk PBUY47
'They Don't Know' / 'Turn My Motor On'

'You Caught Me Out', Oct 1979
Stiff Records, white label 7" single BUY57
'You Caught Me Out' / 'Boys'

'Keep Your Hands Off My Baby', Feb 1981
Polydor, 7" single POSP225
'Keep Your Hands Off My Baby' / 'I Don't Need You'

'There's A Guy Works Down The Chip Shop Swears He's Elvis'
Polydor, 7" single POSP250
'There's A Guy Works Down The Chip Shop Swears He's Elvis' /
'Hard To Believe' / 'There's A Guy Works Down The Chip Shop
Swears He's Elvis' (country version)

'See That Girl', Sep 1981
Polydor, 7" single POSP326
'See That Girl' / 'Over You'

'You Still Believe in Me', Nov 1981
Polydor, 7" single POSP368
'You Still Believe In Me' / 'Queen of the High Teas'

'I Want Out' (Matchbox and Kirsty MacColl), 1983
Magnet, 7" single 105166
'I Want Out'

'Berlin', Aug 1983
North of Watford Records, 7" single NOW100, 12" single
NOWX100
'Berlin' / 'Rhythm of the Real Thing'

'Terry', Oct 1983
Stiff Records, 7" single BUY190, 12" single SBUY190
'Terry' / 'Quietly Alone'

'A New England', Dec 1984
Stiff Records, 7" single BUY216, 12" version BUYIT216, picture
disk DBUY216
'A New England' / 'Patrick' / 'I'm Going Out with an Eighty Year
Old Millionaire'*

'He's On The Beach', Jun 1985
Stiff Records, 7" single BUY225, 12" single, BUYIT225, picture disk DBUY225
'He's On The Beach' / 'Please, Go To Sleep' / 'Please, Go To Sleep (12" extended)'*

'Fairytale Of New York', Nov 1987, reissued in Dec 2005
(The Pogues featuring Kirsty MacColl) Stiff Records, 7" single
'Fairytale Of New York'

'Free World', Feb 1989
Virgin, 7" single KMA1, 10" single KMAN1, 12" single KMAT1, CD single KMACD1, Cassette Single KMAC1
'Free World' / 'Closer To God?' / 'End Of A Perfect Day' (demo)* / 'You Just Haven't Earned it Yet, Baby'* / 'La Fôret De Mimosas'*

'Days', Jun 1989, reissued in Jul 1995
Virgin, 7" single KMA2, 10" single KMAN2, 12" single KMAT2, CD single KMACD2, Cassette single KMAC2
'Days' / 'Happy' / 'El Paso'* / 'Still Life'* / 'Please Help Me, I'm Falling'*

'Innocence', Sept 1989
Virgin, 7" single KMA3, 10" single KMAN3, 12" single KMAT3, CD single KMACD3, Cassette single KMAC3
'Innocence' / 'Clubland'/ 'Don't Run Away From Me Now'* / Guilt Mix* / 'No Victims' (Guitar Heroes Mix)*

'Don't Come the Cowboy With Me, Sonny Jim!', Mar 1990
Virgin, 7" single KMA4, 12" single KMAT4, CD single KMACD4, Cassette single KMAC4
'Don't Come the Cowboy With Me, Sonny Jim!' / 'Other People's Hearts' / 'Complainte Pour Ste Catherine'* / 'Am I Right?'*

'Miss Otis Regrets', Nov 1990, originally on the *Red Hot And Blue*
AIDS benefit album (The Pogues And Kirsty MacColl), Chrysalis
'Miss Otis Regrets' / 'Just One of Those Things'

'Walking Down Madison', May 1991
Virgin, 7" single VS1348, 12" single VST1348, CD singles
VSCDT1348 and VSCDG1348, Cassette single VSC1348
'Walking Down Madison' / 'One Good Thing' / 'Days'* / 'Darling,
Let's Have Another Baby'* / 6am Ambient 12", Club, Urban and
extended remixes*

'My Affair', Jul 1991
Virgin, 7" single VS1354, 12" single VST1354, CD single
VSCDG1354, Cassette single VSC1354
'My Affair' / 'All the Tears That I Cried' / 'Don't Go Near
The Water'* / Ladbroke Groove, Bass Sexy and Olive
Groove remixes*

'All I Ever Wanted', Oct 1991
Virgin, 7" single VS1373, 12" single VST1373, CD singles
VSCDT1373 and VSCDG1373, Cassette single VSC1373
'All I Ever Wanted' / 'Chip Shop' (live)* / 'What do Pretty Girls
Do?' / 'Walk Right Back' (live)* / 'New England' (live)*

'Angel', Dec 1993
ZTT, 7" single ZANG46, 12" single ZANG46T, CD single
ZANG46CD, Cassette single ZANG46C
'Angel' / 'Angel' (Jay's Edit, Apollo 440, Stuart Crichton and Into
the Light remixes)*

'Caroline', Feb 1995
Virgin, 7" single VS1517 CD singles VSCDT1517 and VSCDX1517
'Caroline' / 'Irish Cousin' / 'New England'* / 'The Butcher Boy'* /
'El Paso'* / 'My Affair' (Ladbroke Groove remix)*

'Perfect Day', Jun 1995
Virgin, CD single VSCDT1552
'Perfect Day' (featuring Evan Dando) / 'Tread Lightly' / 'He's On
The Beach' (extended) / 'Terry'

'Mambo De La Luna', Nov 1999
V2, CD singles VVR5010973 and VVR5010978
'Mambo De La Luna' / 'Golden Heart' / 'Things Happen' / Mint
Royale Edit* & Version*

'In These Shoes?', Feb 2000)
V2, CD singles VVR5012183 and VVR5012188
'In These Shoes?' / 'Good For Me' / 'My Affair' (live)* / UR Crazy
Edit* & Remix* / Le Rosbifs mix* / P. Mix*

'Sun On The Water' (Jul 2005)
EMI download only
'Sun On The Water'

•   •   •

Albums

Notes: The main album reissues (*) included additional material,
all of which was previously released (for example single b-sides)
unless otherwise stated.

Desperate Character, Jun 1981
Polydor, LP POLS1035, Cassette POLSC1035

'Clock Goes Round' / 'See That Girl' / 'There's a Guy Works Down the Chip Shop Swears He's Elvis' / 'Teenager in Love' / 'Mexican Sofa' / 'Until the Night' / 'Falling for Faces' / 'Just One Look' / 'The Real Ripper' / 'Hard to Believe' / 'He Thinks I Still Care' / 'There's a Guy Works Down the Chip Shop Swears He's Elvis' (Country Version)

Kite, Apr 1989, reissued* by EMI in Feb 2005
Virgin, LP KMLP1, CD CDKM1
'Innocence' / 'Free World' / 'Mother's Ruin' / 'Days' / 'No Victims' / 'Fifteen Minutes' / 'Don't Come the Cowboy With Me, Sonny Jim!' / 'Tread Lightly' / 'What Do Pretty Girls Do?' / 'Dancing in Limbo' / 'The End of a Perfect Day' / 'You and Me Baby' / 'You Just Haven't Earned It Yet, Baby' / 'La Fôret de Mimosas' / 'Complainte Pour Ste Catherine' / 'Happy'* / 'Am I Right?'* / 'El Paso' / 'Free World' (version)* / 'Innocence' (Guilt Mix)* / 'No Victims' (Guitar Heroes Mix)* / 'You Just Haven't Earned it Yet, Baby' (version)* / 'The End of a Perfect Day' (demo)*

Electric Landlady, Jun 1991, reissued* by EMI in Feb 2005
Virgin, LP V2663, CD CDV2663
'Walking Down Madison' / 'All I Ever Wanted' / 'Children of the Revolution' / 'Halloween' / 'My Affair' / 'Lying Down' / 'He Never Mentioned Love' / 'We'll Never Pass This Way Again' / 'The Hardest Word' / 'Maybe It's Imaginary' / 'My Way Home' / 'The One and Only' / 'Don't Go Near the Water'* / 'One Good Thing'* / 'Darling, Let's Have Another Baby'* / 'My Affair' (Bass Sexy Mix)* / 'Walking Down Madison' (6am Ambient Version)*.

Titanic Days, Feb 1994, reissued* in Feb 2005
ZTT, LP 450994711-1, CD 450994711-2
'You Know It's You' / 'Soho Square' / 'Angel' / 'Last Day of

Summer' / 'Bad' / 'Can't Stop Killing You' / 'Titanic Days' / 'Don't Go Home' / 'Big Boy on a Saturday Night' / 'Just Woke Up' / 'Tomorrow Never Comes' / 'Angel' (Piano Mix)* / 'Fabulous Garden'* / 'King Kong'* / 'Dear John'* / 'Miss Otis Regrets' (live)* / 'Free World' (live)* / 'Touch Me'* / 'Irish Cousin'* / 'Angel' (Single, Stuart Crichton, Into the Light and Apollo 440 mixes)*

Tropical Brainstorm, Mar 2000
V2, CD VVR1009872, Cassette VVR1009874
'Mambo de la Luna' / 'In These Shoes?' / 'Treachery' / 'Here Comes That Man Again' / 'Autumngirlsoup' / 'Celestine' / 'England 2 Colombia 0' / 'Não Esperando' / 'Alegria' / 'Us Amazonians' / 'Wrong Again' / 'Designer Life' / 'Head'

Compilations

Kirsty MacColl, Mar 1985
Polydor, LP SPELP95
'Clock Goes Round' / 'See That Girl' / 'There's a Guy Works Down the Chip Shop Swears He's Elvis' / 'Teenager in Love' / 'Annie' / 'Until the Night' / 'Falling for Faces' / 'Roman Gardens' / 'The Real Ripper' / 'Hard to Believe' / 'He Thinks I Still Care' / 'Berlin'

The Essential Collection, 1993
Stiff Records, CD CD17
'There's a Guy Works Down the Chip Shop Swears He's Elvis' / 'A New England' / 'Patrick' / 'Eighty Year Old Millionaire' / 'See That Girl' / 'Until the Night' / 'Just One Look' / 'He Thinks I Still Care' / 'They Don't Know' / 'Turn My Motor On' / 'Please, Go To Sleep' / 'Terry' / 'Quietly Alone' / 'Teenager in Love' / 'A New England' (12" version) / 'Terry' (12" version) / 'There's a Guy Works Down the Chip Shop Swears He's Elvis' (Country Version)

The One And Only, 1993
Metro CD METROCD063
'A New England' / 'They Don't Know' / 'Terry' / 'Libertango' (with Sharon Shannon) / 'Turn My Motor On' / 'I'm Going Out with an Eighty Year Old Millionaire' / 'Patrick / He's on the Beach' / 'The Manchester Rambler' (Ewan MacColl) / 'Quietly Alone' / 'Please, Go To Sleep' / 'Terry' (12" Mix) / 'Greetings to the New Brunette' (Billy Bragg) / 'A New England' (12" Mix).

Galore, Mar 1995
Virgin, CD CDV2763, Cassette TCV2763
'They Don't Know' / 'A New England' / 'There's a Guy Works Down the Chip Shop Swears He's Elvis' / 'He's on the Beach' / 'Fairytale Of New York' / 'Miss Otis Regrets' / 'Free World' / 'Innocence' / 'You Just Haven't Earned It Yet, Baby' / 'Days' / 'Don't Come the Cowboy With Me, Sonny Jim!' / 'Walking Down Madison' / 'My Affair' / 'Angel' / 'Titanic Days' / 'Can't Stop Killing You' / 'Caroline' / 'Perfect Day'

What Do Pretty Girls Do?, Feb 1998
Hux, CD HUX001 (BBC Radio Sessions, featuring Billy Bragg)
'There's a Guy Works Down the Chip Shop Swears He's Elvis' / 'What Do Pretty Girls Do?' / 'Don't Run Away From Me Now' / 'Still Life' / 'There's a Guy Works Down the Chip Shop Swears He's Elvis' / 'Walk Right Back' / 'Darling, Let's Have Another Baby' / 'A New England' / 'My Affair' / 'Bad' / 'Can't Stop Killing You' / 'Caroline' / 'Free World' / 'He's on the Beach' / 'A New England'

From Croydon To Cuba, Mar 2005
EMI CD Box Set 7243-8-74946-2-6
CD 1: 'They Don't Know' / 'You Caught Me Out' / 'Keep Your Hands Off My Baby' / 'There's a Guy Works Down the Chip Shop

Swears He's Elvis' / 'Hard to Believe' / 'See That Girl' / 'Queen of the High Teas' / 'I Want Out' / 'You Still Believe in Me' / 'Rhythm of the Real Thing' / 'Berlin' / 'Camel Crossing' / 'Roman Gardens' / 'Sticked and Stoned' / 'Terry' / 'A New England' / 'Patrick' / 'He's on the Beach' / 'Innocence' / 'Don't Come the Cowboy With Me, Sonny Jim!' / 'Closer to God?' / 'Fairytale Of New York' / 'Free World'
CD 2:'You Just Haven't Earned It Yet, Baby' / 'Tread Lightly' / 'The End of a Perfect Day' / 'Mother's Ruin' / 'Dancing in Limbo' / 'Days' / 'Still Life' / 'Clubland' / 'Other People's Hearts' / 'Don't Run Away From Me Now' / 'Please Help Me, I'm Falling' / Miss Otis Regrets' / 'Just One of those Things' / 'All the Tears that I Cried' / 'Walking Down Madison' / 'London Bridge is Falling Down' / 'My Affair' / 'All I Ever Wanted' / 'Halloween' / 'We'll Never Pass This Way Again' / 'Count On Me' / 'Dear John'
CD 3: 'Angel' / 'Soho Square' / 'Bad' / 'Can't Stop Killing You' / 'Titanic Days' / 'Tomorrow Never Comes' / 'Caroline' / 'I am Afraid' / 'The Butcher Boy' / 'As Long As You Hold Me' / 'Perfect Day' / 'Sail Away' / 'Libertango' / 'Golden Heart' / 'Mambo de la Luna' / 'In These Shoes?' / 'England 2 Colombia 0' / 'Celestine' / 'Good For Me' / 'Manhattan Moon' / 'Sun on the Water'

The Best of Kirsty MacColl, Aug 2005
EMI, CD CDV3008
'They Don't Know' / 'There's a Guy Works Down the Chip Shop Swears He's Elvis' / 'Terry' / 'A New England' / 'He's on the Beach' / 'Don't Come the Cowboy With Me, Sonny Jim!' / 'Fairytale Of New York' / 'Innocence' / 'Days' / 'Still Life' / 'Miss Otis Regrets' / 'Walking Down Madison' / 'My Affair' / 'Soho Square' / 'Titanic Days' / 'As Long As You Hold Me' / 'Perfect Day' / 'In These Shoes?' / 'England 2 Colombia 0' / 'Sun on the Water'

DVD

From Croydon To Cuba: The Videos, Mar 2005
EMI, DVD 7243-5-44463-9-9

'Terry' / 'A New England' / 'He's on the Beach' / 'Fairytale Of New York' / 'Free World' / 'Days' / 'Innocence' / 'Don't Come the Cowboy With Me, Sonny Jim!' / 'Walking Down Madison' / 'My Affair' / 'All I Ever Wanted' / 'Miss Otis Regrets' / 'Just One of Those Things' / 'Can't Stop Killing You' / 'Mambo de la Luna' / 'In These Shoes?'

Index

331

Index

Index

335

Index